Abortion Rights
and
Fetal 'Personhood'

Edited by

Edd Doerr & James W. Prescott

Abortion Rights and Fetal 'Personhood'

ISBN 0-913111-26-0

Published by

CENTERLINE PRESS
2005 Palo Verde Avenue
Long Beach, California 90815

THIS VOLUME IS DEDICATED TO THE WOMEN AND MEN OF AMERICA AND THE WORLD WHO STRUGGLE TO ADVANCE FREEDOM OF CONSCIENCE AND RELIGIOUS LIBERTY.

Acknowledgments

The conference which produced most of the content of this book would not have been possible without the ideas, suggestions, and hard work of Dr. James W. Prescott. Patricia A. Jaworski's valuable work on the "Thinking about 'The Silent Scream'" documentary was also of major importance.

Financial assistance for putting on the conference and for publishing its papers came from the Unitarian Universalist Social Concerns Grants Panel. Publication was also aided by a grant from the National League for Separation of Church and State. Thanks are due also to the members of Americans for Religious Liberty for their generous support.

Americans for Religious Liberty associate director Maury C. Abraham contributed importantly to putting on the conference, as did ARL administrative assistant Marie Gore, who also transcribed the recording of the addresses.

Thanks also to Harriet F. Pilpel, general counsel for the Planned Parenthood Federation of America, for chairing a panel at the conference, and to John M. Swomley, president of Americans for Religious Liberty and chair of the ACLU Church-State Committee, for his opening remarks at the conference.

The Editors

Edd Doerr is executive director of American for Religious Liberty and vice-president of both the Religious Coalition for Abortion Rights and the American Humanist Association. A former teacher of history, he is the author of six books, including *Religious Liberty in Crisis,* and hundreds of articles.

James W. Prescott, a developmental neuropsychologist and cross-cultural psychologist, formerly was Health Scientist Administrator of the Developmental Behavioral Biology Program at the National Insititue of Child Health and Human Development, National Institutes of Health. He is also a former president of the Maryland Psychological Asssociation.

CONTENTS

Introduction

FEW CONTROVERSIES IN this century have stirred emotions, challenged the political process, or threatened social stability like the one over abortion rights.

Is freedom of choice on abortion a constitutionally protected women's right? Or is abortion the killing of unborn persons, and therefore something to be prohibited by law?

Since the woman's rights movement began getting state legislatures to liberalize abortion laws about 20 years ago -- and especially since the Supreme Court's 1973 *Roe v. Wade* ruling, which held that a constitutional right to privacy covers a woman's right to choose to terminate a problem pregnancy -- bitter battles over abortion have become a permanent feature of the American scene. Congress and state legislatures have fought over proposals to outlaw or sharply curtail access to abortion, bills to require spousal or parental consent, and federal and state Medicaid funding for abortions for poor women. The U.S. Supreme Court has repeatedly been asked to rule on federal, state, and local laws designed to restrict abortion rights to a greater or lesser degree. Demonstrators have sought to close down clinics and/or discourage their clients. Extremists have burned and bombed clinics. Politicians are torn between vocal voters and groups which are either pro-choice or "pro-life." The issue has sharply divided the religious community, both between and within denominations, and the controversy seems unlikely to abate for many years.

In recent years, nearly 1,600,000 abortions have been performed annually in the United States, a rate lower than that of most Eastern bloc and Third World countries. (It is estimated that between 30 and 50 million abortions are performed annually around the world.) About 69% of the women having abortions in the United States are white and 31% nonwhite; 19% are married. In 1983, 61% had had no prior abortions, while 21% had had one. Slightly over 27% of abortions were performed for women 19 and under, 56% for women in their 20s, and 16% for women in their 30s.

Almost half of all abortions take place before eight weeks of gestation, 77% before ten weeks, 90.5% before twelve weeks, and 99.2% before 20 weeks. Only about 100 abortions (less than 0.01%) take place after 24 weeks.

Most abortions, 87%, are performed in non-hospital facilities, while 91% of rural and 50% of urban counties have no abortion facilities at all. Many women have difficulty finding a clinic or other facility, especially after the twelfth week of gestation.

The average charge for non-hospital abortions at ten weeks in 1986 was $238. Since 1977, virtually no federal Medicaid funds have been available for abortions

1

for poor women, though, in 1985, 14 states and the District of Columbia covered the costs of 187,500 abortions for poor women.

Although the fact is not well-known or appreciated, abortion before "quickening" (the point at which a woman first notices fetal movement, at 16-18 weeks of pregnancy) was legal, widely accepted, and apparently far from uncommon throughout this country from the time of the first English settlement in 1607 at Jamestown until state legislatures began banning it, except when necessary to save a woman's life, around the time of the Civil War. As the Supreme Court has noted, states enacted anti-abortion laws in the mid-to-late-nineteenth century for three basic reasons: "a Victorian social concern to discourage illicit sexual conduct"; a concern for the health of women, as abortion was dangerous and did not become safer than bearing children until after antibiotics were in common use toward the middle of the 20th century; and the states' newfound "interest -- some phrase it in terms of duty -- in protecting prenatal life." Historians also have shown that "turf wars" over who was to provide medical care often were involved. Physicians, rather than clergymen, provided the impetus for the restrictive laws. By 1970, however, public and professional opinion had become increasingly supportive of the liberalization of state abortion laws.

The watershed event in the rapid development of abortion rights, of course, was the Supreme Court's ruling in 1973 in *Roe v. Wade*, a case brought by a Texas woman who had been denied approval for an abortion (see Appendix A). After showing that a line of decisions going back to 1891 "recognized that a right of personal privacy, or a guarantee of certain areas or zones of privacy, does exist under the Constitution," with roots of that right found variously in the First, Fourth, Fifth, Ninth, and Fourteenth Amendments, and "in the penumbras of the Bill of Rights," the Court held in *Roe* that the "right of privacy...is broad enough to encompass a woman's decision whether or not to terminate her pregnancy."

"The detriment that the State would impose upon the pregnant woman by denying this choice is apparent," the Court added. "Specific and direct harm medically diagnosable even in early pregnancy may be involved. Maternity, or additional offspring, may force upon the woman a distressful life and future. Psychological harm may be imminent. Mental and physical health may be taxed by child care. There is also the distress, for all concerned, associated with the unwanted child and there is the problem of bringing a child into a family already unable, psychologically or otherwise, to care for it. In other cases, as in this one, the additional difficulties and continuing stigma of unwed motherhood may be involved. All these are factors the woman and her responsible physician necessarily will consider in consultation."

However, while concluding that the constitutional "right of personal privacy includes the abortion decision," the Court held that the "right is not unqualified and must be considered against important state interests in regulation," such as the interest of assuring that abortions are performed only by qualified medical personnel, and, late in pregnancy, a certain interest in potential human life.

The State of Texas argued in *Roe* that a fetus is a "person" within the language and meaning of the Fourteenth Amendment. The Court disagreed, holding that the term "person" in the Constitution nearly always "has application only postnatally." The Court added that, "We need not resolve the difficult question of when life begins. When those trained in the respective disciplines of medicine, philosophy, and theology are unable to arrive at any consensus, the judiciary, at this point in the development of man's knowledge, is not in a position to speculate as to the answer." "In short," the Court concluded, "the unborn have never been recognized in law as persons in the whole sense."

Roe v. Wade thus became the Magna Carta of the abortion rights and women's rights movements. Obviously, however, the story does not end there. A powerful movement, led at first by the bishops of the Roman Catholic Church and joined later by televangelists and ultraconservative religious leaders such as Jerry Falwell and Pat Robertson, began the campaign to overturn *Roe*, or at least to throw as many roadblocks as possible in the way of women seeking to terminate problem pregnancies. The growing pro-choice forces proved sufficiently strong to block passage of constitutional amendments designed either to outlaw abortion or to authorize states to do so. Nonetheless, anti-choice or "pro-life" forces have been powerful enough to stop most federal and state Medicaid funding of abortions for poor women, to deny publicly provided abortions to armed forces and Peace Corps personnel and, dependents, and even to try to cut off federal funding of domestic and international family planning agencies whose activities actually reduce demand for abortions. Social pressures have been responsible for the decisions of many public hospitals not to offer abortion services.

Since 1973, debate over abortion rights has raged incessantly. Catholic bishops, fundamentalist leaders, TV evangelists, and conservative politicians have campaigned vigorously against abortion rights. Other religious bodies and leaders, women's and civil liberties groups, and many politicians have defended freedom of conscience on abortion, though at a much lower decibel level and certainly with a great deal less resources. (See Appendix B for the positions of a number of national religious bodies.)

Where does public opinion stand? Recent major tests of opinion occurred in November, 1986, when statewide referenda on constitutional amendments were held in Massachusetts, Rhode Island, Arkansas, and Oregon. Massachusetts voters, by 58% to 42%, defeated a proposed amendment to the state constitution which would have allowed the legislature to limit or prohibit abortion, eliminate Medicaid funding for abortions for poor women, and prohibit private insurance coverage for abortions. In neighboring Rhode Island, a similar amendment was voted down 65% to 35%. Since Massachusetts and Rhode Island are 50% and 67% Catholic, respectively, and as the Catholic bishops strongly supported the amendments, the votes in the two states clearly showed very strong support for the pro-choice position.

On the same day, Oregon voters rejected by 54% to 46% an amendment aimed not at prohibiting abortion, but only at cutting off state funding for medically necessary abortion and those for victims of rape and incest. In largely fundamentalist Arkansas, voters unexpectedly defeated, by a paper-thin margin, an amendment which would have sought to outlaw abortion by having the state declare constitutionally that personhood begins at conception.

By November 1988, however, some shifts in opinion had occurred. Michigan (58% to 42%) and Colorado (60% to 40%) voters defeated efforts to restore state Medicaid funding for abortions for poor women, while Arkansas voters (52% to 48%) approved an amendment that would outlaw abortion altogether if *Roe v. Wade* is every overturned.

An extensive poll released in January, 1988, by Hickman-Maslin Research, a Washington-based polling group, showed that most Americans favor keeping abortion as a legal option for women who so choose by a 56% to 27% margin. Support for choice was highest in the Northeast (69%), lowest in the South (45%). Support increased with educational level and was higher in urban than rural areas. Democratic (59%) and independent (58%) support was higher than Republican (52%); liberal support higher (79%) than conservative. The pro-choice position was supported by Catholics 52% to 40%, by Baptists 50% to 42%, by other Protestants 56% to 36%, and by "Jewish/other/none" respondents 69% to 26%. White fundamentalists opposed choice 55% to 34%, while southern white fundamentalists opposed it 62% to 29%.

Looking at the question from a different angle, 39% believed that abortion should be available to any woman who wants one, 49% said abortion only should be allowed "under certain circumstances," while only 10% said it should not be allowed. From a still different angle, a constitutional amendment to make abortion illegal was opposed 63% to 31% (Catholics, 60% to 35%; Baptists, 55% to 37%; other Protestants, 64% to 30%; "Jewish/other/none," 73% to 19%; white fundamentalists favored an amendment 50% to 45%).

The entire spectrum of Americans were in strong agreement (78% to 20%) with the statement, "Abortion is a private issue between a woman, her family and her doctor; the government should not be involved." By a 74% to 23% margin, respondents agreed that, "Since nobody knows for certain when life begins, people should follow their own moral convictions and religious teachings on the abortion issue." By 60% to 38%, the poll respondents disagreed with the statement, "Abortion is such an important moral issue that the government has to play a role." The differences between men and women respondents on these questions were negligible.

One year later, in January 1989, the Louis Harris polling organization found that by 57% to 40% the public opposes overturning *Roe v. Wade*, while by 68% to 29% they oppose a constitutional amendment to ban abortion.

Breaking down the 57% to 40% opposition to overturning *Roe v. Wade*, Harris found all regions of the country opposing overturning *Roe*, and that opinion favoring retaining *Roe* increased with educational level: 46% of high school dropouts, 57% of high school graduates, 62% of college graduates, and 82% of advanced degree holders favored upholding *Roe*. Political conservatives supported *Roe* by 53% to 45%, moderates by 58% to 41%, and liberals by 67% to 31%. White Protestants supported *Roe* by 55% to 43%, white Catholics by 56% to 42%, Jews by 90% to 10%, while white TV evangelists' followers opposed *Roe* 53% to 42%.

The bottom line is that most Americans clearly favor keeping abortion as a legal option for women with problem pregnancies.

At the heart of the public policy controversy over abortion is the question of when a fetus becomes a person. A fetus is certainly a living organism from conception on. Genetically, it is human, and it is biologically individually unique, except in the case of identical twins early in gestation. However, when is it to be regarded as a "person" with legal rights?

The "pro-life" movement generally holds that a fetus is a person and should be regarded as a *legal* person from conception. As a publication of the National Right to Life Educational Trust Fund puts it, "From this and all other scientific information, we are compelled to recognize that there is no essential difference between the fertilized ovum we all once were, and the embryo, the fetus, the infant, adolescent and adult we all grew or are growing to be." This essentially religious view has been espoused chiefly by the Catholic bishops, some Orthodox Jewish leaders, and a large number of fundamentalist Protestant clergy, such as Jerry Falwell, Pat Robertson, and the late Francis Schaeffer.

Fundamentalists cite biblical texts to support their view of early fetal personhood, but most biblical scholars would agree with Baptist theologian Paul D. Simmons that there is no clear prohibition against abortion in the Bible, though abortion was certainly common when the Jewish and Christian scriptures were being written.

It should be noted that while the main reason for wanting to outlaw abortion *stated* by anti-choice activists is the protection of "preborn persons," there are other motives for opposing choice which are usually kept hidden for obvious political and public relations reasons. One is the traditional position of the Roman Catholic hierarchy that abortion *and* contraception *and* sterilization are always wrong because they frustrate the procreative purpose of sex. Another motive is the widespread male interest in keeping women subordinated. It is no mere coincidence that the strongest voices against freedom of choice on abortion are men, especially those men who are in leadership positions in religious bodies which oppose ordination of women, which opposed the Equal Rights Amendment, and which often oppose contraception, public school sex education, and even the right of women (and men) to legally terminate failed marriages.

The pro-choice case is much more complicated and nuanced. Opinion varies as to when a fetus becomes a person and as to when and under what circumstances choosing the abortion option may be moral. However, there is a consensus that the decision to continue or to terminate a problem pregnancy legally should be left to the individual woman. The pro-choice position is espoused by a wide spectrum of religious bodies, such as the 30 groups which make up the Religious Coalition for Abortion Rights and by the influential Catholics for a Free Choice. (See Appendix B for the positions of pro-choice religious groups.) Religious support for choice is generally grounded on respect for freedom of conscience, free exercise of religion, and the principle of separation of church and state. From the church-state separation point of view, anti-choice laws would be tantamount to laws "respecting an establishment of religion" forbidden by the First Amendment.

The debate over the legal, constitutional, public policy status of freedom of conscience and choice on abortion, then, hinges largely on the question of when legal "personhood" begins. For this reason, Americans for Religious Liberty

5

sponsored a one-day conference in Washington, D.C., on May 30, 1987, to bring together experts from various disciplines to examine and discuss the "personhood" question.

Representing theology were Catholic theologian Marjorie Maguire, associated with Catholics for a Free Choice, and Paul D. Simmons, Professor of Christian Ethics at Southern Baptist Theological Seminary in Louisville. Fredrica Hodges, then executive director of the Religious Coalition for Abortion Rights, spoke for the thirty Christian, Jewish, and other religious groups which make up that organization. Judith C. Rosen is an attorney in private practice and recipient of the Criminal Defense Bar Association of San Diego Board of Directors Award for her work on fetal "personhood" litigation. Janet Benshoof, an attorney, is director of the American Civil Liberties Union Reproductive Rights Project. Michael J. Flower is Visiting Associate Professor of Biology and director of the Science, Technology, and Values Program at Lewis and Clark College, Portland, Oregon. Michael Bennett is professor and chair of the Department of Neuroscience at Albert Einstein College of Medicine. James W. Prescott is a developmental neuropsychologist and former president of the Maryland Psychological Association. Leigh Minturn is a professor of psychology at the University of Colorado. Lynn M. Morgan is an assistant professor of anthropology at Mt. Holyoke College, South Hadley, Massachusetts. Robert T. Francoeur is Professor of Human Embryology and Medical Ethics at Fairleigh Dickenson University, Madison, New Jersey.

Patricia A. Jaworski, producer of the documentary "Thinking about 'The Silent Scream'", received the Americans for Religious Liberty Distinguished Service Award for her work on the fetal "personhood" issue.

(It should go without saying that the views expressed by each of the authors of these papers are his or her own, and do not necessarily imply agreement with the views of the others.)

It is the hope of the authors and editors that this volume will contribute significantly to public discourse on the abortion rights debate.

What is clear to the editors, after hearing the speakers at this conference and after years of involvement in the abortion rights debate, is that the United States Supreme Court was essentially correct in 1973 in acknowledging a constitutional right to freedom of individual conscience on abortion; that any weakening of that right, either by law or judicial fiat, would violate the constitutional principle of separation of church and state and deal a more severe blow to individual liberty than any in our history; and that, while science cannot settle the issue of when legal "personhood" should begin, it clearly does not support the "theology of fetal personhood" held by those who would subordinate women's rights to the whims of lawmakers only a small minority of whom are equipped by nature to get pregnant.

Edd Doerr
Executive Director
Americans for Religious Liberty

The Assaults on Choice

Fredrica F. Hodges

THROUGHOUT HISTORY, women have been portrayed in many different ways as mothers, as educators and even as symbols of the best hopes and highest aspirations of our society. The Statue of Freedom on the Capitol Dome is a *woman* — the Scales of Justice are held by a *woman* — the Statue of Liberty is a *woman*. Yet as our nation celebrates the 200th anniversary of the U.S. Constitution, women have not yet achieved equal treatment under the law, nor have we been fully accepted by either secular society or the religious community as responsible, moral agents before God — especially when it come to making reproductive health care choices in the context of our own lives.

We are all very familiar with the assaults on the external apparatus of choice — the tools and institutions which allow women a wide range of alternatives in reproductive health care decision-making. We know the horror stories of clinic violence and harassment, the horrendous counselling and evangelizing tactics of bogus clinic operations, and the economic warfare against choice through enactment of the Hyde Amendment and other similar legislation.

But I wonder, have we looked squarely at the other, more insidious, and ultimately more dangerous tactics of the anti-choice movement? More insidious and more dangerous because they are harder to combat; because they are *ideas and concepts* that have begun to seep into the collective consciousness of a nation and to affect the very way the public reasons and thinks about the abortion issue.

Due to time constraints, I will resist covering a litany of such issues and address only two, but ask you to remember that there are more.

The Use and Misuse of God and the Bible

First, the use, or as I prefer to think of it, misuse of God and the Bible. The anti-choice movement which claims it does *not* have a religious base, is fervent in its portrayal of the abortion debate as one between the God-fearing and the Godless. Nothing could be further from the truth.

John Connery, a Jesuit scholar, in his history of the abortion issue, writes:

> "If anyone expects to find an explicit condemnation of abortion in the New Testament, he will be disappointed. The silence of the New Testament regarding abortion surpasses even that of the Old Testament."

Despite this silence of the Bible, countless church-goers across America are being told that the Bible condemns abortion. Why? Because the fundamentalists have proof-texted the Bible to make it say what it is they want it to say. The reality is that the pro-choice religious community can counter their arguments by doing the same thing. In fact, the Religious Coalition for Abortion Rights (RCAR) has done it, but we will never publish it because to do so is to be guilty of the same sin. In your packets is a pamphlet by Dr. Roy Bowen Ward from Miami University in Ohio which makes the point that when he was growing up in the Deep South, conservatives used the Bible to support segregation and when people heard that in the churches, they believed it because it was the Will of God. Of course, society has come to realize that the effort to support segregation with the Bible was a clear misuse of the Bible — and it is exactly the same with the abortion issue.

Therefore, it becomes critically important for RCAR to educate the American public to the fact that within mainline religious America there exists a wide range of theological perspectives on the abortion issue and an equally wide range of opinion as to when abortion is morally justified.

The statement, "Life begins at conception. A fetus is a person and, therefore, abortion is murder," demonstrates most clearly why abortion is fundamentally a religious issue. Despite attempts by opponents of abortion to "prove" scientifically that life begins at conception, most medical and theological authorities agree that such a conclusion can be reached only by religious reasoning.

To this day, even the Roman Catholic Church does not have a position on when the fetus becomes a person. The *Declaration on Procured Abortion* issued by the Vatican Congregation on the Faith in 1974 states:

> "It is not up to the biological sciences to make a definitive judgement on questions which are properly philosophical and moral, such as the moment when a human person is constituted..."

It further notes that at present there is no "unanimous tradition" on "the moment when the soul is infused."

In contrast to the Catholic position, Judaism holds that a separate human life, equal to that of the pregnant woman, does not exist until birth. In 1975, the United Synagogue of America, which represents Conservative Judaism, adopted the following statement:

> "In all cases, the mother's life takes precedence over that of the fetus up to the minute of birth. This is to us an unequivocal principle. A threat to her basic health is moreover equated with a threat to her life..."

To give you another direction in which one might go, Christian ethicist Foy Valentine, in an interview in *Christian Life* magazine, offers still another perspective. "I think life began for humanity with creation at the hands of God...and that all human life is an extension in an unbroken chain from Adam and Eve to every single human being alive today..."

With this wide range of approach within the religious community to the concept of when life begins or when personhood is established, the only way for public policy to respond is "carefully and with flexibility." That is, public policy must recognize the diversity of faith perspectives in this country. It must honor the First Amendment. The Supreme Court in its wisdom recognized this diversity in *Roe v. Wade* because it stated:

> "When those trained in the respective disciplines of medicine, philosophy and theology are unable to arrive at consensus as to when life begins, the judiciary at this point in the development of man's knowledge is not in a position to speculate as to the answer."

God and the Bible are also being used to intimidate women, especially those seeking contraceptive and abortion services who accidentally find themselves in bogus clinics. Intense and deeply personal questions are asked of patients without regard for the purpose of their visit and include: "Do you believe in God?" "Do you believe in the Bible?" "Does your God approve of your lifestyle?" "Are the choices you have made and the ones you are about to make going to affect your eternal life? The Bible tells us no murderer has eternal life."

If the patient does not appear frightened by the religious implications of her possible choices, the medical misinformation she is given is sure to discourage any consideration of abortion — information such as, "the chance of hemorrhaging leading to death is very high"; "50% of women getting abortions have serious complications, and oftentimes this leads to the need for a blood transfusion, and the chances of getting AIDS as a result is increasing," and so it goes.

All of this, of course, is done in the name of God and as a ministry to women, whether we want it or not. The reality is that such facilities do not provide a ministry to women, nor a service to those in need. They simply prey on women at a point in their lives when they are most vulnerable.

It is my belief that the pro-choice religious community must be challenged by the existence of these centers. It must affirm women as responsible moral decision-makers, fully capable of weighing their options in the context of their own faith, and within the sight of God. Women in crisis deserve the best of our diverse religious traditions the best of modern medical technology, the best quality health care, the best in supportive, non-judgmental counselling, and above all, respect.

Anti-Choice Rhetoric

The second area which truly concerns me and one which I think the pro-choice movement must address is the anti-choice rhetoric. The anti-choice groups have been extremely successful in creating a powerful public message, at infusing and diffusing images and ideology into the American social fabric without our even knowing it. Their phrases send quick, often subliminal messages. Their rhetoric is combative and the imagery grotesque. Yet the use of these tactics has begun to have some success in making the American people believe that abortion is murder. Even the polls show it.

The anti-choice rhetoric that "abortion is the murder of an innocent human being" takes its toll; it often inflicts pain, grieving and guilt upon women. It can turn honest self-doubt and grief for a very real loss into destructive anger and self-hate. This became most obvious to RCAR after we ran a TV commercial in St. Louis with a Methodist minister in which he said, "I am a Methodist minister. I am pro-choice. I counsel women. Some have abortions, some don't, but the conflict in their lives is real." The phones rang off the hook. "I want to talk to that Methodist minister. I am a Methodist woman who has been grieving over this decision for fifteen years. I haven't told anyone. I am afraid to talk to anyone, but that is a Methodist minister I can talk to." There are woman out there who have somehow internalized the messages of our opposition — they've internalized them to such a degree that they are living with far more grief and guilt than they should ever have to endure.

Where their rhetoric takes hold, it creates an atmosphere that halts reasonable discourse, informed decision-making, and positive empowering actions on the part of the woman. The anti-choice movement provokes a death of spirit and paralysis of will. Their rhetoric is designed to dis-empower women, to reverse the opportunities and challenge of empowerment which the civil rights and women's movements have provided at great cost, all as a result of the big lie.

The "big lie" — the theory that if you say something often enough *and* connect it with real feeling, people will begin to believe it even when they know in their hearts it is not true — is working. We see the technique used in the assertion that "abortion is the American holocaust." The anti-choice forces capitalize on the revulsion and guilt of our society for the brutality and inhumanity of the Holocaust to build a foundation of guilt.

If the anti-choice forces wish those of us who affirm a woman's right to consider the choice of abortion to see ourselves reflected in the mirror of the Holocaust, then I insist they look at themselves in the very same mirror. The Holocaust was the result of the ascendancy of those who would tolerate no ideological diversity, who would recognize no right to disagree with the principles and social programs of National Socialism, and who were ready to trample every noble notion of democracy and of freedom of conscience and religion beneath the boot of brutal conformity to a single system of belief. The Holocaust teaches us a critical historical lesson. Violence of language leads to violence of deed; violence against property leads inevitably to violence against persons.

Either one or both of these issues — the misuse of God and the Bible as well as the impact of anti-choice rhetoric — may seem insignificant to many, but for those of us who spend a great deal of time in the field, the reality is that the impact is significant, especially in the South and Midwest.

RCAR will try to diffuse the impact of the first, but the entire movement must work together to develop a "pro-choice rhetoric" which will have an equally significant impact on the American public.

Symbiosis, Biology, and Personalization

Marjorie Reiley Maguire

THIS CONFERENCE FOCUSING on fetal personhood is important because underneath all the debates about abortion are conflicting beliefs about the personhood of the fetus. It is well to remember that both sides in the abortion debate are operating from beliefs. It is rare that those basic beliefs are explored to understand their strengths and weaknesses, and to see how they impact on other fundamental beliefs and values in our society.

Personhood is a concept that is incapable of empirical proof. It is not a biological judgment. It is a value judgment our society makes about a being. When we say a being is a person, we are saying that it is a being like us, deserving of the rights, privileges, and respect to which we are entitled as members of the human community. There is no biological moment in human development, from the separate sperm and ovum to the octogenarian, that automatically signals the beginning of personhood. However, we as a society have made a value judgment to treat the offspring of human beings as persons, no matter what their intelligence or bodily deformity. We do this because we have decided that it is worth the financial and human cost. To do otherwise would destroy us as a society. If we relegated some of our offspring to less than personal status, we would raise the fear that the personhood of each of us could be negated by society, by majority vote.

When we go back before birth, however, there is not a similar societal need to recognize fetuses as persons. In fact, the societal need is to not recognize the fetus as a person. That is because a decision by society to automatically call the fetus a person, and give it the safeguards of a person, is not an academic exercise. That decision affects the personhood of a whole class of human beings whom society previously had recognized as persons. It denies the personhood of the woman in whose body the fetus lives, and deprives her of the protection of the law. It denies her personhood because it invades her bodily integrity, which is the basis of her personal autonomy. Our society's law, as interpreted in *Roe v. Wade*, protects the personhood of the woman by protecting her bodily integrity and her personal autonomy.

One of the dangers of focusing on the question of the personhood of the fetus in a conference like this is that it gives us the illusion that we could solve the abortion problem, if only we could decide on the personhood of the fetus. Even if we could reach a moral consensus in our society to consider the fetus a person, it would not mean that the law should outlaw abortion. A "fetus-person" is unlike any other being that we designate as "person," because only the fetus uses the body of another human being for its physical life-support system. That fact radically affects the question of whether a "fetus-person" has a right to life. When we speak of a right to life of persons, we do not mean that the right is so absolute that other persons have an obligation to allow the life systems of their own body to be used to support another person's life.

The right of independently living persons to bodily integrity is illustrated by a legal decision that occurred in Pittsburgh in 1978. Robert McFall was dying of bone cancer. He had a cousin, David Shimp, who had matching bone marrow, which might have effected a cure of the cancer. When Shimp refused to donate the bone marrow to McFall, McFall sought a legal judgment ordering Shimp to donate the bone marrow. The judge in the case (with the good Irish Catholic name of Flaherty), ruled that he could not order the donation of the bone marrow, although he considered it morally revolting that Shimp refused to donate.[1] I believe a similar situation exists with the matter of abortion. Even though there are people who consider it morally revolting for a woman to refuse to allow her body to be used for the life support of a fetus, nevertheless, the law should not order that form of life support, any more than it would order one person to donate blood, bone marrow, or a kidney to preserve the life of another person.

It is a determination to preserve this absolute right to bodily integrity for women that underlies the zeal of the pro-choice side of the abortion debate. The anti-abortion side of the debate misunderstands or misconstrues the pro-choice position on bodily integrity, by characterizing it as defense of property rights over the body. The right to bodily integrity has much deeper and more profound roots than property rights. Our body is not like a coat which we can put on. It is not like a house which we inhabit. Our body is the very fabric of our personhood. It is through our body that we weave the person we are, and, to a large extent, it is our body that will determine the kind of person we can become. If another being controls our body, we have no possibility of self-determination, perhaps the most basic right of a person. Thus, if the law can control a woman's body by prohibiting abortion, it is violating its most basic obligation to the woman. It is doing to the woman what Judge Flaherty could not do to David Shimp.

The anti-choice side of the abortion debate attempts to use similar arguments about bodily integrity to defend the right of the fetus not to be aborted. However, even if the fetus is a person and thus does have a moral right to bodily integrity, the fetus is beyond the protection of the law. The fetus can be compared to a citizen of a totalitarian state whose freedom is taken away by the government. As a free society we would like the inhabitants of foreign countries to experience freedom. However, because we do not want to destroy our own society by imposing democracy on another government, we tolerate systems of government which are different than our own, and even governments which we abhor. Similarly, a woman's body is like the borders of a foreign country. There is

---

1 Alan Meisel and Loren H. Roth, "Must a Man Be His Cousin's Keeper," *The Hastings Center Report* (October, 1978), 5-6.

a sovereign immunity to a person's body that the law transgresses to the nation's detriment. The end cannot justify the means of such an invasion, and citizens begin to fear a law which can ride roughshod over this most basic right of personhood.

Thus, even though there are dangers in a conference such as this on fetal personhood, because it could wrongly suggest that personhood is a question subject to empirical verification, and that *Roe v. Wade* is bad law if a fetus is a person, on balance the exploration of the question of fetal personhood is a valuable intellectual exercise. Many, if not most, people do not believe the fetus is a person, at least in the first trimester of pregnancy, when 91% of all abortions are performed. Moreover, there is a psychological discomfort that is raised by the argument I have made above that the law must permit abortions even if the fetus is a person. Therefore, it is a service to both the common sense impressions and the psychological comfort of most people for the participants in this conference to articulate what qualities we believe are necessary for personhood to exist, and why we believe that a fetus is not automatically entitled to be called by that name of "person."

In the remainder of this paper I will discuss the question of what is a person and when personhood begins. I will develop a relational criterion for marking the beginning of personhood. In brief summary, my position is that what makes a being a person is membership in the human community. The touchstone of personhood is sociality. It is not our brain capacity, or the proper number of chromosomes, but our personal relatedness to others that makes us a person. To use the language of Martin Buber, it is when a being becomes a Thou, rather than an It, that it becomes a person. However, the problem comes in deciding when this membership in the human community, this "Thouness," begins.

Before developing this notion of sociality further, it is necessary to consider the biological side of personhood, both its necessity and its insufficiency. Biology is not unimportant to personhood. Human biology is the necessary but not sufficient condition for including a being in the category of persons. Thus, no matter how much a dog or cat becomes related to a person, and even develops some personal characteristics, we will not call it a person. As I said above, our body is the fabric of our personhood. Without the proper biological substrate, there can be no personhood. I find persuasive the arguments of those participants in this conference who argue that there must be sufficient development of the human fetal brain to speak of a biological reality that is the substrate of personhood, and that such development does not occur until about the seventh month of pregnancy. However, I am not unsympathetic to those who find an earlier biological moment sufficient to undergird a judgment that personhood exists in the fetus. What I would demand in either instance, however, is that the biological reality in question be a social being, a member of the human community, before we call it a person.

The insufficiency of biology for defining human personhood is that a purely biological test of personhood reduces persons to simple biological realities. Maybe it is because I come from a religious tradition that I am uncomfortable with a materialistic approach that sees personhood only in terms of biology. Our Western religious traditions see persons as transcendent, spiritual realities who

13

image God in their personhood. However, it seems to me that in the secular world, even among people who have no religion, persons are viewed as transcendent realities. Secular thinkers may not use soul language when they speak of persons, but there is a recognition that persons have a value that non-personal beings in our world do not have. Similarly, our whole Western ethic, even apart from religion, is built on the idea of the infinite value of the human person.

I am concerned that when persons are defined simply in biological terms, there is the danger of writing off people whose biology somehow does not measure up to the standard, "normal" biology. There's a danger of writing off the retarded and the deformed. I want to avoid that because I think that an important insight in our Western culture and our Western religions is that we have believed in affirming the value of even those who are the weakest among us. I am particularly sensitive to this because I had a child who was genetically damaged, who was severely retarded, and who died a few years ago at the age of ten. I realize what minimal brain capacity he had, and yet I am very aware of how much personhood he had. It was dealing with that dichotomy in my own experience that led me to some of my views on the beginning of personhood.

I find it ironic that the reduction of personhood to biology is not done just by some secular thinkers. Biological arguments for personhood are the favored arguments of most anti-abortionists. They hold that it is an empirical fact that personhood begins at conception because at that moment there is chromosomal conjunction and an individualized genetic package. Many of the adherents of this view are religious fundamentalists who would defend the sacredness and transcendent value of even a newly conceived fertilized egg as well as a fetus. They would probably criticize someone like B.F. Skinner as a materialist, for reducing persons to material realities who can be conditioned like any animal in the sub-human species. The anti-abortionists would claim that persons transcend the material world. Yet, in measuring personhood by chromosomal conjunction and the presence of DNA, the anti-abortionists are unwittingly joining the ranks of the materialists.

Having considered the biological aspect of personhood, we can consider the constitutive side of personhood, sociality. To determine the earliest moment when sociality can begin, it may be helpful to work backwards from the latest possible moment that sociality and personhood can be said to begin. I believe that the latest moment to mark the beginning of sociality is birth. I would argue, and I believe that most people would agree with me, that at least birth marks the beginning of membership in the human community, even if no earlier moment in fetal development does. Birth puts into our midst a being that has come from a member of our species, that looks like us, and that elicits from us a certain sense of obligation. It calls forth personal obligations from us. It is personally related to us as a fellow human, whether we like it or not.

There are philosophers, such as Michael Tooley,[2] who use a criterion for personhood that makes personhood begin even later than birth. Such philosophers would argue that infanticide is not really the killing of a person, that an infant is an extended fetus. Some of the papers presented at this conference dis-

---

2 Michael Tooley, "Abortion and Infanticide," *Philosophy and Public Affairs* 2 (1972), 37-65.

cuss social groups which hold such a belief. However, I think that arguments for recognizing the beginning of personhood at a point later than birth do not track with the common experience and common thinking in our culture. Moreover, I think there would be too many problems in our culture connected with accepting a moment later than birth as marking the beginning of membership in the human community.

It is also feminism that also makes me uncomfortable with locating the beginning of personhood at a moment later than birth. Some of the other participants in this conference are writing about birth ceremonies that are used in some cultures to mark the beginning of personhood or membership in that human community. Without specifically critiquing any of those presentations, I find it negates women's experience and women's part in the personing process to use a point after birth to mark the beginning of personhood. It has been typical of patriarchal culture to fixate on a ceremony other than birth to purify a newborn of women's involvement in the process of its becoming, and to allow the men to take over and assume control of the process. It is not just primitive cultures that do this. Christian Baptism, which is often described as being "born again," can be seen as one such attempt of men to negate the value of the physical birth which came from a woman's body.

In arguing that birth marks the latest possible moment when we should make the value judgment that personhood exists, I am not arguing that life can never be terminated after birth. I am saying that if life is terminated after birth, it is the life of a person that is terminated, not the life of a nonpersonal entity. In the Baby Doe controversies, which raise the question of whether seriously disabled newborns should receive medical intervention that will prolong their life, but also prolong their suffering, the issue is not whether the newborn is a person. The issue is whether we, as a society that values persons, owe all persons life-prolonging medical intervention, or whether allowing death is sometimes the best gift we can give to persons, and the gift most respectful of their dignity. The abortion issue is different. There, a central aspect of the controversy is the question of whether the fetus is a person.

However, our problem in this conference is not to decide whether personhood exists after birth, but whether personhood exists before birth. I would suggest that there is a moment earlier than birth that can mark the beginning of personhood. My position is that the only way a fetus can become a member of the human community, and therefore a person, prior to birth, is if the woman in whose body it exists welcomes it into the human community by her consent to the pregnancy. It is the consent of the woman to continuing the pregnancy that marks the beginning of personhood, no matter how unwillingly that consent is given. It is when she treats the biological reality within her as a Thou, that it becomes a Thou rather than an It. And it is when she treats it as a Thou, that society also has an obligation to treat it as a Thou. Thus, once a woman has accepted a pregnancy, society has an obligation to give her the medical and nutritional care she needs to bring a healthy person into the world at birth.

One woman may rejoice in a pregnancy and consent to it as soon as she knows she is pregnant. Another woman may not consent to the pregnancy and instead seek an abortion. My theory of personhood allows us to think of the first woman as carrying a person within her, while not thereby thinking that the second woman has killed a person by obtaining an abortion. It allows us to talk on one hand of a fetus as a patient, when it is a wanted fetus and the mother is undergoing surgery to correct a problem with the fetus; and yet, on the other hand, we would object to forced surgery on a pregnant woman, even when the surgery is necessary to save the life of the fetus. This theory explains how we could be horrified for the fetus as well as the woman, if someone battered a pregnant woman and caused her to lose a wanted fetus; and yet we are not horrified about the loss of fetal life when when a doctor performs an abortion on a woman who does not want the fetus. It can make us sympathetic to those who want criminal punishment for "fetuscide" in the first case, while the notion of criminal punishment is totally inappropriate in the case of the abortion provider. (This is not to say that punishment for "fetuscide" would be a good public policy when someone causes the death of a wanted fetus.)

To those who search for a neat moment that marks the dividing line between non-person and person, the determinant of personhood that I have proposed may seem wifty and relativistic. However, I have found that using consent of the woman to pregnancy as the marker of the beginning of personhood corresponds to the experience of many women. When I have explained my theory to women, they have agreed with it, telling me that when they had been pregnant with a wanted fetus, or had accepted an initially unwanted pregnancy, they though of the fetus in personal terms. When a pregnancy lacked acceptance or consent they thought of the fetus only as a biological object in their body. Besides corresponding with the actual experience of women, my theory also coincides well with biological information on brain development and symbiosis, as well as with elements of traditional Catholic philosophy and theology.

One of the participants in this conference, Pat Jaworski, has an excellent presentation on the physical development of the brain. One of the things that impressed me about what she has to say is that, even at the basic, cellular level of our being, there is a basis for a paraphrase of John Donne's poem about humans. We can truly say. "no [cell] is an island." The brain does not develop and reach maturity because of the appearance of new individual, isolated cells, but by the relatedness, the connectedness, that develops among the cells. The neurons of the brain do not function in splendid isolation. It is the tendrils going out from each neuron, and the synapses connecting them all, that indicate a mature human brain. Without a minimum level of connectedness, human activity is impossible. This theory of brain development seems to confirm at a biological level that I am correct in my theory that relationship is significant for the beginning of personhood. However, in my theory the personhood of the fetus is not dependent on brain development. I hold that the fetus is a person as soon as there is personal relatedness between the mother and the fetus, even if that is considerably prior to the development of all the physical connections in the fetal brain.

Biology can also provide an interesting complement to my theory in the phenomenon of symbiosis. Symbiosis is a category that is used by biologists to describe the living together of different organisms. There are three kinds of symbiosis, each classification depending on the benefit or harm derived by the host organism from the symbiotic relationship. Commensalism denotes a relationship in which the host organism is neither benefited nor harmed by the symbiosis. Mutualism denotes mutual benefit to both the host and dependent organism. (This is the relationship which the generic word "symbiosis" usually describes.) The third kind of symbiotic relationship, parasitism, signifies a relationship in which there is injury to the host organism and benefit to the guest organism.

At the biological level, a specific symbiotic organism relates in only one way to its partner symbiotic organism. However, at the human level, the symbiotic relationship of pregnancy can be either commensalism, mutualism, or parasitism. Since the host organism in a human pregnancy has a psychic and social dimension to her being, evaluation of benefit or harm to the host organism cannot be measured simply in physical terms. How the woman relates to the pregnancy will determine whether the fetus provides benefit to the woman, or whether it is a parasite on her. When the relationship between mother and fetus is mutually beneficial (mutualism), there is an intertwining of the psychical being, as well as the physical being, of mother and fetus. We could consider the fetus as participating in the mother's personhood. It is for this reason that we can view personhood as beginning when the woman consents to the pregnancy.

The credentials I bring to this conference are not the credentials of a biologist or even a philosopher, but the credentials of a theologian - a Roman Catholic theologian. Therefore, I will end this presentation with some remarks on fetal personhood in the Catholic tradition. It may come as a surprise that it has never been the teaching in the Catholic Church that the fetus is a person from the first moment of conception. Since 1869, the Church has excommunicated women who committed the sin of abortion,[3] but the Church did not simultaneously teach as dogma that the fetus is a person. It could not do so, because Catholic theology considered the presence of a soul as marking the beginning of personhood. The dominant theological theory about the presence of a soul in a fetus had been the theory of "delayed ensoulment." The most influential proponent of this theory in Catholicism was St. Thomas Aquinas, although the theory goes back to Augustine and even Aristotle.

The theory of delayed ensoulment is based on the Aristotelian notion that everything is composed of matter and form. A particular form cannot be combined with just any matter. Matter and form must go together. Form can only be combined with matter that is suited to give expression to that form. In a human being the matter is the body; the form is the soul. According to the theory of delayed ensoulment, the human soul could not be joined to embryonic matter in the early stages of pregnancy, because that matter is not sufficiently developed to receive a human soul. It is not fitting matter for a soul. A human soul can only be infused into a *human* body, and for a body to be human, it has to be able to func-

---

3 Contrary to popular thinking a woman is not excommunicated simply for the fact of having an abortion. She has to commit the *sin* of abortion. In Catholicism there are three requirements for an act to be a sin. It has to be an evil act. (The Church hierarchy would say all abortions are evil acts.) The person doing the act must believe that it is evil. Finally the person must decide to do it anyway, thus going against what their conscience tells them about right and wrong. Thus, the woman who does not believe that her abortion is an evil act has not committed the *sin* of abortion.

tion as a human body. This theory of delayed ensoulment was actually a very modern, evolutionary insight that provides a traditional basis for the kind of developmental view of personhood that I have presented in this paper. (However, the way Thomas Aquinas applied the theory was not helpful. He taught that it only took 40 days to get the body of a male fetus prepared to receive a soul, while it took 80 days to get the body of a female fetus prepared to receive a soul.)

This theory of delayed ensoulment has been so strong in Catholic philosophy that even the present Vatican has not adopted a contrary theory on the beginning of personhood. In its 1974 *Declaration on Procured Abortions* and in its 1987 *Doctrinal Statement on Human Reproduction*, the Vatican Congregation for the Doctrine of the Faith (successor to the Office of the Inquisition) stated that it was taking no position on when the soul is infused into the body, and thus on when personhood begins. The Vatican's position is that the fertilized egg should be treated as if it is a person from the first moment of conception, even though we cannot know whether it is a person or not. Of course the problem with that approach is that it violates the rights of someone whose personhood is not in doubt. We could also treat trees as if they were persons, if it did not detract from the personhood of those we already recognize as persons!

While it has not been the "common and constant teaching"[4] of the Catholic Church that abortion involves taking the life of a person, the Church did condemn abortion as wrong from the early centuries of the Church. However, abortion was not condemned as a sin of murder, but as a sin of contraception, and as the sin of attempting to hide a sexual sin like fornication or adultery. The Catholic Church got its views on contraception, not from its religious roots in Juadaism, but from the very pervasive and influential pagan philosophy of Stoicism. The Stoics taught that it is reason which makes us a person. Passion and emotion identify us with the animals. Since sexuality is passionate and emotional, rather than rational, the Stoics viewed sexuality as a problem. However, they realized they could not completely condemn sexuality, if they wanted the human race to continue. Thus, the Stoics came up with the notion that sexual activity was a good thing for humans to engage in, only if it was for the purpose of procreation. Early Christian philosophers, particularly St. Augustine, adopted this line of thinking from the Stoics, and incorporated it into Christian ethics. Thus, abortion was seen as an extension of other forms of contraception, all of which were viewed as evil. This ancient pagan position on sexuality still pervades the halls of the Vatican, and underlies the Vatican's condemnation of abortion.

Because Catholic teaching on sexuality is infected with this "original sin" of Stoicism, Catholic thought could never fully appreciate the need to respect the bodily contribution of women in the reproductive process. Although Incarnation -- the enfleshment of God -- is a central doctrine in Catholicism, and although a central philosophical doctrine in the writings of Thomas Aquinas is the essential union between body and soul, Catholic teaching has downplayed the

---

4 This language is used by the Catholic bishops to lend authority to the Church's current teaching on abortion. It simply is not the case, as I have briefly shown in this article, that the teaching has been either clear or constant. For a short history of abortion in Catholicism see Daniel C. Maguire, "The Catholic Legacy & Abortion: A Debate," *Commonweal* 114 (1987), 657-62.

importance of embodiment to personhood. Therefore, the Catholic hierarchy has missed the connection between a woman's full personhood and her personal autonomy over her bodily integrity. That is why Catholic leaders have been able too facilely to prefer the potential rights of the fetus to the actual rights of the pregnant woman.

As a theologian, I want to end my presentation in a religious vein. I turn to Judaism for a powerful example of respect for women's welfare within the divine economy of salvation.[5] In The Talmud, the rabbis taught that the fetus was not a person until the head or greater part had emerged in the birth process. Thus, the fetus could be killed for the welfare of the mother, but once the birth process had begun, and the head or greater part of the fetus had emerged, the mother could not be preferred to the half born person because both "persons" were of equal value.

This teaching of the rabbis gave rise to the question of whether abortion could be performed under a broad definition of the "welfare" of the pregnant woman. One such case that arose was the question of whether a woman could abort because of the probability that she would give birth to a defective child. The answer of the rabbis was that a woman could not abort to save her child from future suffering, but she could abort to save herself from the mental anguish of having such a child. The reasoning was that the child's future is in God's hands. The mother's present is in our hands and we have a duty of compassion toward her.

The various sides in the abortion debate would do well to heed the counsel of those rabbis. Present, actual needs take precedence over future, potential needs. The rights of persons take precedence over any rights of potential persons. There can be no respect for "fetal personhood" in a society that does not respect the personhood of the pregnant woman. But there can be no respect for the woman if there is not respect for her personal autonomy over her bodily integrity.

---

5 For my information on Jewish teaching on abortion I have relied on David M. Feldman, "Abortion: Jewish Perspectives," *Encyclopedia of Bioethics*, Vol. I, edited by Warren T. Reich, (New York: The Free Press, 1978), pp. 5-8. See also, Feldman, David M. *Birth Control in Jewish Law: Marital Relations, Contraception and Abortion as Set Forth in the Classic Texts of Jewish Law*. (New York: Schocken paperback, 1974).

The Fetus as Person:
A Biblical Perspective

Paul D. Simmons

DO THE SCRIPTURES of the Old and New Testament teach that the fetus is a person and that abortion is murder? Should evangelical Christians seek to ban all abortions by supporting the Human Life Amendment or similar legislative proposals? Does the Bible treat the unborn as of "equal worth" to the woman morally and spiritually and thus provide "equal protection" under the Law? Can it be shown that the Bible supports the notion that one is a person *from the moment of conception*?

Such questions are basic to the contemporary debate about the moral and legal issues concerning abortion. If the questions above are answered in the affirmative, evangelical Christians will probably support efforts at legislative and judicial levels to overturn *Roe v. Wade*, the 1973 Supreme Court decision legalizing abortion in America. Certainly there are prominent Fundamentalist preachers involved in what has been called The New Religious Right who are working to ban abortion.[1] They claim that the Bible is their authority and assert that God has called them to this action.

Jerry Falwell, founder of the Moral Majority (now Liberty Foundation), has probably been the most effective religious leader in the new coalition. He is joined by Pat Robertson, founder of the 700 Club and erstwhile candidate for the Republican nomination for President of the United States. Numerous other groups led by conservative Christian preachers have joined the effort to outlaw abortion. Christian Voice, Christian Action Council, the Religious Roundtable, American Coalition for Traditional Values, and Concerned Women for America all claim the Bible as the source of their determination to outlaw abortion.

The religious and moral fervor of these zealous Christians has been combined with sophisticated political strategies, effective marketing slogans, and ex-

---

[1] Not all Fundamentalists are involved in activistic politics. Many are still convinced that "politics is dirty business" and compromises Christian convictions and thus remain aloof from the world of organized politics and its strategies to dominate public policy. The term "militant" or "New Right" Fundamentalist is intended to designate those who are deeply committed to and actively involved in efforts to achieve their moralistic and religious goals through political processes. The most prominent example is that of Moral Majority, led by Jerry Falwell, but would include people like Pat Robertson, Jimmy Swaggart, Tim LaHaye and certain leaders in the Southern Baptist Convention.

tensive funding. Abortion is certainly not the only issue pursued by this powerful coalition but it is the major issue on the agenda of the religious groups.[2] The coalition claims to be pro-family, pro-God and pro-America, which has both intrinsic and extensive appeal among American Christians.

The adamant opposition to legalized abortion among these evangelical Christians has also made possible a coalition with traditional Roman Catholicism. For the first time ever in American politics fundamentalist Protestants have combined efforts with conservative Catholics. The reason for the cooperation can be found in their theology of fetal personhood. Harold O.J. Brown argues that "The Bible prohibits the taking of innocent human life. If the developing fetus is shown to be a human being...(or) if human life has begun, then abortion is homicide and is not permissible."[3] Pope Pius XII, arguing from tradition and natural law, declared that "Innocent human life in whatever condition it is found, is withdrawn, from the very first moment of its existence, from any direct deliberate attack."

A Human Life Amendment that declares that Constitutional protection "to life, liberty and the pursuit of happiness" should be accorded a fetus *from the moment of conception*, is thus supported by this coalition. The effects of such a law would go far beyond abortion, of course,[4] but it is perceived as the final solution to an ultimate problem. It is felt that the excesses of elective abortion justify the absolutist position even though such a law would certainly create other difficulties, such as, not permitting abortions even in cases like rape and incest.

The Personhood of the Fetus

The basic theological-biblical question, of course, is that of the personhood of the fetus. New Right Christians contend (1) that the fetus is a person, and (2) that abortion is murder. Francis Schaeffer has been terribly influential among evangelicals and has argued against abortion claiming the Bible prohibits the practice. Along with U.S. Surgeon General C. Everett Koop, he produced a five-episode color motion picture series entitled "Whatever Happened to the Human Race," based on their book by that title. They argue that science proves that one is a person at the moment of conception. "No additional factor is necessary for a later time," say Schaeffer and Koop. "All that makes up the adult is present as the ovum and sperm are united--the whole genetic code."[5] They thus adopt what is called a genetic definition of personhood--a unique code is in fact a unique person and it should be given constitutional protections. Thus, whether a fertilized ovum is in the fallopian tubes of a woman or in a petri dish in a laboratory, it is regarded as a human being made "in the image of God" and deserving legal protection as a person.

---

2 Other issues include opposition to gay rights, ERA, sex eduction, drugs and pornography. They are strongly anti-communist, and advocate prayers in public schools, a hawkish foreign policy, public support for private (religious) schools and free enterprise.
3 Harold O.J. Brown, *Death Before Birth* (Nashville: Thomas Nelson, 1977), p. 119.
4 Certain forms of contraception, such as the IUD, and the newly developed RU-486, would also be instruments of murder.
5 Francis A. Schaeffer and C. Everett Koop, *Whatever Happened to the Human Race?* (Old Tappan, N.J.: Fleming N. Revell, 1979), p. 41.

Proponents of legalized abortion and women who consider or complete elctive abortion are subjected to moral harangue portraying them as "baby killers" and "murderers." Harsh invectives are employed, even drawing parallels to the Nazi genocidal efforts against the Jews. A crusade has developed that often uses morally questionable means in doing battle against what is characterized as the great social and moral evil of the day.

There are several reasons this argument has appeal among evangelical Christians. One is rooted in the powerful emotional attachment that many women feel to the fetus during pregnancy. A relationship develops in which the pregnant woman senses the "otherness" of the fetus and the mother-to-be feels protective and nourishing toward this new life within her. For millions of couples, the fetus is experienced as a person and strong symbiotic ties are felt virtually from the time of conception. No one could possibly convince the couple that what she is carrying is not a person. This experience of a joyous pregnancy and the thrill of anticipated parenthood convince them otherwise.

Second, Christians know that God is the author and giver of life. The Creator has brought all that is into existence out of nothing. The Bible declares that "it is in Him that we live and move, and have our being" (Acts 17:28). Grateful parents understand the passage that says "lo, children are a heritage of the Lord" (Psa. 127:3). Numerous other passages could be cited that express the Christian belief that God the Creator is the source of life.

Third, there is a certain logic to the argument about uniqueness and the genetic code established at conception. No one can deny that each person started with conception. Human life is on a continuum from conception to death. What is started with fertilization develops through various biological stages during gestation, birth, infancy, childhood, adolescence, and adulthood. A person's individual traits are programmed by the particular arrangement of one's DNA code.

Reasons like these are often given by those evangelical leaders who are working to ban abortion. But do these arguments really support the case being made? Profound questions need to be raised as to the basis for these arguments and the manner in which they are applied.

Notice, first of all, the logical problem involved in the genetic definition of personhood, or the notion that a zygote (fertilized egg still in the fallopian tubes of the woman) is a person. Knowing that there is a continuum in development from fertilization to maturity and adulthood does not mean that every step on the continuum has the same value or constitutes the same entity. The best analogy is that of a fertilized hen egg. Given the proper incubation, the egg becomes a chicken and the chicken grows to become a hen or rooster. However, few of us are confused about the entity we are eating when we have eggs for breakfast. An egg--even a fertilized egg--is still an egg and not a chicken.

The genetic definition of personhood confuses potentialities with actualities. Potentialities are certainly important but they do not have the same value as actualities. "An embryo is not a person but the possibility or the probability of there being a person many months or even years in the future," Charles Hartshorne has argued. "Obviously possibilities are important, but to blur the distinction between them and actualities is to darken counsel."[6] The same point is made by John Stott in saying that the decision to abort for reasons of maternal health is "a choice between an actual human being and a potential human being."[7]

The fallacy of believing a zygote is a person is also seen when the argument is reduced *ad absurdum*. Every body cell of a person contains one's DNA, or genetic code. This is why, theoretically at least, persons may be cloned or duplicated. If one uses the genetic definition of person one would have to regard every body cell as a human being since each cell has the potentiality for becoming another person through cloning. Think also of the implications of this definition for surgery or the excision of cancer cells from the body!

The fatal weakness of this argument is its radical reductionism. The easy equation of "person" with "fertilized ovum" (zygote) moves from a terribly complex entity to an irreducible minimum. A zygote is a cluster of cells but hardly complex or developed enough to qualify as "person." A person or human being has capacities of reflective choice, relational response, social experience, moral perception and self-awareness. Both the person and the zygote have "life" and both are "human" since they belong to *homo sapiens*. But neither a zygote nor a blastocyst fully embodies the qualities that pertain to personhood. A great deal more complex development and growth are necessary before the attributes of "person" are acquired.

There can be no argument about whether or not the woman is a person. She bears fully the "image of God" (Gen. 1:27). She is actually, not just potentially, a person. Any discussion of fetal rights to protection, care, and happiness must in no way diminish her constitutional rights. Since she is truly a person, all constitutional rights must be accorded her without question. To do otherwise is to treat her as an object, to de-personalize her and deprive her of God-given rights. The fetus has value but not the same value as the woman; its rights are always relative to and inferior to hers.

Searching the Scriptures

The way in which the Bible is used is also important in the abortion debate. Two principles of biblical interpretation must be kept in mind when using the Bible to provide warrants, backing, or supports for a particular teaching. The first is that the text must be thoroughly examined for its specific meaning. The historical and textual context, the nature of the material, the meanings of terms, and other factors will all need to be assessed in coming to a clear understanding of the meaning of the passage.

The second principle of interpretation/application is that a text or passage cannot be used to settle a technical question that is not specifically dealt with in the text. Literary devices such as metaphor and symbol cannot be pressed into the quest for scientific data, for instance, nor can a passage cast in a celebrative,

6 Charles Hartshorne, "Ethics and the Process of Living," Conference on Religion, Ethics and the Life Process. Institute of Religion and Human Development. Texas Medical Center, March 18-19, 1974.
7 John Stott, "Reverence for Human Life," *Christianity Today*, June 9, 1972, p. 12.

doxological mood be used as if it were a descriptive, systematic, and thus defini-tive explanation of a more technical problem. In short, a text must not be used to draw conclusions that are not germane to the text itself.

These principles are important to bear in mind when searching the Scripture for teaching regarding the personhood of the fetus. Anti-abortion evangelicals are fond of citing over one hundred biblical passages which they regard as teaching that the fetus is a person. An examination of some of the more impor-tant passages reveals the problems involved in such applications.

Psalm 139:13-15 is an oft-quoted text that bears examination:

> "For thou didst form my inward parts (kidneys), thou didst knit (weave) me together in my mother's womb... My frame (bones) was not hidden from thee when I was being made in secret, intricately wrought in the depths of the earth."

Anti-abortion evangelicals take this passage as teaching that the fetus is a person. They further argue that the Psalmist is saying that God caused the preg-nancy and knew him during gestation.

Numerous problems are posed by this interpretation, not the least of which is the fact that the Psalmist was not dealing with the question of abortion. He is free to use poetry and metaphor without trying to be precise or definitive about the point in gestation at which one is regarded as a person. In short, a non-tech-nical, poetic passage is used as if it were a careful, technical and systematic decla-ration regarding personhood. The Hebrews did not think in abstract terms or deal with the stages or processes of gestational development.

Further problems emerge if the passage is taken for its literal meaning. If it is truly a factual or technical statement, scientific understandings of gestation are challenged. The Psalmist's reference to being "wrought in the depths of the earth" reflects the notion that the fetus (or the self) was developed "in the earth" and then introduced into the woman's womb. Plato's *Republic* (III, 414, C-E) recorded the Phoenician myth about people being formed and fed in the womb of the earth, which provides an interesting comparison to if not parallel to the Psalmist's statement.

It is also possible that the passage reflects the Aristotelian idea that the male sperm is the complete seed from which the offspring comes. The male sperm, it was believed, was like the acorn or maple seed. All that is required is a proper in-cubation environment. The woman is only the incubator for the genetic material provided by the man.

The text is a poetic way of celebrating God's love for people. The Psalmist declares that God's love surrounds the person in every corner or dimension of existence. He captures the exhilaration and thrill of religious wonder as he re-flects upon the marvel of one's being in and before God. The person is a creation of the power of God and is doubly blessed when one's being is enraptured by knowing that we are not the power of our own existence and that we can know the Creator who has brought us into being. The 139th Psalm is understandably important in the worship and liturgy of Judaism and Christianity. It enables the believer better to celebrate one's being and relates it to God's caring love.

Those who treat this passage as a definitive, scientific teaching confuse po-etry with prose and a mood of celebration with the need for explanation. The purpose of the passage is to capture the celebrative mood of joy and wonder in being for those who can reflect upon their origins and contemplate what it means to be before God. There is absolutely no intention or purpose in the text to deal with the question of elective abortion or whether the fetus is a person. The speaker reflects the awareness that we all begin prior to birth and that the entire creative process is a source of mystery and awe. All that is is rooted in the creative and mysterious ways of God who brings us into being. It is another declaration of the truth that "it is God who has made us and not we ourselves" (Psa. 100:3).

The passage thus reflects the foundational awareness for the Judaeo-Christian doctrine of God as Creator. God is the source of all that is. He is the power that has transformed organic life from simplicity to complexity through a process of patient sovereignty. The most complex expression of life is found in personal existence--in the self-awareness and reflective self-transcendence of human beings. Knowing anything, however, is to know that we are not self created. Life is not self-generating. Only God can bring something into being out of nothing. The distinctive question for religion is not *how* God has accomplished that miracle--that question belongs to the domain of scientific investigation. The biblical faith affirms that it is *God* who has made us.

A second passage often cited by anti-abortionists is Jeremiah 1:5 where the prophet declares, speaking for God:

"Before I formed you in the belly I knew you; and before you came forth out of the womb, I sanctified you, and I ordained you a prophet unto the nations."

Shoemaker says this passage ascribes personhood to all unborn fetuses.[8] The text will not bear the weight of such an application, however. The passage deals with Jeremiah's calling as a prophet. He is establishing his credentials as one who has been called and appointed by God. His emphatic declaration is that God brought him into being for this very purpose (Cf. Isa. 49:1-5). Thus, the passage is highly personal and specific. It is not a rational discourse on how God creates people or whether every fetus should be counted as a person. Jeremiah declared that God *knew* him, and *consecrated* him. He is making no similar claim for everyone. All this supports his central claim that God is the reason for his existence and the source of his authority to preach as a prophet. Shoemaker's claim that this passage teaches that God causes every pregnancy and that the fetus is a person is bogus interpretation/application for it perverts and distorts the central meaning of the text which deals with prophetic calling, not conception.

A similar problem is posed by the anti-abortion interpretation of Luke 1:41-42 which deals with the meeting between Mary and Elizabeth both of whom were pregnant. Elizabeth, six months pregnant with the one destined to be the forerunner of Jesus, John the Baptist, heard the voice of Mary, who has just discovered that she is pregnant. Luke says:

"And when Elizabeth heard the greeting of Mary, the babe leaped in her womb; and Elizabeth was filled with the Holy Spirit and she exclaimed with a

---

8 Donald Shoemaker, *Abortion, the Bible and the Christian*, (Cincinnati: Hayes, 1976), p. 37.

loud cry, 'Blessed are you among women, and blessed is the fruit of your womb!'"

Again, anti-abortion evangelicals take this as a passage teaching that fetuses are people, focusing as they do on "the babe leaped..."

Problems abound with such an interpretation. The passage makes it clear, for instance, that it is Elizabeth who responds to God's revelation. She did the speaking, declaring the special blessedness of Mary and her child to be. The central point of the passage is theological and practical. It deals with the special role and authority of Jesus. The relation of John to Jesus was a source of considerable confusion during their ministries. The Gospel writers took pains to spell out the fact that John was a forerunner to Jesus, the Messiah, the Son of God. This crucial theological point should not be missed. John was a special servant of God, but was subservient to Jesus, a point emphasized at Jesus' baptism (Matt. 3:13-17; Jn. 1:29-34) and elsewhere (Cf. Mk. 1:4-11; Matt. 11:2-6; Lk. 7:18-23).

It is faulty biblical interpretation to generalize from this passage to the personhood of (every) fetus. Such an approach confuses the intention and meaning of the text with a contemporary debate entirely foreign to the mind of the writer. One might more reasonably use the passage to argue that "quickening" or viability at about the sixth month of pregnancy should be the state of development at which the fetus might be regarded as a person. Even this application is an inference, however, and should not be regarded as a clear teaching of the text in question.

The Biblical View of Person

Nowhere in the Bible is there a clear, precise explanation of personhood. Even so, it provides definitive guidance for the crucial issues of the personhood of the woman and the question regarding the value of fetal life. Notice that the Biblical portrait of person does not begin with an explanation of conception but with a portrayal of God's creating Adam and Eve, the parents of the human race. God created them as male and female. Three texts are of critical importance in understanding the uniqueness of the person-creature. The first is Genesis 2:7, which declares: "Then the Lord God formed man of dust from the ground, and breathed into his nostrils the breath of life; and man became a living soul." The biological aspects of personhood are metaphorically portrayed in terms of "dust" or "clay." God as the origin and giver of life is captured by his breathing life into the clay he has fashioned. The declaration "became a living soul" designated a person as animated flesh. As the person is breathed into, so a person breathes.

The second text distinguishes persons from the animal creation. Genesis 1:27 declares that "God made man in his own image, in the image of God he created him; male and female created he them." The biblical portrait of the uniqueness of personhood centers in the notion of *the image of God*, which is not a physical likeness but a similarity of powers or abilities. These capacities or powers are spiritual, personal, relational, moral and intellectual. Of all the creatures fashioned by God, only people are able to relate to the creator in obedience or rebellion. Only they experience those God-like powers of self-transcendence and self-awareness. People know that they exist and reflect on the meaning of existence. This creature, like God, may be introspective, retrospective and pro-spective. This one may reflect upon the past, anticipate the future and discern the activity of God in his/her personal life and history.

The third text portrays the person as a moral decision-maker. In Genesis 3:22 God says: "behold, mankind is become as one of us, to know good and evil..." To be a person is to be a choice maker, reflecting God's own ability to distinguish good from evil, right from wrong. This passage does not say that people have perfect knowledge of right and wrong as some intrinsic gift from birth. Decisions must be made on the basis of their understanding of God's will. The fact that they "ate of the tree of knowledge of good and evil" means that people are given the burden and responsibility of making decisions that reflect their unique place in God's creation and purposes in history.

The Biblical portrait of person, therefore, is that of a complex, many-sided creature with god-like abilities and the moral responsibility to make choices. The fetus hardly meets those characteristics. At best, it begins to attain those biological basics necessary to show such capacities with the formation of a neo-cortex or no earlier than the second half of gestation.

This distinction seems basic to the Biblical story in Exodus 21:22-25--an important passage for the abortion debate. Here is an account of a pregnant woman who becomes involved in a brawl between two men and has a miscarriage. A distinction is then made between the penalty that is to be exacted for the loss of the fetus and any injury to the woman. For the fetus, a fine is paid as determined by the husband and judges (verse 22). However, if the woman is injured or dies, *lex talionus* is applied: "thou shalt give life for life, eye for eye, tooth for tooth, hand for hand, foot for foot, burning for burning, wound for wound, stripe for stripe" (vs. 23-25).

The story has only limited application to the current abortion debate since it deals with accidental, not willful, pregnancy termination. Even so, the distinction made between the protection accorded the woman and that accorded the fetus under covenant law is important. The woman has full standing as a person under the covenant; the fetus has only a relative standing, certainly inferior to that of the woman. This passage gives no support to the parity argument that gives equal religious and moral worth to woman and fetus.

The one who unquestionably fits the biblical protrayal of person is the woman or mother in question. Certainly, the entire circle of those most intimately involved with the abortion question are persons--considering the data, weighing the facts and values at stake, reflecting on the meaning of this moment, anticipating the future and making some decision. The abortion question focuses the personhood of the woman, who in turn considers the potential personhood of the fetus in terms of the multiple dimensions of her own history, religious beliefs, and the future.

This is a god-like decision. Like the Creator, she reflects upon what is good for the creation of which she is agent. As steward of those powers, she uses them for good and not ill--both for herself, the fetus, and the future of humankind itself. She is aware that God wills health and happiness for herself, for those she may bring into the world, and the future of the human race. Thus, she is engaged in reflecting on her own well-being, the genetic health of the fetus, and the survival of the human race.

Anticipatory Personhood

Some light might also be shed on the abortion debate by distinguishing between actual personhood and anticipatory or attributed personhood.[9] To put it another way, there is both an objective and a subjective side to regarding the fetus as person. Objectively, for instance, the fetus is not a person for it has not acquired the capacities or characteristics that define an entity as a person. Subjectively, however, the pregnant woman or the couple in question may regard the conceptus as a person and provide it with all the respect and protection a person should be accorded.

Couples who want a child and plan a family may and should regard the conceptus as a person. The pregnant woman may joyfully welcome the news that she has a baby on the way. By talking to the fetus, stroking the bulging womb, and celebrating the pregnancy, the child is brought into the circle of the human family. It is not yet a person, but it is already regarded as--it is named and accepted as--a person.

The essential difference between attributing personhood to the fetus and knowing that it is not *actually* a person is the value of the fetus to those involved in the pregnancy. It is not *vitality* but the acceptance, affirmation, recognition, and love for the fetus that grants personhood and assures that it will become a person. The symbiotic bonding between mother and child is the basis for experiencing the fetus as person--as an entity of personal worth. A woman who wants a child and values her pregnancy will be convinced that she is carrying a baby, a person. No other designation conveys the reality of this experience of one who is "other" than the mother. She recognizes it as another self; it is not a "thing" nor simply a part of her body.

This important human phenomenon of attributed personhood is sometimes overlooked by those who support the legal availability of abortion and believe elective abortions are morally justifiable under certain circumstances. The search for objective criteria for personhood often seems cold and calculating to those who have only experienced the joyous, celebrative side of pregnancy. It is unbelievable to them that any woman would choose to terminate a pregnancy. They often react with fear, horror and anger at people they believe to be unappreciative of the value of gestating life.

The mistake made at that point is to confuse anticipatory with *actual* personhood. To experience a fetus as person is not the same as discovering the personhood of the fetus. The fetus is not a person by any objective criteria, but may most certainly be attributed or *ascribed* personhood on highly subjective grounds.

Not every pregnancy results in a personal relationship between woman and fetus, of course. Pregnancy is not always a happy occasion. It may be a destructive experience fraught with horror and threat to the woman. Far from being re-

---

9 See Paul D. Simmons, *Birth and Death: Bioethical Decison Making*, (Philadelphia: Westminster, 1983), pp. 171ff. where the importance of this distinction is applied to considerations regarding biotechnical parenting.

garded as a person to be protected and loved, a conceptus may be experienced as a threat to the woman's well-being (tubal pregnancy, emotional burden), a reminder of sexual abuse (rape or incest), or the dangers attending the processes of conception and gestation (radical fetal deformity).

Extreme caution is necessary when moving from positive experiences that cause people to sing the praises of God when pregnancy occurs (I Sam. 2:1; Gen. 21:16), to conclude that every similar occasion should be equally celebrated. The human experience of pregnancy is tremendously varied and reactions to or understandings of God's activity are understandably different when the occasion is joyous than when it is tragic or burdensome. This problem focuses the issue of divine providence in the human experience of pregnancy under adverse circumstances. If God is to be praised and his glory celebrated when people experience the joys of pregnancy and childbirth, is the experience of pregnancy always to be regarded as the action of divine providence?

Personhood and Providence

What is at issue is the way God is related to the processes of conception and birth or the processes of nature as such. Fundamentalists often portray God as the cause and power of all that is and argue that God is behind all natural events.

Believing that the workings of nature are virtually the actions of God is important for the absolutism of their stance against abortion. Not only is the conceptus held to be of equal value and personhood with the woman, conception is regarded an act of God. The pregnancy would have to be a direct threat to the life of the woman for abortion to be morally justifiable. Then, it would be an act of self-defense. All other pregnancies are to be accepted, regardless of extenuating circumstances as in rape, incest, or fetal deformity.

Shoemaker's argument against abortion in case of rape is typical. He begins with a *non sequitur* about not executing the rapist for the crime and asks rhetorically if we then are to mete out capital punishment upon the innocent unborn? He then sets forth the clinching argument, by saying: "God forbid that we should regard any situation as so tragic that God could not have prevented it if he so chose."[10] He proceeds to apply the same logic to cases of incest and fetal deformity. For him, God makes no mistakes!

In effect, Shoemaker is arguing that God is responsible for the pregnancy by rape. God wills the pregnancy since "he could have prevented it." Logically, Shoemaker would also have to argue that God is responsible for the rape since the rape "could have been prevented" and since the rape was necessary for the impregnation!

What is at stake in the Fundamentalist position is a hyper-Calvinistic stress on the sovereignty of God. It combines theological beliefs about the power and activity of God with a type of "law of nature." As Waltke says, "the causal connection between sexual intercourse and conception...is simply the means whereby God, the first cause of all things, gives his blessing."[11] In other words, however it

10 Shoemaker, p. 30.
11 Bruce K. Waltke, "Reflections from the Old Testament on Abortion," Address to the Evangelical Theological Society, Dec. 29, 1975, p. 11.

happens in nature is the way God does it. No moral significance is made of the fact that between 25 and 50 percent of all pregnancies end without implantation and thus the zygote passes through the monthly menses of the woman. Spontaneous abortion is not morally questionable since God causes these.

This line of reasoning extends to the problem of radical fetal deformity. Shoemaker assures believers in such cases that "God makes no mistakes!" U.S. Surgeon General C. Everett Koop even argues that God creates genetic handicaps! He cites God's speech to Moses in Exodus 4:11: "Who has made man's mouth? Who makes him dumb, or deaf, or seeing, or blind? Is it not I, the Lord?"[12]

Explaining why God would do such things may take one of two forms. Either (1) it is a punishment for sin, or (2) it is an opportunity for Christian growth in spirituality. Shoemaker comforts the woman raped and impregnated by assuring her that "no testings will overtake one except those God has permitted men (sic!) to experience."

Such views of divine providence pose profound problems regarding the use of Scripture and a Christian understanding of the problem of evil. Using God's statement to Moses to explain genetic deformity is a faulty understanding based on bogus exegesis. The context was Moses' reluctance to become God's spokesman, fearing he would not be persuasive. "Dumb," "deaf," and "blind" are metaphors of speaking and understanding God's truth. This passage has nothing whatever to do with genetic handicaps.

Of greater significance is the question of the moral nature of God. Jesus emphatically rejected the notion that God causes evil things to happen to people either as punishment for sin or as a test of faith (Matt. 12:22-26; Luke 11:14-23). The Christian belief is that God is love (1 John 4:8) and that His actions are good not evil (Matt. 19:17). Arguing that God either causes or permits rape or incest and consequent pregnancy, or that God causes every hideous anomaly is to say blasphemous and heretical things about God. Central to the teaching of Jesus was the idea that God is love and goodness. He emphatically denounced and refuted the traditional theology that God caused evil things to happen. He drew a very simple test for deciding: "If you who are evil know how to give good gifts to your children, how much more shall your heavenly Father give good things to those who ask him?" (Mt. 7:11).

For some people, it is more acceptable to portray God as cruel than to suggest he may not be in total control. However, to blame evil on God is to risk confusing the work of Beelzebub with that of the Holy Spirit (Matt. 12:22-36; Luke 11:14-23). Jesus made it plain that an accounting would be made of those who attribute evil to God.

A second problem posed by a Fundamentalist notion of providence deals with the role of persons as stewards in the processes of nature and medical science. People are portrayed as the passive victims of whatever may befall. God only gives strength to bear the tragedy. It is unthinkable, however, to believe that people, made in the image of God, may have to make some god-like decisions re-

---

12 See C. Everett Koop, "Deception on Demand," *Moody Monthly*. May, 1980, p. 27.

garding their stewardship of procreative powers as in abortion. This is "forbidden territory" for human intervention.

However, this religious approach is contradictory. Though it is argued that nature's way is God's way, it is also argued that doctors should intervene to keep nature from terminating a deformed fetus, as in spontaneous abortion. They cannot have it both ways. To adopt the passive, non-interventionist posture is to undermine religious support for all of medical science.

Is it not more consistent to follow the clue given in a doctrine of Christian stewardship? As stewards, people work with God for the good of the entire created world--people, nature, and world alike. Our knowledge of the processes that hinder or help gives a divine mandate to make choices that help rather than hinder. We know that mistakes are made in nature--that genetic codes can become terribly confused. When something goes wrong in nature, we are morally required to correct the problem if possible. Choice not chance becomes the divine mandate. We cannot be indifferent to the anguish and burden of genetic deformities and illnesses. Increased knowledge of genetic processes provides a grand opportunity to help prevent mistakes by nature. Confused genetic codes result in terrible burdens for people. Being responsible stewards of genetic knowledge requires making decisions about the genetic health of children. Until the codes can actually be corrected, abortion for genetic reasons will remain a responsible option many will choose. We may decide to abort as stewards of genetic knowledge and as guardians of the future.

The third problem with the Fundamentalist view of providence concerns its limited and inadequate view of grace. Shoemaker declares that God gives "sustaining grace" to those afflicted with pregnancy by rape or incest or those bearing fetuses which are radically deformed. That God does provide sustaining grace in such situations we do not doubt. But does grace not also give permission to act in spite of ambiguity and with boldness lay hold of the promise of forgiveness?

Karl Barth shows remarkable insight into the power and profundity of the human experience of the grace of God and he pointed to the paradox in the command of God with regard to abortion. He set the subject in the context of "The Protection of Life" and explained "the great summons to halt issued by the command" forbidding the willful taking of human life.[13] Barth thundered God's "No!" to any such action.

However, there is another side to God's command, said Barth. After hearing the "no!" we must be prepared "...to stand by the truth that at some time or other, perhaps on the far frontier of all other possibilities, it may have to happen, in obedience to the commandment that man must be killed by man."[14] Certainly, the life of the unborn is not an absolute value--it is not a person. Nor can the unborn claim to be preserved in all circumstances. God may command the active participation of others in the killing of germinating life.14 When he does, it does not constitutue murder.[15]

---

13 Karl Barth, *Church Dogmatics,* III/4 (Edinburgh: T.T. Clark, 1961), p. 416.
14 Ibid., p. 420.
15 Ibid., p. 421.

It is noteworthy that, while Barth is quoted by anti-abortionists to support their stand, they never mention the fact that he also supported abortion. Barth saw a paradox at the heart of the Biblical view of human stewardship in the protection of germinating life. The freedom to abort is a necessary part of the meaning of the grace of God in the tragic circumstances of life.

Conclusions

Biblical understandings of personhood explain the profound silence of the Bible on the matter of elective abortion. That there are not prohibitions in either the Old nor the New Testaments is rather amazing if the Bible is so clear in its teaching against the practice as New Right Fundamentalists claim. Certainly we know there were harsh penalities for abortion found among surrounding mid-Eastern cultures. The Assyrian code (ca. 1500 B.C.) declared that "any woman who causes to fall what her womb holds...shall be tried, convicted and impaled upon a stake and shall not be buried." The Hebrews knew of such codes which tacitly acknowledge that abortion was practiced.

The absence of specific prohibitions in Scripture could mean either: (1) no Hebrew or Christian ever terminated a problem pregnancy, or (2) abortion was a private, personal and religious matter, not subject to civil regulation. The latter seems the more plausible explanation. Hebrew law gave considerable status to women in contrast to the harsh and repressive attitudes toward woman found in surrounding cultures. Women were equal bearers of God's image (Gen. 1:27) and equal sharers in the tasks of stewardship (Gen. 1:29-30). The emphasis fell upon the woman as one with the god-like ability and responsibility to make choices. As a person before God and others she bears the unique burden of decision making regarding God's will and her procreative powers. The abortion question focuses the personhood of the woman who reflects on the meaning of her pregnancy, considers the data, examines her motives and moral commitments, and anticipates the future. The decision is uniquely hers for the pregnancy is highly personal. It was not socially regulated among the Hebrews except as specified in Exodus 21 (see above).

The same pattern prevailed in the New Testament era. Even Paul, the great apostle who gave directions for moral living to Christians in pagan society, made no mention of abortion. For all his practical guidance, not once does the subject appear in his lists of vices or prohibited actions. Apparently, he regarded abortion as a matter to be dealt with on the basis of faith, grace and Christian freedom. In this matter, the believer is to "work out your own salvation in fear and trembling..." (Phil. 2:12).

The absence of prohibitions against abortion does not mean either that abortion was widely practiced or that there was a cavalier attitude about pregnancy termination. Then as now elective abortion poses substantive issues with which a woman or couple must come to terms. Respect for germinating life, one's own moral and religious beliefs, life plan considerations, and special circumstances will all enter the deliberation. Certainly reasons beyond mere convenience will be needed to offset the gravity of terminating germinal existence. Abortion is seldom to be encouraged but it is not a forbidden option.

Contemporary Christians will do well to follow the biblical pattern in treating the subject of elective abortion. The claim that the Bible teaches that the fetus is a person from the moment of conception is problematic at best. Such a judgment rests on subjective and personal factors, not explicit biblical teachings. The Bible's portrait of person centers on the woman and the man who unquestionablly bear the image of God and live in responsible relation to him.

Further, the absence of civil prohibition--even in a theocratic society!--is a worthy model to follow. The biblical writers' silence reveals a becoming reticence to judge too quickly concerning the morality of another person's choice. It is eloquent testimony to the sacredness of this choice for women and their families and the privacy in which it is to be considered. God's grace is extended to those who accept the responsibilities of parenthood to make difficult choices in the midst of the moral ambiguity of tragic and perplexing circumstances.

A Legal Prespective on the Status of the Fetus:

Who Will Guard the Guardians?

Judith C. Rosen
With the Assistance of
Kate G. Turnbull

"It is required that the thing killed be *in rerum natura*. And for this reason if a man killed the child in the womb of its mother: this is not a felony, neither shall he forfeit anything, and this so for two reasons: first, because the thing killed has no baptismal name; second, because it is difficult to judge whether he killed or not, that is, whether the child died of this battery of its mother or through another cause."

- Sir William Stanford (1509-58), Book One, Chapter 13.

"...[T]he word 'person', as used in the Fourteenth Amendment, does not include the unborn. ...We need not resolve the difficult question of when life begins. When those trained in the respective disciplines of medicine, philosophy and theology are unable to arrive at any consensus, the judiciary, at this point in the development of man's knowledge, is not in a position to speculate as to the answer."

U.S. Supreme Court, *Roe v. Wade*, 410 U.S. 113 (1973).

"Assuming custody over the fetus, and appointing an attorney to represent 'the interests of the unborn child', the Supreme Court of Georgia affirmed a lower court's ruling finding '...that as a matter of fact the unborn child is a human being fully capable of sustaining life independent of the mother' and ordered the mother to undergo a caesarian section without her consent."

Jefferson v. Griffin Spaulding City Hospital (1981) 274 S.E.2d 457.

(Jessie Mae Jefferson delivered vaginally and safely before the decree was implemented.)

A SURVEY OF case law and legislative trends suggests while neither English nor American law had ever regarded the fetus as a person "in the whole sense" before *Roe v. Wade*, that decision precipitated a legal/emotional reconsideration of the fetus' status in the courts and state legislatures. Our judges and lawmakers have failed to heed Justice Blackmun's admonishment: "[o]ur task, of course, is to resolve the issue by constitutional measurement, free of emotion and of predilection."

The trimester paradigm suggested in *Roe* and the court's recognition of the state interest in potential life during the last weeks of pregnancy to restrict and regulate abortion, is being distorted to justify ignorance of customary legal rights of women, characterization of the fetus as "patient", and legislative enactments of feticide statutes and fetal abuse laws.

Indeed, current law suggests a trend to treat the fetus as warranting legal protection for its own sake. Some urge scientific advances and medical technology, giving us a more visible fetus, provides justification to redefine the fetus in the eyes of the law. Others reveal their motivation to overrule *Roe* and outlaw abortion. Still others view the fetus as a helpless victim they must protect. Some frame the issues as the right to privacy vs. the right to life. But few lawmakers exert pressure to enact and fund healthcare systems which will better serve the needs of the pregnant woman and our next generation.

According the fetus personhood status is already creating complicated legal problems. Some women are being subjected to criminal prosecution, loss of job, loss of their child, and even forced surgery. They are labeled neglectful, abusive, and even tort feasor. Misuse of the law in defining the fetus as person has the further detrimental effect of distracting policymakers and healthcare providers from using their creative energies and resources to resolve complex health and societal problems through prenatal care and education - the best protector of fetal health and wellbeing.

Moreover, such an unprecedented clash of rights raises difficult questions requiring creative answers. This conference brings together professionals from four disciplines: theologians, neurobiologists, cultural anthropologists, and lawyers, to discuss the perspective of the fetus as seen from each experience. In so doing, we collectively acknowledge the enormous complexity of the question. But we must do the asking; for others will decide they can be answered simply - and then, who will guard us from the guardians?

As an attorney in private practice, I had the opportunity to represent Pamela Rae Stewart on a volunteer basis on behalf of the San Diego Chapter of the American Civil Liberties Union. Ms. Stewart faced jail and criminal charges for allegedly failing to follow her doctor's advice during her pregnancy. The San Diego County District Attorney filed these charges despite the absence of a fetal abuse statute. This paper presents a perspective on the legal status of the fetus from a review of the cases and commentaries, as well as from first-hand experience representing a woman caught in the fray.

Pamela Rae Stewart was not so much a national heroine as a real human being who suffered anguish and embarrassment under the specter of prosecution while the pundits "analyzed" her life and her motivations.

> Ever since the District Attorney's office decided to accuse Pamela Rae Stewart of abusing her yet to be born fetus, she has been stripped of her privacy and dignity.
> The El Cajon woman has been pinched and poked in the public spotlight, her motives and judgment questioned.

...The limelight brought Stewart only humiliation. Reporters examined and discussed the prenatal warning her doctors supposedly gave her. They held back nothing, not even the details of her last sex act before the baby was delivered.

Pamela Rae Stewart had been reduced to an object of national debate.
- *The San Diego Evening Tribune.* November 11, 1986 editorial.

No paper on the legal perspective of the fetus can avoid the landmark decision *Roe v. Wade*. Those legal commentators fearing academic demise found lifeblood in that decision. A wealth of comment, analysis, and prediction has followed setting out the legal status of the fetus. This paper, then, does not redo what is already available, but presents an overview of the cases that best illustrate the current issues and a bibliography to serve as resource.

First, a brief review of the caselaw before *Roe v. Wade*, a discussion of *Roe* and later United States Supreme Court cases reaffirming its significant points will be briefly summarized. Some recent lower court decisions and state legislative enactments since *Roe* will be described that best illustrate the current trend to give the fetus legal status. But, as will be seen, current decisions appear to avoid constitutional analysis of competing interests, misconceive *Roe v. Wade*'s holding, and inappropriately rely on decisions and policy in one area of the law as precedent for another; they make bad law. Finally, there will follow a discussion of the implications if the state courts and legislatures continue this trend.

Some courts' willingness to respond to emotional outcries and rush to judgment reflects a certain legal egocentricity. Doing all we can to protect our next generation requires a more complex interdisciplinary approach; this conference is a far wiser alternative.

The Legal Status of the Fetus Before *Roe v. Wade*

The rights and protection accorded the fetus prior to the Surpeme Court's *Roe v. Wade* decision have been summarized and discussed by a number of commentators.[1] Before 1973, courts addressed the legal status of the fetus, depending upon the area of law in question, but in no sense did the fetus achieve personhood status. The limited recognition of the fetus was not the result of heated judicial debate about whether the fetus was a "person", but rather a reflection of the policy goals inherent in different areas of the law.

American courts first considered the status of the fetus in property and inheritance disputes. When a fetus existed at the time of death of the testator, the

---

1 See, for example, Loisell, Abortion, The Practice of Medicine and the Due Process of Law, 16 UCLA L. Rev. 233 (1969); Means, The Law of New York Concerning Abortion and the Status of the Fetus, 1964-1968; A Case of Cessation of Constitutionality, 14 N.Y.L.F. 411 (1968); Means, The Phoenix of Abortional Freedom: Is a Penumbral or Ninth-Amendment Right About to Arise from the Nineteenth-Century Legislative Ashes of a Fourteenth-Century Common Law Liberty?, 17 N.Y.L.F. 335 (1971); Quay, Justifiable Abortion - Medical and Legal Foundations, 49 Geo. L.J. 395 (1961); King, the Juridical Status of the Fetus: A Proposal for Legal Protection of the Unborn, 77 Mich. L. Rev. 1647 (1979); Johnsen, the Creation of Fetal Rights: Conflicts with Women's Constitutional Rights to Liberty, Privacy, and Equal Protection, 95 Yale L.J. 599 (1986); Shaw and Damme, Legal Status of the Fetus in Genetics and the Law II (A. Milansky, G.J. Annas, eds. 1980); Nelson, "Forced Medical Treatment of Pregnant Women: 'Compelling Each to Live as Seems Good to the Rest'" 37 Hastings L.J. 703 (1986).

fetus was considered eligible to inherit provided it was subsequently born alive.[2] If a man were to die unaware of the existence of a fetus, it was assumed he would want the resulting child to benefit from his estate.

Thus, at common law, the court's concern was with effectuating the intent of the deceased, not with the personhood of the fetus. This policy is reflected in the current Uniform Probate Code: "Relatives of the decedent conceived before his death but born thereafter inherit as if they had been born in the lifetime of the decedent."[3]

Similarly, in the criminal law, the fetus was not recognized as a "person". In fact, at English common law, terminating a fetus was not an indictable offense. However, by the eighteenth century, English courts were willing to uphold convictions for homicide if the victim was a "quick" fetus, who was born alive and who survived and breathed for a short period of time, only to subsequently die as the result of injuries inflicted prenatally.

The requirements of quickening and live birth are deeply rooted in history and have an evidentiary basis as well. The notion of quickening was based on St. Augustine's belief that the human embryo was inanimate for an indeterminable time after conception, but then became animate, after which the destruction of the embryo was murder and punishable by death. To this theory St. Thomas Aquinas added the refinement that life is demonstrated by two actions, knowledge and movement. He theorized that soul is the first principle of life and soul entered the body of the embryo at the time of first movement. Bracton subsequently equated the perceptible movement in the womb with quickening. The concept of quickening led to the common law rule stated by Blackstone that "life...begins in contemplation of law as soon as the infant is able to stir in the mother's womb."

Abortion law in the United States evolved from the English common law position: no indictment would lie for aborting a consenting woman before quickening, but would lie for such an act after quickening.[4] In 1821, Connecticut became the first state to enact abortion legislation; it applied only to those women who were "quick with child". It was not until 1860 that abortion before quickening was made a crime in the state. In 1828, New York adopted legislation

---

2 See, e.g., *Cowles v. Cowles*, 56 Conn. 240, 13 A. 414 (1887); *Christian v. Carter*, 193 N.C. 537, 137 S.E. 596 (1927).
3 Uniform Probate Code, Section 2-108 (1983); see also, *Matter of Peabody*, 5 N.Y.2d 541, 158 N.E.2d 841 (1959)
4 See, Means, The Law of New York Concerning Abortions, *supra*, note 1 at 426.
There was a long period during which English and American women enjoyed a common law liberty to terminate at will an unwanted pregnancy, from the reign of Edward III to that of George III. This common law liberty endured, in England, from 1327 to 1803; in America, from 1607 to 1830. "If the mother destroy hir childe newely borne, this is Felonie of the death of a man, though the childe have no name, nor be baptised. And the justice of peace may deale accordingly. But if a childe be destroyed in the mother's belly, is no manslayer nor Felonie to be imprisoned upon this statute." (William Lambarde "Offices of the Justices of Peace" (1581).)
From time immemorial until 1803, abortion was and always had been, in England, a crime at canon law, of purely ecclesiastical cognizance. Thus, abortion was not a felony because it was a purely ecclesiastical offense, and always had been, even in Anglo Saxon times. In 1661, the common law privilege against self incrimination was extended to the canonical tribunals. Therefore, it became impossible even for the Church of England to compel a religiously observant woman to testify against herself by giving evidence of fetal life prior to an abortifacient act, and without such evidence, conviction of such a canonical crime, though still theoretically possible, had become a practical impossibility. Means, "The Phoenix of Abortional Freedom: Is a Penumbral or Ninth-Amendment Right About to Arise from the Nineteenth-Century Legislative Ashes of a Fourteenth-Century Common Law Liberty?", 17 N.Y. Law Forun 336 (1971).

that served as a model for early anti-abortion statutes. The statute barred destruction of an unquickened fetus as well as of a quick fetus; however, destruction of a quick fetus was second degree manslaughter, the other only a misdemeanor.

Between 1830 and 1850 a number of states followed New York's lead and enacted anti-abortion statutes. As the court noted in *Roe v. Wade,* most of the statutes "dealt severely with abortion after quickening but were lenient with it before quickening."[5]

By the end of the 1950s, a large majority of the jurisdictions banned abortion, however and whenever performed, unless done to save or preserve the life of the mother.[6]

The Supreme Court addressed the issue of the policies behind restrictive abortion statutes in its opinion in *Roe v. Wade.* While clearly there was no single intention of the various state legislatures, the Court found that the states were attempting to protect women from what was once a dangerous medical procedure. The status of the fetus has undergone fundamental change in the area of tort law. In 1884, Holmes wrote that "[a]n unborn child has no existence as a human being separate from its mother; therefore it may not recover for the wrongful conduct of another."[7] The courts used a number of rationales for denying recovery to a child for harm inflicted in utero. Some courts simply held that the fetus was a part of the woman, not a separate individual.[8] Since, in many instances, a third party would have no notice that the fetus existed, the courts held a third party could owe no duty toward the fetus.[9] Additionally, courts feared that a cause of action might lead to fraudulent or spurious claims,[10] or claims brought on behalf of the fetus against the mother.[11]

The major changes in tort law came primarily as a result of challenging the notion that the fetus was a part of the mother. In *Bonbrest v. Katz,*[12] the court permitted recovery for prenatal injuries if the injury occurred after viability and the fetus was subsequently born alive. The court pointed out that a viable fetus can live apart from its mother and so should not be considered a part of her. Later courts focused on the need to compensate a living person wrongfully injured rather than on the legal status of the fetus. "If in the meanwhile those processes [which will ultimately result in a human being] can be disrupted resulting in harm to the child when born, it is immaterial whether before birth the child is considered a person in being."[13]

---

5 410 U.S. 113, 139 (1973).
6 See Comment, A Survey of the Present Statutory and Case Law on Abortion: The Contradictions and the Problems, 1972 U. Ill. L.R. 177.
7 *Dietrich v. Inhavitants of Northampton,* 138 Mass. 14 (1884).
8 "That a child before birth is, in fact, a part of the mother, and is only severed from her at birth, cannot, we think, be successfully disputed. The doctrine of the civil law...that an unborn child may be regarded as *in esse* for some purposes, when for its benefit, is a mere legal fiction, which, so far as we have been able to discover, has not been indulged in by the courts of common law to the extent of allowing an action by an infant for injuries occasioned before its brith." *Allaire v. St. Luke's Hospital,* 56 N.E. 638, 640 (1900).
9 *Drobner v. Peters,* 232 N.Y. 220, 133 N.E. 567 (1921).
10 *Stanford v. St. Louis - San Francisco Ry. Co., et al.,* 108 So. 566 (1926) ("...many cases might arise...where the recovery would be based upon the merest conjecture or speculation as to whether or not the prenatal injury was the cause of the death or condition of the child.")
11 *Allaire,* 56 N.E. at 640 ("If the action can be maintained, it necessarily follows that an infant can maintain an action against its own mother for injuries occasioned by the negligence of the mother while pregnant with it.")
12 65 F.Supp. 138 (D.D.C. 1946).
13 *Smith v. Brennan,* 31 N.J. 353, 157 A.2d 497 (1960).

Thus before *Roe*, the law recognized that the fetus had certain limited rights, such as inheritance, and was entitled to certain projections, such as the right of recovery, if born alive, for prenatal injury. But as our highest court concluded after reviewing the early cases, "Neither English nor American law has ever regarded the unborn as legal persons in 'the whole sense'."

Roe v. Wade

The *Roe v. Wade* decision overturned a Texas criminal law which made it a crime to procure an abortion except to save the life of the mother.

The court held that the fundamental right of privacy "is broad enough to encompass a woman's decision whether or not to terminate her pregnancy." But, the court stated:

> "[t]he pregnant woman cannot be isolated in her privacy. She carries an embryo and later a fetus... As we have intimated above, it is reasonable and appropriate for a state to decide that some point in time another interest, that of the health of the mother or that of potential human life, becomes significantly involved. The woman's privacy is no longer sole and the right to privacy she possesses must be measured accordingly."

While the court found that states had a compelling interest in the potential life of a fetus after viability - when it could survive on its own - it did not find that fetuses have a right to life at any time in their gestation. The court specifically held that a fetus is not a person within the language and meaning of the Fourteenth Amendment[14], and it specifically declined to resolve the difficult question of when life begins.

The court defined viability as the point at which the fetus is "potentially able to live outside the mother's womb, albeit with artificial aid" and "observed that [v]iability is usually placed at about seven months (28 weeks) but may occur earlier, even at 24 weeks." The court explained:

> "[w]ith respect to the state's important and legitimate interest in potential life, the 'compelling' point is at viability. This is so because the fetus then presumably has the *capability of meaningful life outside the mother's womb*... If the state is interested in protecting fetal life after viability, it may go so far as to proscribe abortion during that period *except when it is necessary to preserve the life or health of the mother.*"

Thus, even in the comparatively narrow context of abortion regulation, *Roe v. Wade* made clear that the State's interest in a woman's life and health predominates. Indeed, as one commentator noted "[a]s a matter of constitutional law, ...the State's interest in protecting fetal life is not so compelling as to be absolute. Rather, this interest is limited by the mother's right of privacy and by her own interests in the preservation of her own life and health. Consequently, it is simply

---

14 The Fourteenth Amendment states: All persons born or naturalized in the United States and subject to the jurisdiction thereof, are citizens of the United States and of the State wherein they reside. No State shall make or enforce any law which shall abridge the privileges or immunities of citizens of the United States; nor shall any State deprive any person of life, liberty, or property, without due process of law; nor deny to any person within its jurisdiction the equal protection of the laws.

wrong to assert that *Wade* grants the State unqualified authority to protect the fetus or an unlimited power to prohibit abortions after viability."[15]

In fact, "[t]he *Roe* decision has served as a key precedent in the rapid expansion of legal protection for individual rights of personal autonomy and bodily integrity in an increasing number of contexts, expecially medical decision making. Yet even as *Roe* has emerged as a guarantor of constitutional protection in gender neutral, non-abortion contexts, it has been increasingly subjected to a crabbed and mechanical interpretation in cases involving women's reproductive freedom. ...[A]s political and medical preoccupation with the fetus has increased, *Roe* has come to be used as a legal weapon against pregnant women - invoked as authority not only for restrictions on their liberty but even for actual physical invasions such as court ordered caesarian sections."[16]

Since *Roe v. Wade* made clear that the woman's interest in her health and life continues to outweigh any asserted state interest in potential life after viability, that case cannot be read to authorize serious invasions of woman's life, health and personal autonomy. To do so "...represents a serious distortion of that landmark case."[17]

Nevertheless, current caselaw suggests that *Roe v. Wade* is so misconceived. The following section will detail recent caselaw and acts of state legislatures which treat the legal status of the fetus as warranting protection for its own sake. The misinterpretation of *Roe* and the judicial emotional reaction to fetal rights advocates, has resulted in a number of recent cases and statutes which appear to accord legal personhood to the fetus. The issue as framed by those who claim to be protectors of the fetus, actually put the fetus more at risk.

Recent Developments in the Law and the Legislatures

While the United States Supreme Court continues to reaffirm *Roe v. Wade*, some courts and state legislatures misconceive its holding and analysis. Perhaps they do so since while the high court continues to recognize and acknowledge the woman's rights to privacy in the abstract, it continues to deliver mixed messages. This is particularly true for poor women who suffer from absence of Medicaid funds and decent public services and for teenage women who in many states are hindered by parental consent or notification requirements.[18]

Thus, some lower courts assert that the State's interest in potential life at viability justifies ignorance of the pregnant woman's interests altogether. These decisions virtually ignore our highest court's continued explanation that viability is a necessarily fluid concept "the determination of which must be a matter for the judgment of the responsible attending physician". *Planned Parenthood of Central Missouri v. Danforth*, 428 U.S. at 64, 96 S.Ct. at 2839, *Colautti v. Franklin* (1979) 430 U.S. 395, 397, 99 S.Ct. 675.

---

15 Nelson, "Forced Medical Treatment of Pregnant Women", *supra* at p. 742.
16 Gallagher, Janet. "Fetal Personhood and Woman's Policy", *Women, Biology and Public Policy*.
17 Hubbard, Ruth. "Legal and Policy Implications of Recent Advances in Prenatal Diagnosis and Fetal Therapy", 7 Women's Rights Law Reporter 3:201-218, Spring 1982, hereinafter Hubbard.
18 (See, for example, *Harris v. McRae*, 448 U.S. 297 (1980).

"Because of the number and imposition of these variables, the probability of any particular fetus obtaining meaningful life outside the womb can be determined only with difficulty. Moreover, the record indicates that even if agreement may be reached on the probability of survival, different physicians equate viability with different probabilities of survival, and some physicians refuse to equate viability with any numerical probability at all."

Colautti v. Franklin, supra, 439 U.S. at 396.

And, some lower courts ignore that a different analysis is required *outside* the context of abortion where a woman choses to carry her pregnancy to term.

Court Ordered Obstetrical Interventions[19]

A recent survey investigated the scope and circumstances of court ordered obstetrical procedures in cases in which a woman had refused therapy deemed necessary by a physician for the sake of the fetus and reported alarming statistics:

"Court orders have been obtained for caesarian sections in eleven states, for hospital detentions in two states and for intrauterine transfusions in one state. Among 21 cases in which court orders were sought, the orders were obtained in 86%; in 88% of those cases, the orders were received within six hours. Eighty-one percent of the women involved were Black, Asian, or Hispanic, 44% were unmarried, and 24% did not speak English as their primary language. All the women were treated in a teaching hospital clinic or were receiving public assistance."[20]

The report acknowledged that "[a]mong the most harrowing experiences for obstetricians is the refusal of therapy by a pregnant woman. For physicians who are specially trained in monitoring fetal well being, such refusals may appear callous or irrational."[21]

The commentators conclude that "[c]ourt ordered interventions may ultimately cause more problems than they solve. They rest on dubious legal grounds, they expand rather than limit physician's liability, and could adversely affect maternal and infant health."[22]

The report is based upon lower court decisions which are often unpublished and do not represent the state of the law. Some of these decisions pervert the state's interest after viability. But as *Thornburgh, supra*, makes clear, any state interest in the potential life of the viable fetus must be subordinated to the health and safety of the pregnant woman.

Other courts misapply rationales applicable in one area of the law to justify their decisions in a completely different context. Thus, for example, some courts in justifying forced caesarian sections rely on the expansion of liability for wrongful fetal death in tort law. However, even though wrongful death statutes

---

19 The alleged necessity of many caesarian sections has come under increasingly critical scrutiny. See, for example, The Caesarian Birth Task Force, National Institutes of Health Consensus Development Statement on Caesarian Childbirth, 357 *Obstetrics and Gynecology* 537 (1981); Guillenim, Babies by Caesarian: Who Chooses, Who Controls?, 11 *Hastings Center Report* 15 (June 1981), cited in *Hubbard* at pp. 213-214.

20 Kolder, M.D., Gallagher, and Parsons, M.D., "Court Ordered Obstetrical Interventions" *New England Journal of Medicine* 316:1192-6 (May 7, 1987) (hereinafter *New England Journal*).

21 *Id.*

22 *Id.*

may permit recovery for the loss of a pregnancy, such decisions represent efforts to compensate prospective parents for their loss rather than recognition of the fetus as a person. Most cases in negligence and malpractice suits for prenatal injuries require live birth so that the right to recover damages belongs not to the fetus but to a live-born independent person.

Furthermore, some court-ordered caesarian cases misinterpret precedent. For example, in Colorado, the court assumed jurisdiction over the fetus in the juvenile court to take physical custody of the pregnant woman and order her to undergo a caesarian section. In so doing, the Colorado trial court relied on *People v. Estergard*, 169 Col. 445, 457 P.2d 698 F(1969), which held that the juvenile court had jurisdiction to determine paternity prior to birth and to order support payments. In *Estergard*, however, the court had viewed itself as implementing the clear legislative purpose of the paternity law by preventing the father from evading responsibility for support by simply leaving the state before the birth. Moreover, there was not, as there is in the caesarian section cases any conflict between the interests of the pregnant woman and the fetus.

Similarly, reliance upon two blood transfusion cases - a 1964 New Jersey Supreme Court case - *Raleigh Fitkin - Paul Morgan Memorial Hospital v. Anderson*, 42 N.J. 421, 201 A.2d 537, cert. denied, 377 U.S. 985 (1964), and *In Re President of Georgetown College, Inc.*, 331 F.2d 1000 (DC Cir.) cert. denied, both upholding orders authorizing blood transfusions to nonconsenting patients is also specious. Specifically, *Raleigh Fitkin*, decided in 1964, reflects neither the reassessment of the pregnant woman's constitutional rights provided by *Roe v. Wade* in 1973, nor the notion that the right to privacy includes the right to refuse treatment affirmed by the New Jersey Supreme Court in *In Re Quinlan*, 70 N.J. 10, 355 A.2d 647.

The *Georgetown College* decision likewise fails to reflect the values articulated later in *Roe v. Wade*. The case was decided by a single circuit judge and the appellate court denied rehearing since the woman had received the transfusions and left the hospital. Of interest, Circuit Judge (former Chief Justice) Burger would have dismissed the petition for want of a justiciable controversy because the hospital had no legally protected right warranting judicial interference. This, he maintained, was not an area for judicial action, being among "*those matters which are strictly a private concern and thus beyond reach of all governmental power*". Cases involving Jehovah's Witnesses often result in court ordered medical treatment as a vehicle for meeting the patient's religious scruples. For example, in *Georgetown College*, Judge Skelly Wright stressed that "her religion merely prevented her consent to a transfusion...thus the effect of the order was to preserve for Mrs. Jones the life she wanted without sacrifice of her religious beliefs." Furthermore, the patient in *Georgetown College* was incompetent.[23]

The use of the courts to order forced surgery or caesarian sections not only misapplies precedent and takes *Roe* out of context, but flies in the face of a general legal trend toward honoring individual decision making in the area of medical care. It has long been recognized that touching someone without his or her

---

[23] For additional discussion of the caesarean section cases, see Annas, Forced Caesarean: The Most Unkind Cut of All, 12 *Hastings Center Report* 16 (June 1982). Annas expresses concern that court orders may be employed as a weapon by obstetricians "to bully women [the doctor] views as irrational into submission".

consent can result in criminal charges or in a civil lawsuit. Doctors may not operate, or carry out medical procedures, without a patient's consent. A doctor who fails to obtain such informed consent can be sued.[24]

In recent years, courts have recognized that individual rights may override whatever social interest there may be in forcing a patient to undergo medical treatment. Some of these cases involve fatally ill patients' rights to forego invasive or painful procedures that might prolong but cannot save their lives. Others arise out of treatment refusals motivated by individual religious convictions or other strongly held beliefs.[25]

As Professor Regan has pointed out, the notion that one individual's body can be invaded and appropriated to the purposes of another is jarringly alien to the Anglo-American legal tradition.[26]

Thus, a number of state courts have held that the right to refuse medical treatment as protected by the right to privacy extends to situations where the treatment is necessary to preserve the patient's life. As one court stated, "The constitutional right to privacy, as we conceive it, is an expression of the sanctity of individual free choice and self determination as fundamental constituents of life. The value of life...is lessened...by the failure to allow a competent human being the right of choice." *Superintendent of Belcherton State School v. Saikewicz*, 373 Mass. 728, 742, 370 N.E.2d 417 (1977).

Feticide - Cases and Legislation[27]

As indicated elsewhere, at common law, the definition of "person" for purposes of the criminal law was one who had been born alive. Most state courts which have ruled on the question of whether a homicide statute which refers only to "persons" can be interpreted to include fetuses have held that it cannot, thus incorporating the born alive rule. In several of the states, however, where a court accepted the born alive rule, the legislature later enacted amendments adding fetuses to the homicide law or enacting separate feticide statutes after the court's decision. California, for example, passed a law defining feticide as homicide after its Supreme Court barred such prosecutions.[28]

---

24 Courts have held unconstitutional even isolated instances of the type of intrusions to which a pregnant woman is subjected in a court ordered surgery case. For example, the state may not compel criminal suspects to undergo certain medical procedures. In *Rochin v. California*, the court held that the forcible pumping of a criminal suspect's stomach violated the individual's 14th Amendment due process rights, and was "conduct that *shocks the conscience*." 342 U.S. 165, 172 (1952) (emphasis added). This was true despite the fact that the individual was a criminal suspect, police officers witnessed the suspect swallow two pills which they believed to be narcotics, the stomach pumping involved an isolated instance of intrusion, and the court stressed it must review criminal convictions "with due humility".
25 In *Re Osborne* (1972), a Jehovah's Witness injured in an accident refused blood transfusions. His decision was based on religious beliefs. The court refused to order treatment.
However, in *In Re President of Georgetown College, Inc.* (1964), the judge was intent on preserving the patient's religious scruples by taking judicial responsibility for the procedure.
26 See Regan, Rewriting *Roe v. Wade*, 77 Mich.L.Rev. 1569 (1979).
27 Hunter, "Feticide - Cases and Legislation", May 5, 1986 Memorandum ACLU.
28 In *Keeler v. Superior Court*, 2 Cal.3d 619, 470 P.2d 617 (1970), the California Supreme Court decided that a viable fetus, though stillborn as the result of an assault upon its mother, was not a "human being" for purposes of the murder statute. Shortly after *Keeler*, the California legislature amended its homicide statute by adding "a fetus" to the list of possible murder victims. California Penal Code Section 187(a) (West Supp. 1986). The legislature did specify that the statute would not apply when death of a fetus resulted from an act "solicited, aided, abetted, or consented to by the mother

Sixteen states have adopted the born alive rule,[29] and that same number have enacted feticide statutes.[30] Few of these statutes have been challenged as to their constitutionality. In *People v. Apodoca* (1978) 76 Cal.App.3d 479, 142 Cal.Rptr. 830, the California homicide law was upheld against the challenge that it was impermissibly vague because it was not limited to fetuses after viability. The Court of Appeals found it unnecessary to decide that question since the fetus at issue was past the point of viability. No other constitutional question was raised. Georgia's feticide statute was challenged unsuccessfully on the grounds that use of the word "quick" to define the parameters of criminal liability was unconstitutionally vague. In *Brinkley v. State* (1984) 253 Ga. 541, 322 S.E.2d 49, the Georgia Supreme Court approved the usage of the word "quick" and upheld the statute.

Some alternative statutes have focused on the attack against the woman rather than the fetus.[31]

In 1986, feticide bills were enacted in Minnesota, and introduced in Kentucky, Missouri, Nebraska, Virginia, and West Virginia.

Just as misinterpretation of the state's, interest in the fetus after viability was used to justify court ordered surgery, many feticide bills rely on the concept.

Nan Hunter of the ACLU's Reproductive Freedom Project comments that "[a]ll such laws lack an objective standard to determine whether the defendant knows or should know a woman is pregnant. Viability, however, is not a useful concept in the feticide context. Viability occurs at different points in different pregnancies and requires medical expertise to diagnose. Further, it has little relationship to the visible onset of pregnancy. For some women, a pregnancy may not be obvious to the non-expert or unfamiliar eye even past the initial point of viability. For others, a different body type might indicate pregnancy at a much earlier stage. Except in the very last stages of pregnancy, no one other than a physician could be expected to know the fetus is viable. And, if the point of the law is to deter attacks against pregnant women, the assault should be penalized if the pregnancy was known or obvious, regardless of whether the fetus was yet viable."[32]

---

of the fetus". And a later decision interpreted the term "fetus" to refer only to a "viable unborn child". *People v. Smith*, 59 Cal.App.3d 751, 129 Cal.Rptr. 498 (1976).

29 These are: Alabama, Alaska, Colorado, Georgia, Hawaii, Kentucky, Louisiana, Maine, New Jersey, New York, North Dakota, Ohio, Rhode Island, Tennessee, Texas and West Virginia. (In Louisiana, the court held that live birth was required and a fetus was not a human being under Louisiana's murder statute. *State v. Gyles*, 313 S.2d 799 (La. 1975). After *Gyles*, legislators passed a new statute that defined a "person" for the purpose of the criminal code, as including a human being from the moment of fertilization and implantation. (Louisiana Rev. Stat. Ann. Sec. 14.2(7) (West Supp. 1986)). However, a later court did not interpret this law as actually extending to the homicide law. In this decision, *State v. Brown*, 378 S.2d 916, the court refused to extend the homicide statute despite the intervening legislation. The court reasoned that if the homicide laws are to be amended to include feticide, the amendment must be clear and must comport with a woman's right to voluntary abortion. Thus, all terminations of fetuses could not be designated as murder.

30 They are: California, Florida, Georgia, Illinois, Indiana, Iowa, Michigan, Minnesota, Mississippi, Missouri, New Hampshire, Oklahoma, Utah, Washington, Wisconsin, and Wyoming.

31 Examining the fact patterns of cases, it is obvious that assaults against pregnant women often occur in situations common to battering or abusive relationships. In *Keeler v. Superior Court, supra*, the defendant attacked his former wife immediately after her visitation period with the children of their marriage, demanding she stay away from the children if she was pregnant. In *People v. Greer* (1980) 79 Ill.2d 203, 402 N.E.2d 203, the defendant spent much of the day drinking in a local bar before saying he was going home to "beat the hell out of my old lady". One of the dissenting judges in that case, although arguing that the death of the fetus should be considered murder, declared that "[w]e are here concerned with the violent attack upon the person to the point where the fetus was fully viable." In *Hollis v. Kentucky* (1983) 652 S.W.2d 61, the defendant attacked his estranged wife.

32 Hunter, Memorandum, *supra*.

Janet Gallagher, of the Civil Liberties and Public Policy Program at Hampshire College in Amherst, proposes that the most effective way to deal with deliberate or wantonly reckless behavior which results in the loss of a pregnancy is to classify the attack on the pregnant woman as aggravated assault, or - if the local statutory scheme allows - to employ a victim impact analysis or enhanced sentencing procedures to impose appropriately heavier sentences. In any event, she urges such statutes should be "drafted carefully".[33]

In deciding whether a person in a vehicular homicide statute includes the fetus, two states expressly refused to apply civil law precedent to the criminal statutes. Thus, the Ohio Supreme Court in *State v. Dickinson*, while recognizing "person" to include fetuses for the purpose of recovery in civil wrongful death actions, refused to apply this broad definition of "person" to a criminal statute; "It must be noted...that the definition of a word in a civil statute does not necessarily import the same meaning to the same word in interpreting a criminal statute. The result may be desirable, but criminal statutes, unlike civil statutes, must be construed strictly against the state."[34]

When faced with the identical issue, the Michigan Supreme Court in *People v. Guthrie*, while noting that Michigan's wrongful death statute had been interpreted to include the unborn, refused to change the definition of "person" in a vehicular homicide statute; "It is one thing to mold, change and even reverse established principles of common law and civil matters. It is quite another thing to do so in regard to criminal statutes."[35]

In *Commonwealth v. Cass* (1984) 392 Mass. 799, 467 N.E.2d 1324, a four-three majority of the Massachusetts Supreme Judicial Court overturned the "born alive" rule and held that a viable fetus is a "person" within the meaning of the vehicular homicide statute. Relying heavily on a 1975 decision in which it interpreted "person" to include the viable unborn for the purposes of civil wronful death actions, the court in *Cass* saw no reason to apply a different definition to the term in this criminal action. The second ground for the court's decision in *Cass* was a simple assertion by the court that the judiciary has the power to redefine words in criminal statutes.[36]

In *State v. Horne* (1984) 282 S.C. 444, the South Carolina Supreme Court's decision to overturn the born alive rule was presented in a two-page opinion which avoided most of the controversial issues.

Three other jurisdictions that have considered the issue since 1983 have all upheld the born alive rule.[37]

---

[33] Gallagher. "Statutes Involving the Criminal Death of Fetuses", Memorandum, January 22, 1986.
[34] *State v. Dickinson* (1971) 28 Ohio S.2d 65, 70, 275 N.E.2d 599.
[35] *People v. Guthrie* (1980) 97 Mich.App. 226, 232, 293 N.W.2d 775.
[36] These two grounds have been criticized by at least one commentator. (See Carroll, "*Commonwealth v. Cass*", 7 Western New England Law Review 309 (1984).)
[37] *Hollis v. Kentucky*, 652 S.W.2d 61 (1983); *State ex. rel. Atkinson v. Wilson* (1984) 332 S.E.2d 807; *State v. Soto*, - (Minn. 1985).

Fetal Abuse and Neglect

All states have statutes prohibiting child abuse and neglect.[38] Statutes allowing the state to assume custody and control of a born child have been used as the jurisdictional basis for judicial orders compelling a pregnant woman to submit to treatment for the sake of her fetus. For example, a 1981 incident of a court ordered caesarian section in Atlanta, Georgia, arose from the pregnant woman's religious objection to surgery and blood transfusions. The hospital sought court intervention. Doctors testified that the woman had a complete placenta previa, a condition in which the placenta blocks the birth canal. There was, claimed the doctors, a 99% certainty that the fetus could not survive vaginal delivery and there was at least a 50% chance that the woman herself would die at an attempt at vaginal delivery. A Georgia court, convinced by doctors' presentations, declared that the near term fetus was "a human being fully capable of sustaining life independent of the mother" and that it "lacked proper prenatal care and subsistence." The Georgia courts granted temporary custody of the fetus to the government's social service agencies that had brought the court case, and gave them full authority to make all decisions, including given consent to the surgical delivery".[39] Their temporary custody ended in an unexpected manner some two weeks later when the woman's placenta shifted and she gave normal birth to a 7 pound 2 ounce girl.

One child neglect statute expressly defines the term child to include a fetus.[40]

Conversely, in California, a court of appeals expressly declined to include the fetus within a child neglect statute, finding the legislature did not so intend.[41]

Nevertheless, in that same state, where there was no legislative enactment directed toward fetal abuse or neglect, and a clear decision indicating the neglect laws did not include the fetus, in San Diego, California, Pamela Rae Stewart was charged under a 115 year old misdemeanor child support statute with failing to provide adequate prenatal care to her fetus and further alleging this caused the death of her child. Even without statutory authority for the unprecedented charge, the prosecutor twice tried to discover all of Ms. Stewart's confidential medical records, asserting there was no patient/physician privilege in a criminal proceeding. Given the highly private and confidential nature of the medical records, the court agreed with the defense that the discovery matter be stayed pending a determination whether the complaint was legitimate. Ultimately, the trial court agreed the legislature never intended for the statute to be used to pun-

---

38 For a complete list and analysis of these statutes, see Katz, Howe and McGrath, Child Neglect Laws in America, 9 Fam.L.Q.1 (1975) (cited in Nelson, "Forced Medical Treatment of Pregnant Women: 'Compelling Each to Live as Seems Good to the Rest'", The Hastings Law Journal 37:703, 725 at fn. 71 (May 1986)).
39 *Jefferson v. Griffin Spaulding County Hospital*, 247 Ga. 86, 274 S.E.2d 457 (1981).
40 New Jersey Statutes Annotated, Section 3:4C-11 (West 1981).
41 *Matter of Stephen S.*, 126 Cal.App.3d 26, 178 Cal.Rptr. 525. The court strongly disapproved of the prosecutor's action in that case. A pregnant woman, Kay S. had requested judicial review of a mental health committment and the matter had been set for hearing. The prosecutor expressly declined to proceed under the mental health committment action, and instead the Department of Social Services sought to take jurisdiction of the fetus - which of course included jurisdiction over her. As a result, Kay S. spent two months in custody at which time the appelalate court dismissed the appeal since the child had been born, however, sharply criticizing the methods used. "We disapprove of the use of the juvenile court proceedings in the instant case which effectively detained the mother for approximately two months in circumvention of the state's mental health laws."

ish a pregnant woman and therefore dismissed all charges against Pamela Rae Stewart, concluding "she committed no crime."[42]

One day after the Pamela Rae Stewart case was dismissed, a California State Senator introduced a "fetal abuse" bill. (SB 1070) Faced with significant challenges by the ACLU, the California Medical Association, the California Nurses Association, and other healthcare providers, the author of the bill has, at this time, withdrawn his bill from consideration by the Senate's Judiciary Committee for further amendment. The bill may resurface next year.

In Michigan, a court held that evidence of a woman's prenatal abuse or neglect could be considered during neglect proceedings instituted by the state to deprive her of custody of her newborn child.[43] The court also held Mother X's confidential medical records could be discovered, even though there were state and federal statutes protective of confidentiality of such records.

Tort Law: Recovery for Wrongful Life, Wrongful Death, and Prenatal Injuries[44]

The issues whether a fetus is a person for purposes of recovery of damages for tortious conduct inflicted upon the body of the pregnant woman or by the pregnant woman herself, clearly evidences the confusion in the law in this area. A majority of jurisdictions hold that a viable fetus is a person whose death is compensable under a wrongful death statute.[45]

Several states take the position that a stillborn fetus never achieves the status of a "person" and therefore no liability arises for causing its death.[46]

---

42 The prosecutor relied on California Penal Code Section 270 since it included a 1925 amendment that for the purposes of this section a person is a "child conceived but not yet born." In 1925 when the amendment was adopted, Section 270 could be applied to the mother only under extremely limited circumstances. A mother became subject to the provisions of that section only if the father died or became incapacitated. If the prosecution had then argued that the legislature intended the amendment to apply to cases like Ms. Stewart's, then it would have been in the curious position of arguing that the legislature intended her to be sent to jail for conduct leading to the death of her child if her husband happened to be dead, but intended her to be immune to prosecution if he happened to be alive. At that time, that statute only applied to fathers reflecting the social expectations and responsibilities of female parents and of male parents with respect to the financial support of their children. Acting as amicus in the Stewart case were: The California Chapter of the National Organization for Women, San Diego Chapter of National Organization for Women, Action Committee for Abortion Rights, American Association of Obstetricians and Gynecologists, District 9, Committee to Defend Reproductive Rights, Equal Rights Advocates, Inc., National Campaign to Restore Abortion Funding, Pregnancy Rights Organization/Privacy Rights Organization and the Women's Lawyers Association of Los Angeles. In addition, the California Medical Association and other healthcare providers supported dismissal of the Stewart case, fearing prosecutions would drive women away from prenatal care, causing great risk to themselves and their fetuses.
43 *In Re Baby X* (1980) 97 Mich.App. 111, 293 N.W.2d 736.
44 The right of a third party to recover damages for the death of another human being did not exist at common law. In England, the courts did not allow a civil recovery because an individual found liable for a homicide was himself put to death, with his belongings forfeited to the crown. Thus, there were no assets remaining from which to pay off a subsequent civil judgment. (See *Moragne v. States Marine Lines* (1970) 398 U.S. 375, 382-84.) However, every state has enacted wrongful death legislation, thus permitting a civil cause of action.
45 For a summary of the law under wrongful death statutes, see NOTE, "Wrongful Death of a Fetus: Does a Cause of Action Arise When There is No Life Birth?" Villanova Law Review 31:669 (1986) (hereinafter Wrongful Death NOTE). For a discussion of the caselaw in the wrongful life context, see Tort Law 72 ABA Journal 46 1986. For a discussion of the history and the elements of the tort of "wrongful life," see Azzolino v. Dingfelder: Wrongful Life - The Ultimate Tort, 1985 Det.C.L.Rev. 921.
46 Those states permitting recovery for wrongful death of a viable fetus are: Washington, DC, Alabama, Arizona, Connecticut, Delaware, Georgia, Idaho, Illinois, Indiana, Kansas, Kentucky, Louisiana, Maryland, Massachusetts, Minnesota, Mississippi, Missouri, New Hampshire, New Mex-

The various state courts have analyzed the legislative intent and have looked to other legal contexts to determine whether a cause of action is allowable. A number of state courts have recognized wrongful death actions for the destruction of fetuses for the explicit purpose of compensating parents. For example, in *Vulk v. Baldazo*, 103 Id. 570, 651 P.2d 11 (1982), the court held "[i]t is clear, therefore, that [the wrongful death statute] confers upon parents a cause of action for the wrongful death of a 'child' and thus protects the rights and interests of parents and not those of the decedent child."[47] Recognizing a wrongful death action to compensate parents for the loss of their expected child also seeks to deter and punish the tortious conduct. In *Eich v. Town of Gulf Shores* (1974) 293 Ala. 95, 300 S.2d 354, suit was allowed "because the punitive nature of our wrongful death statute demands the punishment of the tortfeasor" and in *Vaillancourt v. Medical Center Hospital* (1980) 139 Vt. 138, 425 A.2d 92, the court held "[u]nder such a rule, there is the absurd result that the greater the harm, the better the chance of immunity, and the tortfeasor could foreclose his own liability." Similarly, in *Dunn v. Rose Way Inc.* (1983) 333 N.W.2d 830, the plaintiff's wife, unborn child and two year old daughter were all killed in an automobile accident. The father was permitted to recover and the court focused on the legal status of the parent's right to sue rather than that of the fetus.

Recently, however, those courts permitting recovery have focused on identifying the fetus rather than the parent as the locus of the right when there is no live birth. This represents "a dangerous conceptual move."[48] For example, in *Amadio v. Levin* (1985) 509 Penn. 199, 501 A.2d 1085, the parents of the decedent alleged that the negligence of four treating physicians caused their full term child to be stillborn. The majority asserted that since recovery is allowed in instances of prenatal injury, this implicitly means that an unborn child is an "individual" with a right to be free from prenatal injuries; if a fetus is an individual at the time of the injury, it is also an individual at the time those injuries cause death.[49] A Louisiana case permitted recovery since, "A human being exists from the moment of fertilization and implantation (*Danos v. St. Pierre*, 402 S.2d 633, 639 (Louisiana 1981)) and in West Virginia a court held a fetus is a person for wrongful death statute is "technically correct in view of the fact that 'biologically speaking' such a child is, in fact, a presently exising person, a living human being." *Baldwin v. Butcher*, 155 W.Va. 431, 438-39, 184 S.E.2d 428, 432, (1971).

Most courts holding the minority view -- that recovery should not be permitted -- argue that to find legislative intent to include the fetus under a wrongful death act is to improperly create a cause of action not provided for by statute or in the common law. Indeed, in California, the California Supreme Court held

---

ico, North Dakota, Ohio, Oklahoma, Oregon, Pennsylvania, Rhode Island, South Carolina, Texas, Vermont, Washington, West Virginia, and Wisconsin.

Those states denying recovery are California, Florida, Iowa, New Jersey, New York, North Carolina, and in Alaska, the District Court held no recovery is permitted for the wrongful death of a nonviable death of a fetus but has not decided the issue with regard to viable fetuses.

47 By comparison, the North Carolina Supreme Court, noting the compensatory nature of its wrongful death statute, denied recovery stating, "It can hardly be seriously contended that the death of a fetus represents any real pecuniary loss to the parents." *Gay v. Thompson* (1966) 266 N.C. 394, 146 S.E.2d 425.

48 Johnsen, Dawn E. "The Creation of Fetal Rights: Conflicts with Women's Constitutional Rights to Liberty, Privacy, and Equal Protection", 95 Law Journal 599 (January 1986).

49 NOTE, Wrongful Death, *supra*.

the use of the word "person" evinced the clear intent to preclude any cause of action for the death of a fetus. (See *Justus v. Atchison* (1977) 19 Cal.3d 564, 565 P.2d 122.) Other courts have relied on the ground that damages are too speculative. Some courts have pointed out that sufficient compensation is available in the parent's own cause of action. In *Graf v. Taggert*, 43 N.J. 303, 204 A.2d 140 (1964), the court held the mother could bring her own action for both mental and physical injuries. Another court in New York held recovery for wrongful death of the fetus would be a windfall given that the mother has a cause of action for her own injuries and the father may sue for funeral expenses and loss of consortium.

Wrongful birth or wrongful life causes of action allege that because a health-care professional did not provide accurate information or accurate testing, an unhealthy fetus was conceived or brought to term. The parents complain they would have chosen to abort had they known of the problem and the action is brought on behalf of the injured child.

Some courts think that allowing damages for wrongful life would disavow the sanctity of a less than perfect life,[50] but the California Supreme Court has said:

"[i]t is hard to see how an award of damages to a severely handicapped or suffering child would disavow the value of life or in any way suggest that the child is not entitled to the full measure of legal and non-legal rights and privileges accorded to all members of society."[51]

In *Turpin*, the California Supreme Court denied general damages to a child born deaf, returning to the unascertainable damage rationale of earlier cases, but did allow the child to recover extraordinary expenses for specialized teaching, training, and hearing equipment she would incur due to her deafness.

The court reasoned:

"[i]n an ordinary prenatal injury case, if the defendant had not been negligent, the child would have been healthy; thus, as in a typical personal injury case, the defendant in such a case has interfered with the child's basic right to be free from physical injury caused by the negligence of others. In this case, by contrast, the obvious tragic fact is that plaintiff never had a chance "to be born as a whole, functional human being without total deafness"; if defendants had performed their jobs properly, she would not have been born with hearing intact, but - according to the complaint - would not have been born at all."

The California Supreme Court denied recovery for general damages because "(1) It is simply impossible to determine in any rational or reasoned fashion whether the plaintiff has in fact suffered an injury in being born impaired rather than not being born, and (2) even if it were possible to overcome the first hurdle, it would be impossible to assess general damages in any fair, nonspeculative manner." California has statutorily barred wrongful life suits.[52]

At least ten states have specifically allowed, or indicated that they will allow, recovery to a live born child for her prenatal injuries sustained during viability.[53]

---

50 *Berman v. Allen*, 80 N.J. 421, 404 A.2d 8 (1979).
51 *Turpin v. Sortini*, 31 Cal.3d 220 at 233, 643 P.2d 954 (1982).
52 California Civil Code Section 43.6(a) (West 1982).
53 See Beal, "Can I Sue Mommy?" Analysis of a Woman's Tort Liability for Prenatal Injuries to Her Child Born Alive, 21 San Diego Law Review 325, 331-32, note 42 (1984). See also Schedler, G.

One case has declined to hold as a matter of law whether a child may sue his mother for taking tetracycline during her pregnancy, allegedly resulting in the discoloration of the child's teeth. Suit was also brought against the physician. *Grodin v. Grodin and Dr. Cohen*, 102 Mich.App. 396, 301 N.W.2d 869 (1980). Dr. Cohen had assured Mrs. Grodin it was impossible for her to become pregnant and thus she continued to take tetracycline. Eventually, Mrs. Grodin saw another doctor who told her she was in fact seven or eight months pregnant, at which point Mrs. Grodin stopped taking the medication. Mrs. Grodin asked the lower court to dismiss the complaint against her citing intrafamily tort immunity. The appellate court sent the matter back to the trial court to determine whether Mrs. Grodin's conduct was a reasonable exercise of parental discretion. If her conduct was reasonable, she would be immune from suit and absolved from liability.

Fetal Rights vs. Maternal Rights?: Implications

As illustrated by the caselaw set out above, when the interests of the fetus and mother are harmonized, a legitimate desire to protect the rights of the pregnant woman and fetus emerges. Thus, for example, permitting wrongful death actions on behalf of the fetus serves to compensate parents for the loss of their expected child and to deter and punish the tortious conduct. Similarly, some feticide laws protect pregnant women from physical attack and from the harm of having their pregnancies involuntarily and violently terminated by third parties. Holding third parties responsible for the negligent or criminal destruction of fetuses is therefore consistent with, and even enhances, the protection of pregnant women's interests and fetal health.

Some legislatures and courts, however, have focused the locus of the right on the fetus rather than the woman, creating a clash of rights and interests.

"It makes no sense, biologically or socially, to pit fetal and maternal rights against one another. Indeed, legal rights do not offer a proper framework for assessing the situation of a pregnant woman and her fetus. As long as they are connected, nothing can happen to one that does not affect the other. ...To argue rights of the fetus *versus* those of the mother ignores this organic unity and substitutes a false dichotomy, though one that is habitual in Western, mechanistic thought, in which we speak of head versus heart, hand versus brain, and mind versus body. *But these are false metaphors,* and the mistake leads to absurd conclusions when one tries to argue rights of one part against those of the other. As long as a fetus is attached to the pregnant woman, her body maintains its life and her body wall bars access to it. ...It also does not make social sense to juxtapose fetal and maternal 'rights.' Who is the winner in the contest of 'rights'...?

"Surely not the fetus any more than the mother. Since infants are born in a state of utter dependency, and since our present social arrangements are such that the mother usually is the one who must respond to the infant's needs, it makes no better sense to set mothers and

"Women's Reproductive Rights: Is There a Conflict With The Child's Right to be Born Free From Defects?" *The Journal of Legal Medicine*, 7:357 (1986).

infants up as antagonists before or after birth. If physicians refuse to treat pregnant women and their fetuses as organic wholes, newborns will be in trouble, no matter what heroic measures of fetus-saving physicians institute against the wishes of prospective mothers."[54]

The use of the courts as enforcers for doctors' orders in forced surgery cases is especially startling. The inquiry must be whether doctors can use or invade a non-consenting woman's body for the sake of another patient, fetal or born. If the rationale for forced caesarian sections is to be accepted, will forced fetal surgery and fetal therapy be next? "As 'choices' become available, they all too rapidly become compulsions to 'choose'the socially endorsed alternative. In this realm, it is amazing how quickly so-called options are transformed into obligations that, in fact, deprive us of choice."[55]

In light of the grave constitutional issues involved, courts should hesitate to allow judicial authority to be invoked in disputes between a pregnant woman and her doctor. As George Annas points out, the delivery room does not lend itself to calm reflection on judicial precedent or the furture implications of a decision.[56] Indeed, as reported in the New England Journal of Medicine, most court orders were handed down in six hours.[57]

A most alarming result when fetal rights are pitted against maternal rights is in the area of criminal law. Thus, for example, even though no law made fetal abuse a crime, in San Diego, California, Pamela Rae Stewart spent six days in jail while bail was being discussed. To lock women up in pregnancy prisons will do nothing to promote fetal health. Indeed, during the pendency of the Pamela Rae Stewart case, women, particularly those of high risk, stayed away from prenatal care altogether.

> "The case involving Pamela Rae Stewart, an El Cajon woman who was charged in the death of her newborn infant because she allegedly took drugs during her pregnancy, drove women further underground, [Dr. Suzanne Dixon, a pediatrician at UCSD Medical Center] said. A judge eventually dismissed the case and Stewart was not prosecuted. That fear is particularly bad in San Diego County, Dixon said. There is a fear that if you're doing drugs and pregnant you're going to go to jail. *We don't need those kind of problems!*"
> *San Diego Union*, March 31, 1987, p. B-1.

Those who advocate punishment for pregnant women who abuse substances during their pregnancy also fail to recognize other dangers in creating this adversarial relationship between mother and fetus. Indeed, experts in treating substance abusing mothers warn this could lead to a "legacy of state custody".[58]

Furthermore, enactment of fetal abuse and neglect laws would mandate reporting by the pregnant woman's physician. In addition to the obvious constitutional breaches of rights to privacy, and against unreasonable searches and seizures, such reporting would destroy the confidential relationship between patient and physician. The result is that pregnant women would not seek prenatal

---

54 Hubbard, p. 215-216.
55 Hubbard, p. 210.
56 Annas, *supra.*
57 *New England Journal, supra.*
58 Jessup, Marty and Roth, Robert, "Clinical and Legal Perspectives on Prenatal Drug and Alcohol Use: Guidelines for Individual and Community Response" (1987).

care for fear that everything they say to their doctors could and would be used against them in a court of law.

"The language of 'fetal rights' is dangerous. It draws upon and reinforces deeply misogynist attitudes. Ultimately, fetal wellbeing is not well served by an ideological insistence on framing pregnancy health issues as conflicts between two separate, anatagonistic entities. Policy makers and healthcare providers would do better to encourage an attitude toward pregnancy that emphasizes a woman's respect and care for the fetus, not as subordination to the unborn, but as affirmation of herself and of her choice to become a mother."[59]

Conclusion

A review of caselaw before and after the historic decision *Roe v. Wade* indicates that current lawmakers and state legislators are binding themselves in mere abstract terms and legal fictions, and blinding themselves to human lives and realities.

Thus, when the issue is framed as fetal rights vs. maternal rights, court decisions and legislative enactments reveal not so much interest in the fetus as an interst in substituting their judgment or a doctor's for that of the pregnant woman for conduct they don't like. Selective prosecution is repugnant in our state of laws.

Framing the issues as an abstract clash of rights ignores obvious biological, social, and practical realities, Thus a pregnant woman can be accused of a nonexistent crime and spend time in jail, confidential medical records can be subject to surveillance and state intrusions, a pregnant woman may be strapped to an operating table and chemicals injected into her against her will, and an incarcerated pregnant woman waiting to be shackled may be delayed getting to the hospital to deliver safely.

Thus, it is up to us to raise the social consciousness of our lawmakers and judges; it is up to us to protect our next generation. Let us not ignore the realities of women's lives. The fetus is in the uterus and the uterus is in the body of a woman. Her rights and her choices must be affirmed and respected. We must reach out to those in trouble, counsel them, teach them, so that their choices are more ethically and morally responsible. At the same time, we must advocate access for this population for good nutrition, healthcare, housing, education, and safe work environments.

We must educate the courts to avoid the abstract issues of fetal rights vs. maternal rights and speak to them of nurturing and caring and affirmation. We must teach them a new language of analysis.

> No one lives in this room
> without confronting the whiteness of the wall
> behind the palms, blanks of books
> photographs of dead heroines.
> Without contemplating last and late
> the true nature of poetry. The drive to
> connect. The dream of a common language.[60]

---

59 Gallagher.
60 From Origins and History of Consciousness by Adrienne Rich. *The Dream of a Common Language*, W.W. Norton & Co., Inc., New York (1978)

Bibliography

Journal Articles & Texts

Andrews, The Legal Status of the Embryo, 32 *Loyola Law Review* 357 (1986).

Annas, Forced Caesarians: The Most Unkindt Cut of All, 12 *Hastings Center Report* 16 (1982)

Beal, Can I Sue Mommy? Analysis of a Woman's Tort Liability for Prenatal Injuries to Her Child Born Alive, 21 *San Diego L.Rev.* 325 (1984)

Bross and Meredyth (1979) Neglect of the Unborn Child. 3 *Child Abuse and Neglect.*

Carroll, *Commonwealth v. Cass*, 7 Western New England L.Rev. 309 (1984)

Chavkin, Woman as Baby Vehicle, 7 *Women's Rights Law Reporter* 219 (1982)

Defining Human Life: Medical, Legal, and Ethical Implications (M. Shaw and A.E. Doudera, Editors, 1983).

Doudera (1982) Fetal Rights, It Depends. *Trial* April 39

L. Edelstein, The Hippocratic Oath 10 (1943)

Gallagher, "Prenatal Invasions and Interventions: What's Wrong with Fetal Rights", 10 *Harvard Women's Law Journal* 9-58 (1987)

Gallagher, Statutes Involving the Criminal Death of Fetuses, Memorandum, Jan. 22, 1986

Glantz, *The Legal Aspects of Fetal Viability in Genetics and the Law II* (A. Milunsky, G.J. Annas, eds. 1980)

Guillenim, Babies by Caesarian: Who Chooses, Who Controls? 11 *Hastings Center Report* 15 (1981)

Harrison, B. (1983) *Our Right to Choose: Toward a New Ethic of Abortion.* Boston: Beacon

Hubbard, Legal and Policy Implications of Recent Advances in Prenatal Diagnosis and Fetal Therapy, 7 *Women's Rights Law Reporter* 201 (1982)

Hunter, Feticide - Cases and Legislation, *ACLU Memorandum*, May 5, 1986

Johson, The Creation of Fetal Rights: Conflicts with Women's Constitutional Rights to Liberty, Privacy and Equal Protection, 95 *Yale L.J.* 599 (1986)

Kader, The Law of Tortious Prenatal Death Since Roe v. Wade, 45 *Mo. Law Rev.* 639, 641 (1980)

Katz, Howe and McGrath, Child Neglect Laws in America, 9 *Fam.L.Q.* 1 (1975)

Keeton, Dobbs, Keeton, Owen, Prosser and Keeton on the Laws of Torts, 5th ed. (1984) at p. 370, n. 32, listing states that consider fetuses to have died in utero to be persons under wrongful death statutes

King, The Juridical Status of the Fetus: Proposal for Legal Protection of the Unborn, 77 *Mich. Law Rev.* 1647, 1672 (1979)

Kolder, Gallagher and Parsons, Court Ordered Obstetrical Interventions, 316 *New England J. of Med.* 1192 (May 7, 1987)

L. Lader, Abortion 75-77 (1966)

The Law and the Unborn Child: The Legal and Locial Inconsistencies, 46 *Notre Dame Law* 349, 3544-360 (1971)

Leonow, The Fetus as a Patient Emerging Rights as a Person. 9 *American Journal of Law & Medicine* 1 (1983)

Louisell, Abortion, the Practice of Medicine and the Due Process of Law, 16 *UCLA Law Rev.* 233 (1969)

Means, The Law of New York Concerning Abortion and the Status of the Fetus, 1664-1968: A Case of Cessation of Constitutionality, 14 N.Y.L.F. 411 (1968)

Means, The Phoenix of Abortional Freedom: Is a Penumbral or Ninth Amendment Right About to Arise from the Nineteenth Century Legislative Ashes of a Fourteenth Century Common Law Liberty? 17 *N.Y.L.F.* 335 (1971)

Milbauer, b. (1983) The Law Giveth: Legal Aspects of the Abortion Controversy New York: Aginium

Mohr, J. (1978) *Abortion in America.* New York: Oxford University Press (summary of 19th century legislation and court decision)

Nelson, Forced Medical Treatment of Pregnant Women: 'Compelling Each to Live as Seems Good to the Rest,' 37 *Hastings L.J.* 703 (1986)

Note, Live Birth: A Condition Precedent to Recognition of Rights, 4 *Hoffstra Law Rev.* 805, 825 (1884)

O'Brien, M. (1983) *The Politics of Reproduction.* Boston: Routledge and Kegan Paul.

Parness, Social Commentary: Values and Legal Personhood. 83 *W.Va. Law Rev.* 487 (1981)

Petchesky R. (1984) *Abortion and Women's Choice.* New York: Longman.

Quay, Justifiable Abortion - Medical and Legal Foundations, 49 *Geo. L.J.* 395 (1961)

Regan, Rewriting *Roe v. Wade,* 77 Mich. L.Rev. 1569 (1979)

Robertson, J. (1982) The Right to Procreate and In Utero Therapy. *Journal of Legal Medicine* 3, 33

Schedler, Women's Reproductive Rights: Is There a Conflict with the Child's Right to be Born Free From Defects? 7 *J. of Legal Medicine* 357 (1986)

Shaw and Damme, *Legal Status of the Fetus, in Genetics and the Law.* II (A. Milunsky, G.J. Annas, eds. 1980).

Warner, M. (1976) *Alone of All Her Sex: The Myth and Cult of the Virgin Mary.* New York: Alfred Knopf

Westfall, Beyond Abortion: The Potential LIfe of the Human Life Amendment. 8 *American Journal of Law & Medicine* 97 (1982)

Cases

Abele v. Markle, 351 F.Supp. 224 (Ct. 1972); also appealed. C.f. *Cheany v.State*, ___ IN ___, 285 N.E.2d at 270

Abrams v. Foshee, 3 Iowa 274 (1856)

Allaire v. St. Luke's Hospital, 184 Ill. 359 56 N.E. 638 (1900)

Baldwin v. Butcher, 155 W.Va. 431, 184 S.E.2d 428 (1971)

Bombest v. Kotz, 65 F.Supp. 138 (D.D.C. 1946)

Brinkley v. State, 253 Ga. 541, 322 S.E.2d 49 (1984)

Burns v. Alcala, 420 U.S. 575 (1975)

Byrn v. New York City Health & Hospitals Corp., 31 N.Y.2d 194, 286 N.E.2d 887 (1972)

Christian v. Carter, 193 N.C. 537, 137 S.E. 596 (1927)

Colautti v. Franklin, 430 U.S. 395 (1979)

Commonwealth v. Bangs, 9 Mass. 387, 388 (1812)

Commonwealth v. Cass, 467 N.E.2d 1324 (1984)

Commonwealth v. Parker, 15 Mass. (9 Matc.263 (1845)

Cowles v. Cowles, 56 Conn. 240, 13 A. 414 (1887)

Curlender v. Bioscience Laboratories, 106 Cal.App.3d 811, 165 Cal.Rptr. 477 (1980)

Danos v. St. Pierre, 402 So.2d 63 (La. 1981)

Dietrich v. Inhabitants of Northampton, 138 Mass. 14 (1884)

Douglas v. Town of Hartford, 542 F.Supp. 1267 (D. Conn. 1982)

Drobner v. Peters, 232 N.Y. 220, 133 N.E. 567 (1921)

Dunn v. Rose Way Inc., 333 N.W.2d 830 (Iowa 1983)

Edwards v. State, 40 Fla. 527 (1898)

Eich v. Town of Gulf Shores, 293 Ala. 95, 330 S.2d 354 (1974)

Eggart v. State, 40 Fla. 527 (1898)

Elliot v. Brown, 361 S.2d 546, 548 (Ala. 1978)

Endresz v. Friedberg, 24 N.Y.2d 478, 486, 248 N.E.2d 901, 905 (1969)

Evans v. Olson, 550 P.2d 924 (Okla. 1976)

Foster v. State, 182 Wisc. 298, 196 N.W. 233 (1923)

Gray v. State, 77 Tex.Cr.R. 221, 178 S.W. 337 (1915)

Grodin v. Grodin, 102 Mich.App. 396, 301 N.W.2d 869 (1980)

Harberson v. Parke Davis, Inc., 98 Wash.2d 460, 656 P.2d 483 (1983)
Harmon v. Daniels, 525 F.Supp. 798 (W.D. Va. 1981)
Harris v. McRae, 448 U.S. 297 (1980)
Hoener v. Bertinato, (1961) 67 N.J. 517, 171 A.2d 140
Hollis v. Kentucky, 632 S.W.2d 61 (1983)
In Re Baby X, 97 Mich.App. 111, 293 N.W.2d 736 (1980)
Jefferson v. Griffin Spalding Country Hospital Authority, 247 Ga. 86, 274 S.E.2d 457 (1981)
Keeler v. Superior Court, 2 Cal.3d 619, 470 P.2d 617 (1970)
McGarvey v. Magee-Women's Hospital, 340 F.Supp. 751 (WD Penn. 1972)
Matter of Peabody, 5 N.Y.2d 541, 158 N.E.2d 841 (1959)
Matter of Stephen S., 126 Cal.App.3d 26, 178 Cal.Rptr. 525
Miller v. Bennett, 190 Va. 162, 50 S.E.2d 217 (1949)
Mitchell v. Commonwealth, 78 Ky. 204 (1979)
Mone v. Greyhound Lines, 368 Mass. 354, 331 N.E.2d 916 (1975)
Montana v. Kentucky, 366 U.S. 308 (1961)
Montana v. Rogers 278 F. 2nd 68 (CA 7 1960)
O'Grady v. Brown, 654 S.W.2d 904 (Mo. 1983) (en banc)
People v. Apodaca, 76 Cal.App.3d 479, 142 Cal.Rptr. 830 (1978)
People v. Guthrie, 97 Mich.App. 226, 293 N.W.2d 775 (1980)
People v. Smith, 59 Cal.App. 3d 751 (1976)
Planned Parenthood of Central Missouri v. Danforth, 428 U.S. 64
Poole v. Endsley, 371 F.Supp. 1379 (N.D.Fla. 1974). Affirmed in part 516 F.2d 898 (5th Cir. 1975)
Raleigh Fitkin-Paul Morgan Memorial Hospital v. Anderson, 42 N.J. 421, 201 A.2d 537 (1964)
Renslow v. Mennonite Hospital, 67 Ill.2d 348, 367 N.E.2d 1250 (1977)
Roe v. Wade, 410 U.S. 113 (1973)
Smith v. Brennan, 31 N.J. 353, 157 A.2d 497 (1960)
Smith v. Gafford, 31 Ala. 45 (1857)
State v. Alcorn, 7 Idaho 599, 64 P.2d 1014 (1901)
State v. Brown, 378 S.3d 916
State v. Cooper, 22 N.J.L. 52 (1849)
State v. Dickenson, 28 Ohio State 2d 65, 275 N.E.2d 599 (1971)
State v. Gyles, 313 S.2d 799 (La. 1975)
State v. Murphy, 27 N.J.L. 112 (1858)
Superintendent of Belchertown State School v. Saikewicz, 378 Mass. 728, 370 N.E.2d 417 (1977)
Thornburgh v. American College of Obstetricians and Gynecologists, ___U.S.___, 106 S.Ct. 2169
  (1986)
Turpin v. Sortini, 31 Cal.3d 220, 643 P.2d 954, 182 Cal.Rptr. 337 (1982)
Vaillancourt v. Medical Center Hospital, 139 Vt. 138, 415 A.2d 92 (1980)
Verkennas v. Corniea, 229 Minn. 365, 38 N.W.2d 838 (1949)
Volk v. Baldazo, 103 Idaho 570, 651 P.2d 11 (1982)
Wallace v. Wallace, 120 N.J. 675, 421 A.2d 134 (1980)
Womack v. Buchhorn, 384 Mich. 718, 187 N.W.2d 218
Woods v. Lancet, 303 N.Y. 349, 102 N.E.2d 691 (1951)

Code Sections

42 U.S.C. 606(b) (West Supp. 1986)
California Health and Safety Code, Section 25956 (West 1984)
CFR Sections 46.203(b), 46.203(c) (1985)
New Mexico Statutes Ann., Section 30-3-7 (Supp. 1985)
Uniform Probate Code, Section 2-108 (1969)

Fetal "Personhood" and the Law
A Comment on Judith Rosen

Janet Benshoof

HISTORICALLY THE FETUS has never been treated as a separate person or a person at all. Legal rights, if any, have come into play only after a live birth. Certainly the Founding Fathers never considered fetuses as citizens or persons. By contrast, although black people and women certainly suffered legal disability under the law, their basic legal personhood was already fixed in the common law.

The characterization of a fetus as a person or as an entity that has legal status has been changing in the last ten years to what I believe to be an alarming degree, insofar as women's rights are concerned. Even though the rights of a woman versus that of a fetus in a nonabortion context have not been constitutionally adjudicated by the Supreme Court, one nonetheless sees discussions of the legal status of the fetus all across the legal landscape. I believe that it is worth noting these developments in the legal culture and looking at some of their underlying causes.

A perusal of recent legal literature reveals the following:

Actions for the wrongful death of a fetus in the womb have moved beyond simply compensating the woman for the loss of her pregnancy and begun to characterize the fetus as a human life; there has been increased recognition of the legal status of the fetus in the criminal law. For example, in 1986, Massachusetts was the first state to hold that the vehicular homicide statute applied also to fetuses. Therefore, the person who caused the accident was criminally charged not only with the death of the pregnant woman but with the death of the fetus, as well. This move, unprecedented at the time, has spawned would-be imitators; there is an increasing recognition of the fetus set over and against the pregnant woman carrying it, as we see cases of authorities forcing caesareans, forcing blood transfusions, or even going so far as criminally charging a woman because she did not follow the proper prenatal care.

The notion of fetal personhood has begun to appear even so far afield as the workplace, in the context of occupational safety. While the federal government has steadily relaxed regulations on companies and failed to enforce strict occupational safety laws, it has at the same time encouraged discriminatory application of these laws by subjecting women to strict regulation in the workplace because of their pregnancy or their potential pregnancy. For example, a few years ago, the ACLU represented five women in Virginia who had been sterilized against their will in order to keep their jobs at the American Cyanamid Company. And the company's rationale was that in order for them to keep their jobs they would either have to show that they were sterile or become sterilized, because the jobs involved potential harm to a fetus. As unions have begun to sue to stop the use of pesticides and other dangerous chemicals, one can envision a judge who has allowed limited use of, say, a pesticide order that pregnant women could not be workers. Thus, instead of cleaning up the workplace for all people, men and women, government may simply choose to exclude pregnant women or potentially pregnant women from certain jobs because of possible harm to the fetus, reminiscent of the stringent requirements and restrictions that barred women from access to the workplace 100 years ago.

There are several reasons why these developments are taking place right now. One reason is the activity of the Right to Life movement. Those who want to outlaw abortion or to pass a "human life" amendment to the Constitution realize as a strategic matter that the more humanness that can be attributed to the fetus, the more legal status can be accorded the fetus in child custody law and inheritance law and in negligence law and tort law, the better chance there may be to ultimately pass a "human life" amendment.

A second reason is that the language of tort law cannot keep pace with its own doctrinal development. The fact that fetuses have been granted more legal rights results in part from sloppy legal conceptualization by judges who fail to realize the implications of how they write their decisions, even if those decisions are coming out with a result that people of good will would all support.

A third reason is that technology plays an increasingly major role in defining relationships, as it varies the number of ways of having children and the increased number of parents a child could have. Looking at surrogacy, for example, the fetus does become somehow separate from the mother because of the contract involved, particularly now that the technique of embryo transplant has been perfected, where the embryo is put in a woman who is not the genetic parent at all. In other words, we have a situation where the egg comes from the mother and the sperm from the father, and the resulting embryo is put into yet a third party, the woman who will carry the fetus to term. Those kinds of techniques separate the fetus from the woman in a way that makes it more possible for people to visualize and for the law to conceptualize the two separate persons.

At the same time, the logic of technological development and scientific discovery that drives doctors and scientists is animated by the operative belief that if it is possible to do something, one should do it, sometimes with unexpected and frightening results. For example, some states have begun to disallow the use of so-called "living wills" (which grant a loved one the authority to choose to terminate life support systems in the event of a coma or profound disability) by pregnant women. In other words, if you are injured in a car accident and you are pregnant, the state can take over and keep you alive forever. What this means is that becoming pregnant can cost a woman her right to have a medical surrogate carry out her wishes. In other words, you're not treated as a competent adult if you're a woman and potentially could become pregnant. This simply would not be the case were it not for recent advances in life-sustaining technology. Recently, I had a revealing exchange with a physician, who is also an ethicist heading the ethics department in a major teaching hospital in New Jersey, who talked about the fact that they were now keeping alive women who were in accidents up to 30 weeks of pregnancy and then attempting a caesarean. And he said that no matter what kind of living will the woman had signed, they would ignore it, that this advance in technology was wonderful, and besides, what does it matter what the unconscious woman wanted when she was conscious?

Hand in hand with technological development, there is also a sort of gung-ho cultural context that doctors operate in, that if they can do it, they must do it, and they want to do it. I do not think that many of those same doctors would treat a man who had a car accident that way and take out his heart immediately because they could now do heart transplants. On the contrary, they would be very careful to see that he signed an organ donation card. They would be much more respectful of that, but somehow a woman who has a fetus inside her is different and no matter how or why she became pregnant -- maybe it was involuntary, maybe she was raped -- her living will is inoperative.

Since *Roe v. Wade* is the touchstone of legal discussion in this area, I would like to close with some reflections on what *Roe v. Wade* means, and on the tensions that are now in the Supreme Court over where *Roe* is going.

First of all, *Roe v. Wade* said that the fetus was not a person for the purpose of constitutional rights. Beyond that, the Court said it was not competent to make the decision about whether or not a fetus was a person, and took note of the religious and moral debate around the status of the fetus. This does not mean that the Court was unaware of the biological facts of fetal development. Rather, the Court recognized that biology as such does not stand alone, that biology has whatever value we attribute to it, notwithstanding attempts by the anti-abortion movement to end discussion by invoking biological facts when in truth that is where discussion only begins. The Court recognized that what we were dealing with are questions of religion, of conscience, and not just biology, and that by not saying that the fetus was a person, it was leaving it for individual people to make their own conscientious decisions.

Roe v. Wade did not say that women have the right of privacy across the board and that they can have an abortion at any point in pregnancy under any conditions. Justice Blackmun, who wrote the opinion, did talk about the fetus as such in that he said that in the third trimester, or after viability, (that is, when the fetus could live on its own), a state could, if it wanted to, outlaw abortion, but even then a woman's life or health prevailed. Now presumably under all the definitions of health the Supreme Court has used, even after viability a woman can get an abortion if her mental or physical health may be impaired. The interesting thing is that while roughly half the states in the country do limit post-viability abortions and roughly half the states do not, there is absolutely no difference in the incidence of late abortions between these two groups, absolutely none. Our research, and research by the Centers for Disease Control in Atlanta, yield the result that virtually no abortions are being performed after the fetus has reached viability.

Nevertheless, the thought of post-viability abortions makes a lot of people queasy even though they can find none in practice. I have learned from experience that the kinds of abortion one finds even near the time of viability are the most heartbreaking. They are women who found adverse results from amniocentesis, or teenagers who are trying to get the money because Medicaid doesn't pay for abortions -- situations of that sort, even at around the twentieth week of pregnancy, and 99% of all the abortions in this country are done before 20 weeks of pregnancy. Now the Supreme Court's language in recognizing that after viability a state could choose to prohibit abortion in some circumstances, has led judges to extend that reasoning to the nonabortion context. This is an especially dangerous development. For example, in New York State, a judge recently ordered a blood transfusion for a woman who was a Jehovah's Witness and felt that was against her religion, when she was 18 weeks pregnant, well before viability, and the whole basis of his reasoning was *Roe v. Wade.* He said that if the state can prohibit abortion after viability because of its compelling interest in the fetus, then even before viability it can order something, albeit not as intrusive as prohibiting abortion, such as a forced transfusion. In fact, the two contexts are wholly different, and in fact it is constitutionally threatening to adopt the *Roe* reasoning into the non-abortion context because that opens up a whole Pandora's Box.

Within the judicial community, there seem to be some pro-choice judges who are still very adamant about keeping the fetal status in the third trimester and retaining the viability concept. For example, in 1983, in *Planned Parenthood v. Ashcroft,* the Supreme Court upheld a law requiring that a second physician to help the fetus be present during a late abortion. This was definitely done for the fetus, not for the woman. Also, although we have so far won cases that restrict the kind of abortion a woman can have late in pregnancy, the Supreme Court has indicated that if you could perform an abortion that would save the fetus without additional harm to the woman it would probably uphold that as constitutional, but it has yet to confront that question in practice.

In the final analysis, I believe that the concept of viability is both dangerous and ultimately misguided. Abortion rights should be framed in terms of women's privacy and equality interests. In that light, anti-abortion laws violate rights to liberty and bodily integrity, which have a long history in this country. Ultimately, we all have to look at anti-abortion laws as real impediments to women's equality. If women are not going to be defined by biology, then biology cannot be used against them in anti-abortion legislation.

Thinking About *The Silent Scream*

An Audio Documentary Produced by

Patricia Jaworski

Interviewed in the documentary are Isaac Asimov, Michael Bennett, Patricia Gold-man-Rakic, Clifford Grobstein, and Dominick Purpura. Ms. Jaworski served as both narrator and interviewer in the documentary.

Jaworski: In January, 1985, the twelfth anniversary of the Supreme Court's decision to legalize abortion, the Pro-Life Movement released the film *The Silent Scream*.

Silent Scream Soundtrack: "Now for the first time, we have the technology to see abortion from the victim's vantage point. Ultra-sound imaging has allowed us to see this, and so for the first time, we are going to watch a child being torn apart, dismembered, disarticulated, crushed and destroyed by the unfeeling steel instruments of the abortionist."

Jaworski: Dr. Bernard Nathanson narrates *The Silent Scream*. The film, using ultra-sound, shows an abortion on a twelve week old fetus. Dr. Nathanson, as he describes the fetus's reaction to the abortion instrument:

Silent Scream Soundtrack: "Now the heart rate has speeded up dramatically, and the child's movements are violent at this point. It does sense aggression in its sanctuary. It is moving away. One can see it moving to the left side of the uterus in an attempt, a pathetic attempt to escape the inexorable instruments which the abortionist is using to extinguish its life. Now the heart has again perceptibly speeded up. We can time this at approximately 200 beats per minute, and there is no question this child senses the most mortal danger imaginable."

Jaworski: *The Silent Scream* has been recognized as a powerful film. Viewers, regardless of their stand on abortion, have reacted with strong and mixed emotion. The film has received widespread media attention, has had formal viewings at the White House, and has been seen by Congressmen and about 150 million people.

My name is Pat Jaworski, and today, we will be *Thinking about the Silent Scream*. We will not focus on the emotional impact of abortion, nor will we discuss woman's rights. Today, we will look at abortion from a new perspective -- one that might allow us to judge the *Silent Scream* -- *and* give us information on an issue which troubles many people.The concern of many, is whether the fetus is a person -- a conscious, thinking person -- aware of pain and capable of feeling terror during an abortion. This concern has been brought to the forefront by *The Silent Scream,* and by other actions of the Pro-Life Movement. As a result, the question of *when personhood begins,* is now critical. Since 1981, the Pro-Life Movement has introduced at least four bills in Congress that declare that a person begins at conception -- and in *The Silent Scream,* the fetus is constantly referred to as a person.

Silent Scream **Soundtrack**: "Now this little person at twelve weeks is a fully formed, absolutely identifiable human being. He has had brain waves for at least six weeks, his heart has been functioning for perhaps eight weeks, and all the rest of his human functions are indistinguishable from any of ours."

Jaworski: If we are to look at the fetus as a person and as a *fully formed human being, having human functions indistinguishable,* from ours -- consciousness, feelings, thought -- then we cannot ignore the one part of the human body that is needed to sustain these qualities.

Asimov: Now, we thoroughly realize that the brain is the center of thought, it is the center of emotion and without the brain, we are merely a lump of thoughtless meat that might respond automatically in some simple ways as an amoeba might. But nothing more.

Jaworski: Dr. Issac Asimov, who has a Ph.D. in chemistry, and is the author of *The Human Brain* and over 300 other books on science and science fiction, explains that for centuries, the center for humanness was thought to be the heart.

Asimov: In ancient times, the most important and obvious organ was the heart. It beat, it constantly beat, it never stopped day or night, and when it did stop, you were dead. Furthermore, it obviously adjusted itself to your moods. If you worked a great deal, it sped up. When you slept, it slowed down. If you were enraged or frightened, it would speed up. If you relaxed it would slow down. It was the obvious organ for life, emotion, feeling...

Jaworski: Other parts of the body have also been given responsibility for these qualities, including the blood.

Asimov: We still speak of someone being hot-blooded when they act out of emotion, or cold-blooded if they act simply out of intellectual thought. Another organ was the spleen, and we still speak of people venting their spleen when we mean that they express their anger or spite. And in all this, nothing much was said about the brain -- and Aristotle himself, who was the greatest philosopher of ancient times thought that the brain was simply a device that cooled the blood that passed through it.

Jaworski: There is now no question that the brain is critical to personhood. If there is no brain, or if the brain is not functioning, then an abortion does not destroy a consciously aware, thinking, feeling fetus. On the other hand, if a complete brain does exist -- from conception, or as early as twelve weeks -- and the fetus is an aware, thinking being, capable of feeling terror during an abortion, then there is a tiny person in the womb, and abortion could conceivably be considered murder.

Today you will hear from four scientists who have a great deal of expertise on the human brain. Amongst them, they have spent more than 60 years researching the brain. These scientists -- from Albert Einstein, Stanford, the University of California, and Yale -- will give us information on such questions as -- at what point does a fetus have a brain, when does the brain start to function, and when do the qualities of personhood -- such as thought, feelings, and conscious awareness -- begin? Because the interviews were done before *The Silent Scream* was released, and because of the sensitivity of the subject, the scientists edited their portions of the script for factual correctness.

Jaworski: Does the brain even exist at conception?

Bennett: No!!

Jaworski: Dr. Michael Bennett, Chairman of the Neuroscience Department at the Albert Einstein Medical School. Dr. Bennett actively teaches, writes, and directs research on the brain.

Jaworski: If there's no brain at conception, can there be a person at conception ?

Bennett: Certainly not, there's no person there.

Jaworski: Can there be a person without a brain?

Michael Bennett: No, no way. You can't be a person without a brain, you can't be a dog without a brain, you can't be a cat without a brain, or a chicken without a brain.

Jaworski: The mature human brain has around *100 billion brain cells*, called nerve cells or neurons. Neuron after neuron -- thousands of them are connected in chain-like fashion. The first neuron passes information to the second, the second to the third, and so on. Not only are there thousands of neurons in a chain, there are thousands of chains, and neurons in one chain can connect with neurons in hundreds of other chains -- forming a vast communications network. It's estimated that there are *one hundred trillion* connections between neurons in the brain. How and when all of this develops is the fascinating question behind the science of developmental neurobiology.

Jaworski: Dr. Patricia Goldman-Rakic is Professor of Neuroscience at the Yale Medical School. Dr. Goldman-Rakic has been doing research in developmental neurobiology for over 20 years.

Goldman-Rakic: Well, the premise of all of modern neurobiology is that the brain is the organ of consciousness. The brain is the organ of sensation, perception, conscious experience.

Jaworski: What about thought?

Goldman-Rakic: Including thought. There is no thought without brain.

Jaworski: The human brain does not exist without neurons. Brain neurons do not exist prior to four weeks in utero. They are created from the end of the first month in utero until several months after birth -- but *the peak period* for their creation is from two to five months in utero. However, the existence of neurons does not mean the existence of a developed functioning brain.

Goldman-Rakic: The brain is unique in that the cells undergo a process of migration. So when a cell is born, its nowhere near having finished it's developmental course. It now must move from it's place of origin to a distant location and that can take, in some cases, weeks.

Jaworski: The bulk of migration occurs from two to six months in utero. The first two steps -- the creation of the neurons, and migration -- contribute to the phenomenal growth of the brain in the early fetal months. As the billions of newborn neurons accumulate and push outward, *they are shaping* the internal and external structure of the brain. What's the third step?

Goldman-Rakic: This step usually takes place after this cell reaches its final target, and it's in its location -- and then it starts to develop specialized appendages.

Jaworski: Now, when I've seen pictures of neurons, there's sort of a central body, and out from that central body come all these tree-like branches...

Goldman-Rakic: Those are called dendrites. The cell has to grow its dendrites. You have a main branch, and then you have limbs growing out from that branch. Some cells have larger dendrites than other, more complex, more bushy. Now at the same time is the outgrowth of the axon of that cell. And let us say we are talking about a cell which is going to command a leg muscle to move. That cell has to grow an axon all the way from the top of the brain to the lumbar region of the spinal cord. That can be several feet.

Jaworski: How long does it take for a neuron to grow all these branches?

Goldman-Rakic: Well, we're talking days and weeks, and months.

Jaworski: It is during this third step that neurons will form, not only their dendrites and axons, but what is perhaps their most critical parts -- the synapses. It isn't until *synaptic connections* are built that one neuron can pass information to other neurons.

Goldman-Rakic: The whole goal of the development of neurons is to achieve what we call synaptic connections, in which the part of one cell actually becomes, if I can sort of use loose terminology, wired to another cell. It's only by achieving the proper connections that one can get proper behavior. For example, the retina which receives visual information from the environment should send this information to the part of the brain that is capable of processing visual information, and not to the part of the brain which will be receiving auditory information. So proper wiring is essential.

Jaworski: Synapses start to form from about the third month in utero, but most are formed after birth. In fact, synapses continue to be built for years after birth. Besides the creation of the neurons, migration and the development of the dendrites, axons, and synapses, the brain must go through even more steps before it can properly function.

Dr. Clifford Grobstein, a developmental biologist who is the former head of the Stanford University Biology Department, and is now at the University of California at San Diego, makes an important point concerning the development of the brain:

Grobstein: It's important to recognize that this general process goes on at different rates in the different parts of the brain. And of course, what we are particularly interested in is the cortex where so much of what appears to be related to volitional behavior, choices, thought, cognitive processes, and so on, goes on.

Jaworski: You mean the cerebral cortex?

Grobstein: The cerebral cortex.

Jaworski: Dr. Dominick Purpura is a neurologist and neuroscientist, former dean of the Stanford University Medical School, and current dean of the Albert Einstein Medical School. Dr. Purpura has been researching the development of the human brain since 1974 when he started doing research on mental retardation.

Purpura: The things that seem to be very important are a certain minimum number of nerve cells in the cerebral cortex, a certain level of development of these nerve cells, and a certain minimum number of synaptic connections. Which says then, that if you don't have that number of neurons, or that amount of connections, you're not going to be able to produce the qualities of humanness, personhood.

Jaworski: So you place the beginning...

Purpura: Of the capacity for personhood in the middle of the last trimester.

Jaworski: So prior to that, you would say there is no person.

Purpura: There is no person.

Jaworski: Does that mean that personhood is there at seven months in utero?

Purpura: It says that if there's a time at which it could begin, this is the point. It can't begin earlier. We're putting the boundary condition, a limit, the minimal time for personhood to begin, the minimal time -- it's not three months, it's not two months, it's seven months.

Narrator: So there is no person at conception?

Purpura: No possibility.

Jaworski: There is no possibility of a person at one month?

Purpura: None, none -- not through the first trimester, not through the second trimester even. And, at 28 to 29, 30 weeks, yes, yes, suddenly, something, the windows opening now.

Jaworski: Prior to this, there is a noticeable lack of axons, dendrites, and synaptic connections in the cortex. Around the 28th week, there is a dramatic change:

Purpura: It's the point at which the rate of dendritic growth is at its maximum, and when synapses are starting to form, and the rate of synapse development is occurring at the greatest speed in the cerebral cortex.

Jaworski: A few weeks later, critical changes are seen in the fetal brain wave pattern. By thirty-one weeks, the brain waves become organized, and finally start to make sense, says Dr. Purpura. Yet *The Silent Scream* claims that the twelve week fetus has already had brain waves for six weeks?

Purpura: Any electrical activity recorded from the brain is called a brain wave. One can record all kinds of oscillations back into the second or third week of embryonic life, but one can record all kinds of wild electrical oscillations from a couple of nerve cells sitting in culture, too. That doesn't mean anything. It only means that all cells have electrical potentials. The human liver cell has electrical potentials in it. It can generate, if you will, certain types of quote "brain waves," But those cells are concerned with digestive enzymes. So the presence of electrical activity is common to virtually all cells.

Jaworski: Although electrical activity can be recorded early in utero, it's around thirty-one weeks that brain waves become meaningful. A few weeks later, the first signs of wakefulness and sleep are seen.

What about some of the other statements made in *The Silent Scream*? At one point, Dr. Nathanson is using some models showing the outside shape of fetuses ranging from four to twenty-eight weeks in utero:

Silent Scream **Soundtrack:** "As you can see, there is no revolutionary or dramatic change in the substance of this person throughout this developmental stage. Now this little person at twelve weeks is a fully formed, absolutely identifiable human being."

Jaworski: If you look at the fetus from the outside only, what Dr. Nathanson is saying may appear correct. But if you look at what's going on inside, you realize that there *are phenomenal changes* occurring. The fetus is not fully formed at twelve weeks in utero, and in fact, is undergoing dramatic and revolutionary changes at this time. The billions of neurons are still being created, they will be traveling for weeks to their destinations, and once there, they will be growing the trillions of dendrites and synapses that they will need to function. As this is happening, the whole brain is being shaped.

The feeling that abortion might be causing a fetus to feel pain and terror is a legitimate concern, and this feeling is expressed by Dr. Clifford Grobstein.

Grobstein: If we are concerned about the possibility, about doing anything to a developing human being, we do not want to invade any possible consciousness or selfness or produce any pain or discomfort, then we have to err on the side of caution.

Jaworski: Throughout *The Silent Scream,* movement is the only evidence used to infer that the fetus is feeling pain and terror. It has been argued that the movements seen in the film are caused by the abortion instrument pushing the fetus around. But just suppose that the movements are not a result of this -- could *The Silent Scream's* explanation be true? Dr. Dominick Purpura:

Purpura: Movements can occur at the very earliest stage; for example, reflexes of the spinal cord are demonstrable in the very earliest stages -- the reflex movements that occur when even the mother feels life. You may have twitches and these twitches can cause the muscle to move in different ways -- so movement itself, movement is the poorest judge, the poorest criterion for personhood.

Jaworski: And as Dr. Purpura points out, even simple organisms such as the single-cell parmamecium and sperm move.

Dr. Clifford Grobstein agrees. In 1981, he wrote an interesting book -- with a very difficult title -- called *From Chance to Purpose: An Appraisal of External Human Fertilization*. In the book, Dr. Grobstein discussed movements of the fetus. Movements have been detected as early as eight weeks in utero.

Grobstein: In therapeutic abortions, that is, where it was necessary for health reasons to abort the fetus - if it was stimulated in the mouth area, there were reactions of the head, turning movements of the head. Now that kind of responsiveness would be referred to as a reflex -- and that suggests that it always occurs in exactly the same way, and that it certainly doesn't involve any volition, or will, on the part of the responding organism.

Jaworski: How about the third month -- the end of the first trimester ?

Grobstein: The kind of reflexes that one can elicit at that stage are somewhat more complex. On the other hand, these are still the kind of behaviors that I think almost all neurophysiologists and students of behavior would call reflexive, automatic, whatever term you want to use. So that, I would say that at three months when the fetus hasn't progressed beyond that level of behavior, one would probably conclude that at that point there is not anything present of the sort that we would associate with a person.

Jaworski: No one wants to cause a fetus to feel pain or terror, but it has to be realized that a brain must exist before pain and terror can be felt -- structure always precedes function -- and not only must the brain exist, it must reach a certain level of development. The scientific evidence reveals a basic flaw in *The Silent Scream's* major premise. If indeed, the fetus is a conscious, feeling, little person -- at conception, or as early as twelve weeks -- then why does the complex process of building the brain occur? Why would nature bother to create the billions of neurons, have them travel for weeks, build trillions of special appendages -- some of which are feet long -- for no reason? Nature goes through this process, because the brain is needed before personhood can exist in the fetus.

For many years, debate centered around the question of when human life begins. But there is no beginning to human life on today's earth -- it is passed from generation to generation. Human life does not begin with the fertilized egg.

Is the fertilized egg living?

Clifford Grobstein: Yes.

Jaworski: Is the unfertilized egg living?

Clifford Grobstein: Yes.

Jaworski: Are the millions of sperm that are produced and wasted also living?

Grobstein: Yes.

Jaworski: Then these are all forms of human life.

Grobstein: Yes, they are all human and alive.

Jaworski: Then any time we waste a sperm or an egg, we are terminating life.

Grobstein: Yes, we are certainly terminating life. Yes.

Jaworski: So then one could argue that as soon as a young woman starts ovulating, that they should start having sex and getting pregnant as soon as possible.

Grobstein: Yes, yes. If you accept the logic of the people who are trying to argue that, if it's alive and human, then it's got to be sacred, and particularly if it has the capability, the potential to become an individual, a person, then you have to protect it. Then in that case, yes, every time, a young woman ovulates without having had intercourse, she has failed to achieve the potential of the egg.
Incidentally, men waste many more gametes than woman.

Jaworski: You mean sperm? Millions and millions every time.

Grobstein: Millions and millions and millions.

Jaworski: Dr. Michael Bennett, also commenting on the beginning of human life:

Bennett: I think one would have a hard time saying exactly when human life began -- how many millions of years ago. What I'm saying is that human life started back there.

Jaworski: It doesn't start with the fertilized egg.

Bennett: The egg is living, the sperm is living. The sperm swims around. It's got to be alive. The unfertilized egg is quite active. You can cause it to divide artificially; you can cause it to respond. It's doing a lot of protein synthesis, it's breathing, it's metabolizing, synthesizing protein. It's doing lots of things. The unfertilized egg is clearly a living cell. It's a human cell, it has all the information in it to make a human.

Jaworski: Because human life is a continuum, the critical question then becomes -- at what point in the continuum does personhood begin -- and the answer to this question offers us important guidelines in the abortion issue.
The evidence concerning the development of the brain directly contradicts the claims made in *The Silent Scream* -- and in light of this evidence, the contents

of the film have to be re-evaluated. Although *The Silent Scream* may still have a strong emotional impact when viewed, the evidence -- from scientists who have expertise in this area -- has to be considered. And the evidence should be taken into account on any decisions about abortion -- including decisions on bills in Congress that declare that a person exists at conception. There is no person at conception -- and to declare a person as beginning at conception flies in the face of all the scientific evidence.

You've been listening to *Thinking About The Silent Scream*. *Thinking About The Silent Scream* was written and produced by Pat Jaworski. Edited by Deborah Gaines, Narrative Direction - Kathy Healy. Sound Engineering - Peter Bochan. And thanks to some people who have given a lot of support while producing this show: Pam Bayless, Karen Clark, Tim DeBaets, Kathy Healy and Niss Ryan. This is Pat Jaworski.

Neuromaturation and the Moral Status of Human Fetal Life

Fetal personhood: an intrinsic property or a matter of multiple attributions?

THE QUESTION "When does human life begin?" has become the well-known and controversial encapsulation of a central issue in the conflict over abortion--the moral status of embryonic/fetal life. From one perspective the question as put is thought to frame the issue adequately. In this view personhood is a matter of natural objectivity; we are simply *presented* with the fact of full humanness or personhood--an *intrinsic* and *scientifically discoverable* property emerging during the course of a continuous ontogenetic process. However, there is a problem with this notion of intrinsic personhood, and it is deciding which of several different suggested properties is the one "real" answer to when a particular and personal human life has begun. Is it possession of the unique human genome achieved after fertilization, loss of embryonic ability to twin (i.e. developmental individuality) roughly two weeks later, appearance of fetal motility at six to seven weeks of gestation, emergence of unmistakably human form a few weeks later still, first awareness, or birth? In deciding, one must give reasons for one's choice and thereby necessarily introduce "extra-biological" dimensions as part of the choosing. As a result, the biological indicators come to serve as little more than the material referents for these reasons. The recognition that reasoned choices among contending properties must be made has led many to focus precisely on those reasons, and to claim that the properties whereby we understand and value prenatal personhood are not those discoverable by science but those *constituted* within a social fabric, and most properly by those who are directly involved with the fetus before and after its birth (Solomon, 1983, p.220).

Harrison (1983), for example, claims that our evaluation of embryonic and fetal human life is a complex exercise of moral agency in the face of a precise moral question: "When shall we predicate full human value to developing fetal life?" Such predication or attribution is clearly a socially constitutive act *extrinsic* to the fetus. It is not, however, an act unconcerned with the changing nature of the fetus or its intimate and dependent relation to the woman nurturing it. Thus, as we exercise this moral agency we are counselled to take into account "developmental criteria for stipulating the degree of similarity to existing human beings required for counting fetal life as *a* human life" while attending to "the moral reasons for and against viewing prenatal life as morally continuous or discontinuous with existent humanity" (Harrison, 1983, pp. 208-209). That is, we are to *look for developmental differences which make a moral difference.*

Given the view expressed by Harrison, how do we engage in the process of predication? If we cannot begin with scientific facts about prental ontogenesis, if the meaning or definition of personhood is simply not something arrived at empirically, then it must be decided upon. The justification for a choice of developmental criterion must originate elsewhere and earlier, within our moral communities. Thus, we look toward the embryo or fetus from the vantage point of existent humanity, having already chosen one or more criteria--about ourselves--as anchors of a possible moral continuity with the developing fetus. These prior choices of criteria thereby condition the nature of our moral gaze.

While several such criteria have been suggested (and noted above), perhaps the most compelling of prenatal criteria are those related to the central nervous system (CNS). This is so because the CNS materially underpins the development of several capacities we socially construe as of moral importance to us: (1) awareness (expecially of pleasure and pain); (2) a discrete and sustainable bodily existence achieved through birth which enables a transition in the manner of nurturance and occasions "'a convenant of caring' that *creates* personal existence"; (Harrison, 1983, p.223;) (3) a rich meshwork of neocortical circuitry whose post-natal "remodeling" (see below) may in part reflect the neuro-embodiment of an emerging personal existence lived in interaction with others; and finally, those Engelhart (1983, p.184) associates with persons in the strict sense (i.e. persons of the sort we hopefully are): (4) sense of self, (5) ability to exercise rationality, and (6) capacity to choose freely and responsibly. Thus, our moral sensibilities turn our gaze to a collection of important, neurally-enabled capacities warranting attention. It is at that point scientific methodologies and tools can sometimes be used to tell us *when* there emerges a nervous system of sufficient material complexity to embody those capacities (already) judged as morally pertinent. Knowing when, we are (perhaps) better prepared to fashion the bridge of moral continuity spoken of by Harrison.

A brief chronicle of human embryonic/fetal neuromaturation: knowing when integrative transitions occur

Although the process of human development from newly fertilized ovum to birth is properly considered a continuum of change, it is an uneven continuum. There are periods of developmental transition during which integrative functions appear and increasingly complex embryonic and fetal properties emerge. This general observation is true of neuromaturation as well. Thus, if we adopt the position that the integrative activities of the prenatal CNS are an important consideration for our possible ascription of moral standing, we must ask *which* integrative functions are of moral significance and *what degree of neural development* must be evidenced before we are advised to "draw the line" that encompasses particular fetal lives within our moral communities and protects them from harm?

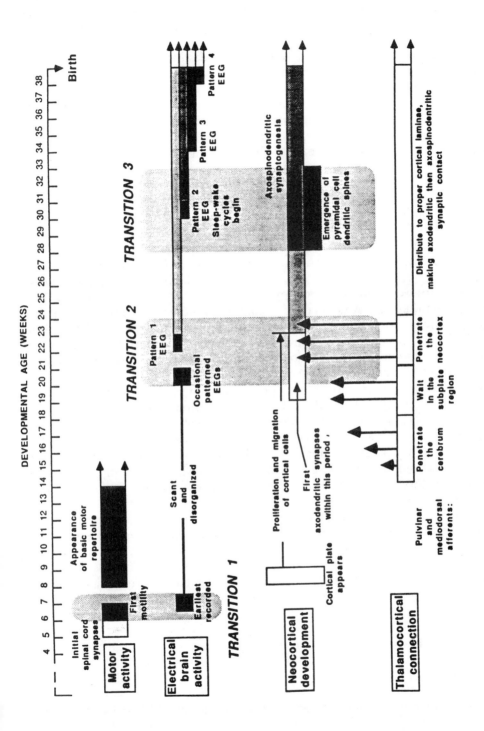

FIGURE 1. Neuromaturational Processes During Fetal Human Life

First, it is important to understand that the development of the nervous system can be followed as a sequence of processes (Flower, 1985), not all of which may be of comparable moral significance. The earliest developmental event is the appearance of *unspecialized* (or *presumptive*) neural cells; these are different from other embryonic cells in that only they are destined to produce the CNS as ontogenesis proceeds. There then follow two further changes, developments which begin at different times and proceed at different rates in various parts of the CNS (a circumstance that makes it difficult to speak about neuromaturation of the fetal CNS as a whole). First, presumptive cells begin preparing to function as nerve cells; they *differentiate* by changing their morphology and biosynthetic activities. This differentiation enables the second major change, a *cooperative assembly into supercellular arrays.* Neural cells synapse ("hook up") with one another, producing information-carrying circuits. As is probably obvious, the last of these developmental processes will eventually come to interest us most, for it is neural circuitry that makes possible the integrative function of the nervous system.

However, it is useful to look first at earlier events and then proceed in the direction of greater complexity. As the human embryo develops, when is there first "something neural" to observe, characterize, and talk about scientifically? During the third week of human development it is already possible to identify that portion of the embryo which is the presumptive or rudimentary forerunner of the future CNS; at this time, however, there are no functional nerve cells. In the fifth week (Figure 1), maturing neurons can be found in the cervical (neck) region of the embryonic spinal cord (Okado, 1981, pp.212, 215); they are sufficiently specialized that the simplest sort of supercellular circuits (reflex arcs) can be established soon thereafter, serving to support rudimentary fetal motility. At this time, also, there are undoubtedly differentiating neurons in the developing brainstem region (Humphrey, 1978). However, if we look for the neocortex we will not find it even in rudimentary form. It is put in place by processes of cellular proliferation and migration that do not begin until the eighth week and last through the fifth month of development. And even when most of the neocortical cells are in their proper place at five months, the multicellular assemblage does not yet constitute a functioning cellular array, for these neocortical cells have yet to fully differentiate. For instance, if we look for indications of neocortical cellular specialization (evidenced morphologically by the production of long cellular extensions known as axons and dendrites, and by the appearance of multiple synaptic targets or "spines" on the latter) we will find relatively few before 20 weeks. Many weeks later, with the relatively sudden emergence of these specialized cellular morphologies and synaptic points-of-contact, a rapid and quantitatively enhanced formation of complex neocortical circuitry is enabled.

Looking at specific neuromaturational processes

The Earliest Events

If at three weeks of development there are no functional nerve cells, how much time passes before neural function (of some sort) appears? We can ask when electrical activity is first detectable and when there first appear functions (such as motility) known to be dependent on neural maturation. In both cases the answer is the same: about the sixth-to-seventh week (Figure 1). As was noted earlier, there is not even the hint of a neocortex at this time; thus, the electrical activity observed (Borkowski and Bernstine, 1955) does not indicate higher brain function. However, such activity may be a manifestation of early embryonic brainstem function.

What of prenatal motility? What degree of neuromaturation is required to support it? Very little, as it turns out. When observed ultrasonigraphically, the late-stage embryo of six weeks can be seen to exhibit occasional and "just discernible movement"; a week later, a "startle" response emerges. Over the next six to seven weeks a relatively complex repertoire of spontaneous motor activities emerges (de Vries *et al*, 1982); the fetal limbs and head move about, breathing movements occur, and swallowing and sucking are observed. The "control" of this activity might conceivably reside in the relatively simple neural circuitry of the spinal cord, as Robertson (1985) has suggested in his account of the later cyclic motor activity of post-mid-gestation fetuses. However, as the development of younger fetuses proceeds, the various motor activities exhibit temporal patterns of expression which differ one from the other (de Vries et al, 1985), possibly indicative of some measure of modulatory influence "higher" than the spinal cord. It has been suggested (Flower, 1985) that the earliest modulator of such activity is the brainstem (serving, for example, to integrate rudimentary sensory input from such sources as fetal muscle "stretch receptors," small "sensors" embedded in muscle tissue and triggered by muscle contractile activity to send electrical impulses to the CNS). This suggestion of a general integrative function (Transition 1 in Figure 1) is made more reasonable by the recent observations of Visser and colleagues (1985). They found that anencephalic fetuses lacking the brainstem region exhibited considerable *but abnormally patterned* motility when compared to that of anencephalic fetuses with intact brianstem. They also noted that substantial motility (though again unorganized) was possible even in anencephalics in which only abnormally situated nests of spinal cord neurons were present. Thus, little neural circuitry was necessary for movement, but an intact brainstem was associated with normal *patterns* of fetal activity.

Of what significance is this putative brainstem integrative function? Is it, if real, in any way an attractor of our moral concern? At this very early time do we have morally justifiable reasons for establishing a moral bridge expressed through an imputation of some form of fetal personhood? In virtue of what actions on our part would we define the imputation? As the brainstem is not the same thing as the neocortex we can be certain that the patterned changes in fetal motility are not the result of intention; they are not indicative of any sort of conscious awareness and need not draw our moral attention for that reason. However, are there other reasons to attend to a fetus of this stage? At least one philosopher thinks so. Tauer (1985, p.258-259) has argued that "...if integration through the brainstem is a valid hypothesis...it seems reasonable to describe the late first trimester fetus's relationship to tactile stimuli and to its own movements...as fetal 'experience'." While such experience is not conscious as we have noted, Tauer suggests (p.259) that "it is comparable to other nonconscious experience in its significance for psychological life." This is so for Tauer because she counts the foundations of later personal traits (self-consciousness, rationality, and self-determination) as begun when integrative brain pathways are first established, including those of the brainstem. In other words, Tauer advances a "whole brain" conception of personal prenatal becoming. She suggests (citing Mittelman, 1960, p.104-105) that "intrauterine events may be 'physiological antecedents of later happenings...traces that in some way are equivalents of later memory traces...'." *If* such speculative traces do exist and *if* they influence (even in part) later neural capacities of moral significance then one can understand why Tauer would attribute to fetuses older than six weeks a status she calls the *psychic sense of person*. For Tauer, an integrative foundation is being laid down, one that in some (undoubtedly indirect) way may affect the person-to-be. But what kind of respect does she argue is due a fetus with such a status? Or asked differently (to emphasize the constitutive nature of status-giving), what actions of ours would realize that status in practice?

Crucial for the attribution of psychic personhood is the *realized* potential of such fetuses to become persons in the strict sense. The status of psychic personhood is morally relevant only if fetal "experience" is continuous with and determines the development of personal psychological characteristics of a person like you and me--that is, only if a full pregnancy is anticipated and completed. Thus, *Tauer's argument for psychic personhood* (as she recognizes) *is not one on the basis of which we would proscribe abortion during the first trimester.* Instead--and certainly of importance--Tauer's argument for attributing psychic personhood to a human life during its seventh week of prenatal development is relevant to the question of--and is constituted by--the care and nurturance necessary to protect the normal integrative embodiment of a CNS crucial for continued creation of a personal existence. That is, even if the speculative claims of (later-effective) "memory trace-like" experience as early as six to seven weeks of gestation can be sustained, the notion of psychic personhood instructs us only as to our proper relationship to a fetus that will develop to birth: we ought to avoid injurious intervention (e.g. experimentation or traumatic therapeutic measures) and to care for the fetus's normal development through proper maternal nutrition, avoidance of undue stress, harmful chemicals and the like, thus protecting a future person. Of course, such a concern for protective behavior would come into play before six to seven weeks of gestation because *earlier* processes of CNS (and other organ-system) development are subject to developmental mishap as evidenced by such abnormalities as anencephaly and spina bifida. While Tauer would surely be concerned about such outcomes and the avoidance of conditions producing them, her arguments concerning psychic personhood--as we have seen--are directed to those processes of CNS emergence involving the formation of integrative pathways which might exert some type of "memory" effect. Such concern surely entails not only responsible maternal care but also an *enabling societal concern*, one that ensures the availability of proper prenatal services to all women seeking to care well for the fetal lives their bodies sustain. Thus we find, perhaps surprisingly, that the early events of human neuromaturation--as stated thus far-- may have much to do with how we view and support full-term pregnancies while having nothing to do with the morality of early abortions.

Emergence of the neocortex: As noted earlier, neocortical development requires many months. The cells of the neocortex are produced by a zone of proliferative cells located some distance from the site of neocortex formation, thus prospective neocortical cells must actively migrate to their final position--a process that begins at about 52-54 days of embryonic development (Molliver et al, 1973, p.406; Marin-Padilla, 1983, p.34). Continuing for more than three months, this process of cell proliferation and migration produces a succession of neocortical cell layers within which neurons of different function specialize and begin forming synapses, the interconnections that produce a supercellular form of organization: neocortical circuitry. The first of these synapses are formed some time between 19 and 22 weeks of development (Molliver et al, 1973, p.404), although most neocortical synaptogenesis occurs over an extended period of time beginning at about the 28th week (Purpura, 1975, p.45-46, examining the visual neocortex), a time after which the key neuronal classes of the neocortex exhibit on their dendritic extensions the tiny projections or spines which are the necessary "targets" for establishing neocortical circuitry which is *morphophysiologically equivalent* to that of a full-term neonate.

Of greater importance for our purposes here, perhaps, is Purpura's observation that such dendritic spine development "does not represent a continuous process traceable to early fetal phases of dendritic differentiation." Thus, for example, while neocortical cells of 24 to 27 week fetuses have already begun formation of dendritic extensions, they possess no dendritic spines (Purpura, 1975, p.46). Rather, they begin to appear "suddenly" at around the 28th week. This rapid appearance of dendritic spines is an example of what was earlier termed an "uneven continuity," a developmental transition (Transition 3 in Figure 1) occurring over a relatively short time period (in this case, the seventh month of pregnancy). This observation should not be taken to mean that prior to 28 weeks the visual region of the neocortex is inactive. In fact, preterm infants exhibit electrical activity in the visual neocortex (visual evoked responses or VERs) as early as 24-25 weeks of gestation (i.e. after the time of appropriate thalamocortical connection to be noted below). In the particular situation studied by Purpura and his colleagues, the transition in synaptic capability (and thus supercellular circuit-forming capacity) was associated with a qualitative change in this functional VER activity to that characteristic of a full-term neonatal VER (i.e. attainment of morphophysiological equivalence as an outcome of neuromaturational events of the seventh gestational month).

In short then, at least one region of the neocortex, that one processing visual information, exhibits a rather sharply-bounded developmental emergence of dendritic spines that in turn enables a quantitative leap in synaptic connectivity. Whether other regions of the neocortex follow a similar time-course of synaptic transition--that is, whether this time period might reflect a nearly *qualitative* shift in over-all neocortical capability--is not known with certainty. However, recent observation of simultaneous or *isosynchronous* synapse production in *diverse* regions of the cortex of non-human primates at a stage of neuromaturation comparable to that studied by Purpura is suggestive of this possibility (Rakic et al, 1986). If fetal humans exhibit this self-same isosynchronous synaptic transition then we might expect that Transition 3 (Figure 1) leads to a neocortex exhibiting qualitative different capabilities.

What sensory input is there for the neocortex to process?

It would hardly be controversial to argue that we are most likely to attend to fetuses whose level of neuromaturation supports (we suspect) some determinable form of awareness. After all, aware is how we are (if not asleep, anaesthetized, or in a coma). And to be aware--unless there is some form of awareness that is sub-cortical--there must be a synaptically interconnected neocortex and sensory input to it. How and when is the latter achieved?

Nearly all input to the neocortex passes through the thalamus, an important multi-component structure that modulates qualitatively different "types" of sensory input prior to passing them on to appropriate regions of the sensory neocortex. Without functional thalamocortical connections, the neocortex is nearly isolated and, in any case, not in receipt of the sort of neural information which when processed is represented as sensation. Thus, we can change the question posed above: do we have any knowledge of the developmental time-course over which thalamic neurons send out extensions to and connect with the neocortex? Studies by Kostovic and Goldman-Rakic (1983) and Dostovic and Rakic (1984) indicate that two regions of the thalamus (the pulvinar and mediodorsal) produce fibers that penetrate the neocortex at least as early as the 22nd or 23rd week (Transition 2 in Figure 1) but probably not much earlier. It is possible that the first neocortical synapses detected by Molliver and co-workers (1973) number among them initial contacts between neocortical cells and sensory-input fibers--although at present there is no evidence that his is (or is not) the case. It is possible that other regions of the thalamus send extensions toward the forming neocortex at earlier times. If they do, however, any synaptic interconnection could not involve the neocortex proper (for, as we have just seen, no neocortical synapses are seen earlier than 19 weeks of gestation). The thalamocortical axons might target cells which lie "beneath" the overlying neocortex (the so-called subplate region) as the former "await" maturation of their eventual targets in the neocortex itself--a situation suggested to occur in the maturation of the neocortex of other mammals (Chun, Nakamura and Shatz, 1987). As indicated above, most of neocortical synaptogenesis--including the bulk of those thalamocortical connections linking the "sensory outside" to the neocortical neurons which underpin a possible "awareness within" --are established many weeks later. Thus, beginning at perhaps 21 to 23 weeks of gestation there is a transition to a neocortex potentially in receipt of sensory input.

Neocortical Activity At and After Mid-Gestation

In spite of the evidence we have just examined, we cannot as yet define what degree and kind of neocortical synaptogenesis is necessary and sufficient to support particular complex CNS functions, including some degree of awareness. We can, however, follow the emergence of increasingly complex electroencephalograms (EEGs) as well as the behavior of premature fetal-infants, and note the "resemblance" of both to those of older infants.

Prior to mid-gestation, the electrical activity associated with brain function is relatively unorganized and does not exhibit patterns suggesting the type of activity characteristic of much older fetuses or newborn infants. After mid-gestation, however, a series of increasingly complex EEG pattern changes occur. Thus, Transition 2 is characterized not only by initial neocortical synaptogenesis and arrival of sensory input channels but by the first manifestation of patterned (but intermittent) brain waves as well. Gertler (1986) has recently suggested that this first appearance of neocortical activity constitute what he terms "brain birth." However, what sort of brain birth is this? Normal postnatal brain function is characterized by *continuous* electrical activity. An activity pattern of this sort is not present from the time the first neocortical cells begin making synaptic contact; rather, the change in EEG pattern to one of continuous electrical activity occurs at about 30 weeks of gestation--the period designated here as Transition 3. Furthermore, this latter EEG pattern marks the distinction between fetal wakefulness and sleep (Spehlmann, 1981). It is maybe significant that this latter activity transition occurs as the number and type of neocortical synapses changes between 28 and 32 weeks of development, perhaps representing the functional outcome of the suggested isosynchronous shift in pattern of neuronal connectivity noted earlier.

This period of transition is highlighted by other observations as well. Premature fetal-infants of 28-32 weeks gestation have been characterized (Gesell, 1971) as "loosely articulated and flaccid mannikins"; they are limp and torporous if stimulated. Only several weeks later does this torpor give way to a genuine wakefulness when the newborn is stirred to activity, just about the time (roughly 34-36 weeks of gestational age) EEG patterns change once again and there emerge so-called "behavioral states"--stable, synchronously recurrent constellations of activities (motility, breathing and heart rate) that had previously changed independently of one another (Prechtl and O'Brien, 1982; Nijhuis *et al*, 1982).

Looking at what has been said, *it seems we may have the greatest difficulty deciding what to make of the period of time from 20 to 30 weeks*, the interim between Transitions 2 and 3. At the outset of this time period the neocortex is a collection of individual neurons; at the "end," an interconnected collective exhibiting continuous electrical activity and participating in cycles of fetal sleep and wakefulness. If we are wont to speak seriously of fetal personhood, we will surely focus on this time period, a time frame which brackets the second-to-third trimester "division." Of crucial importance, of course, is whether we look to the earliest events and talk of a personhood-entitling "brain birth" as Gertler has suggested, or whether we turn our attention to the (perhaps) qualitative shift in neocortical connectivity and emergence of sleep/wake cycles occurring near this period's end, thereby requiring as a developmental difference which makes a moral difference a fetal neocortex exhibiting morphophysiological properties similar to those of full-term infants. Whatever tentative choice we might make as between Transitons 2 and 3, it is clear the course of fetal ontogenesis bracketed by these transitions is one about which we need much more information.

The "Finishing Touches" of Neuromaturation

Neuromaturation is not a process ending at birth. For example, Huttenlocher (1979) and Huttenlocher *et al* (1982) have followed the process of neocortical synaptogenesis from the 28th week of gestation to early adolescence. They found that the number of synapses increases rapidly during the last weeks of prenatal development and up until about one year of age after which time there is a gradual loss of synapses (especially during early childhood), with the synaptic number characteristic of adults reached by early adolescence.

What does such a decrease represent?

In other organisms, a comparable "paring back" of synaptic connections in some regions of the neocortex has been interpreted as an *activity*-or *experience dependent* stabilization or "tailoring" of some neural pathways at the expense of others. If a similar neurodevelopmental plasticity is the case in humans as well, one might consider the eventual "fine-tuning" of neocortical connectivity during childhood as a "lived accomplishment." If fine-tuning does occur, it would be unlikely the experiential dimension is the whole story. Thatcher and colleagues (1987, pp.1110-1113) have recently demonstrated age-dependent changes in neocortical EEG activity from birth through adolescence. From these observations they conclude (p.1113) that during human cortical development "there is a genetically programmed unfolding of specific corticocortical connections at relatively specific postnatal ages." Combining these views, one could say (not at all surprisingly) that as each of us lives our early years, the experiencing of our world "shapes", at least in part, the neocortical pathways so crucial to developing personhood. Neuromaturation and emergent personhood are thus as inextricably intermeshed as are the myriad neuronal circuits that comprise the human central nervous system.

Where has our investigation of embryonic and fetal neuromaturation led us?

Observations of neuromaturation suggest the possibility of three significant integrative transitions during ontogenesis of the prenatal human CNS. The first appears to involve the brainstem's modulatory effect on patterns of fetal motility emerging during the first trimester. It has been argued here and by Tauer (1985), however, that this integrative function is not one which would lead us to predicate a sort of fetal personhood barring abortion in the first trimester. The second transition is undoubtedly more complex. It includes the arrival in the neocortex of sensory-input fibers from the thalamus--a minimal requirement for establishing even the possibility of awareness at the neocortical level. The third transition is marked by the emergence of continuous EEG activity and wake/sleep cycles; it may also be characterized by a rather abruptly initiated period of dendritic spine formation, thereby providing the capacity for a type of synaptogenesis characteristic of more mature neocortical circuitry and (perhaps) establishing the first material possibility of neocortical functions comparable to those of normal, full-term infants--including, one might presume, the first manifestation of awareness. Thus, if we return to those neocortical capacities most likely to engage our moral attention as we prepare to ascribe a protected status of fetal personhood (i.e. possible awareness and/or a discrete and sustainable bodily existence regularly achieved through birth), we might be led to conclude that it is probably not until after 28 weeks of gestation that the fetal human attains a level of neocortex-mediated complexity sufficient to enable those sentient capacities the presence of which might lead us to predicate personhood of a sort we attribute to full-term newborns.

Bibliography

Borkowski, W.J., and Bernstine, R.L. (1955). Electroencephalography of the fetus. *Neurology* 5: 362-365.

Chun, J.J.M., Nakamura, M.J., and Shtaz, C.J. (1987). Transient cells of the developing mammalian telencephalon are peptide-immunoreactive neurons. *Nature* 325: 617-620.

de Vries, J.I.P., Visser, G.H.A., and Prechtl, H.F.R. (1982). The emergence of fetal behavior. I. Qualitative aspects. *Early Human Development* 7: 301-322.

de Vries, J.I.P., Visser, G.H.A., and Prechtl, H.F.R. (1985). The emergence of fetal behavior. II. Quantitative aspects. *Early Human Development* 12: 99-120.

Englehardt, H.T. (1983). Viability and the use of the fetus. In W.B. Bondeson *et al* (eds.), *Abortion and the Status of the Fetus*, D. Reidel Publishing Company, Dordrecht, Holland, pp. 183-208.

Flower, M.J. (1985). Neuromaturation of the human fetus. *Journal of Medicine and Philosophy* 10: 237-251.

Gertler, G.B. (1986). Brain birth: a proposal for defining when a fetus is entitled to human life status. *Southern California Law Review* 59:1061-1078.

Gesell, A. (1971). *The Embryology of Behavior*, Greenwood Press, Westport, Connecticut.

Harrison, B.W. (1983). *Our Right To Choose: Toward a New Ethic of Abortion*, Beacon Press, Boston.

Humphrey, T. (1978). Function of the nervous system during prenatal life. In U. Stave (ed.), *Perinatal Physiology*, Plenum, New York, pp.651-683.

Huttenlocher, P.R. (1979). Synaptic density in human frontal cortex: developmental changes and effects of aging. *Brain Research* 163: 195-205.

Huttenlocher, P.R., de Courten, C., Garey, L.J., and Van Der Loos, H. (1982). Synaptogenesis in human visual cortex--evidence for synapse elimination during normal development. *Neuroscience Letters* 33: 247-252.

Kostovic, I. and Goldman-Rakic, P.S. (1983). Transient cholinesterase staining in the mediodorsal nucleus of the thalamus and its connections in the developing human and monkey brain. *Journal of Comparative Neurology* 219: 413-447.

Kostovic, I., and Rakic, P. (1984). Development of prestriate visual projections in the monkey and human fetal cerebrum revealed by transient cholinesterase staining. *Journal of Neuroscience* 4: 25-42.

Marin-Padilla, M. (1983). Structural organization of the human cerebral cortex prior to the appearance of the cortical plate. *Anatomy and Embryology* 168: 21-40.

Mittelmann, B. (1960). Intrauterine and early infantile motility. *Psychoanalytic Study of the Child* 15: 104-127.

Molliver, M.E., Kostovic, I., and Van Der Loos, H. (1973). The development of synapses in cerebral cortex of the human fetus. *Brain Research* 50: 403-407.

Nijhuis, J.G., Prechtl, H.F.R., Martin, C.B., and Bots, R.S.G.M. (1982). Are there behavioral states in the human fetus? *Early Human Development* 6: 177-195.

Okado, N. (1981). Onset of synapse formation in the human spinal cord. *Journal of Comparative Neurology* 201: 211-219.

Prechtl, H.F.R. and O'Brien, M.J. (1982). Behavioral states of the fullterm newborn. The emergence of a concept. (In H.F.R. Prechtl ed.), *Psychobiology of the Newborn Infant*, Blackwell, Oxford, pp.53-73.

Purpura, D.P. (1975). Morphogenesis of visual cortex in the preterm infant. In M.A.B. Brazier (ed), *Growth and Development of the Brain*, Raven Press, New York, pp. 33-49.

Rakic, P., Bourgeois, J.P., Eckenhoff, M.F., Zecevic, N., and Goldman-Rakic, P.S. (1986). Concurrent overproduction of synapses in diverse regions of the primate cerebral cortex. *Science* 232: 232-235.

Robertson, S.S. (1985). Cyclic motor activity in the human fetus after mid-gestation. *Developmental Psychobiology* 18: 411-419.

Solomon, R.C. (1983). Reflections on the meaning of (fetal) life. In W.B. Bondeson et al (eds.), *Abortion and the Status of the Fetus*, D. Reidel Publishing Company, Dordrecht, Holland, pp. 209-226.

Spehlmann, R. (1981). *EEG Primer*, Elsevier-Holland, New York.

Tauer, C.A. (1985). Personhood and human embryos and fetuses. *Journal of Medicine and Philosophy* 10: 253-266. Thatcher, R.W., Walker, R.A., and Giudice,S. (1987). Human cerebral hemispheres develop at different rates and ages. *Science* 236: 1110-1113.

Visser, G.H.A., Laurini, R.N., de Bries, J.I.P., Bekedam, D.J., and Prechtl, H.F.R. (1985). Abnormal motor behavior in anencephalic fetuses. *Early Human Development* 12: 173-182.

Personhood From a Neuroscientific Perspective

Michael V.L. Bennett

DR. FLOWER'S PAPER describes the development of the human brain and relates its development to that of "personhood". The concern with the brain as an indicator of whether a developing organism can be endowed fully with the qualities of a human being can be rationalized by comparison with other organs. There is none, not heart, kidney, lung or spleen, that we cannot transplant, do without, or replace artificially. The brain is the essence of our existence. If, in fiction, a brain is transplanted from one body to another (which is not a realistic possibility because of the multiplicity of connections required), personhood goes with the brain and does not reside within the recipient body (which is not to deny that the body influences and indeed is necessary for brain function).

The recently adopted criteria for death provide a further example of the centrality of the brain. The vital signs of heartbeat and respiration are no longer considered a valid indicator of human life, and electroencephalographic techniques permit us to determine whether there is brain activity or chance of its resumption; if a person is brain dead, he or she is dead.

The concept of brain death requires implicitly that there be brain life, and Dr. Flower's presentation may be examined in that respect as well as in terms of personhood. The developing brain is recognizable very early in development as a distinct structure, and for it to develop normally the woman carrying the embryo or fetus should not subject it to drugs or other exogenous compounds. Not until much later, at least the seventh month, does the brain develop the interconnections that are required for adult functioning. Obviously, however, the brain of a seven month fetus is not capable of functioning at the level of the brain of an adult or even of an infant of six months to one year of age. The brain still has a great deal of development ahead of it, and anatomical techniques on which Dr. Flower's presentation depends are inadequate to recognize these changes. Some changes, such as myelination or partial loss of synapses can be resolved; other changes at a biochemical level are not resolvable at present. In either case, given the brain's complexity, their relevance to changes in function will be difficult to determine.

If there is no person at the seventh month, but only the neural connectivity that permits one to develop, can one determine when there is a person? From a months or year or two when the baby is beginning to recognize its parents, feel fear, joy and anger, and to put its feelings into words. Personhood develops over a prolonged period. This fact does not deny that a newborn infant thrives on, and indeed requires, the loving care that its parents give it because they regard it as a person. The bonding of parent to offspring begins well before birth before development of the brain to the extent that personhood is possible. The distress and even devastation of miscarriage attests the early love that a parent can feel for an anticipated person well before a person is really there. The biological value of devotion to one's offspring need not be documented, and whether it is genetic or culturally determined in humans does not alter the fact that it is a strong drive.

If one would permit abortion before personhood developed and one accepts that an infant is definitely not a person until, say six months to one year of age, would this argument justify infanticide? The answer is absolutely not. The absence of personhood in an early infant would permit infanticide if personhood were the only consideration, but this is not justification of infanticide, and there are many other considerations. The strong biological or sociological parenting drive, empathic response and societal interests provide ample motivations, reasons and sanctions against infanticide.

Although the seven month fetus or full term infant may not yet be endowed with personhood, there is no doubt that it is learning. A charming but almost frightening observation is that newborn infants prefer their mothers' voices to those of strangers; they have been listening there in utero. (What else have they heard?) Recognizing its mother's voice, although a higher level of functioning than usually ascribed to infants, is not personhood. In general, one's pets and domestic animals can make the same distinction. This early learning does suggest the range of nurturing behavior that influences the infant's development and coming personality.

The question of personhood or moral status of the developing embryo, fetus or infant has been made more crucial with increasing medical skills in the procedures of in vitro fertilization at one end and treatment of pre-term infants at the other. It is possible to fertilize mammalian eggs, including human eggs, outside the female body and to grow them through many cell divisions before introducing them into a prospective mother (who need not be the source of the eggs). Since the technique generally produces many more eggs than the desired number of infants, there are often left over embryos (which can sometimes be successfully put on hold by freezing to liquid nitrogen temperatures). To ascribe the properties of personhood to these embryos would be without scientific basis.

At the other end of the process, it is becoming possible to save much younger fetuses (or infants). Sufficient maturation of the respiratory system and its neural control are required, but newborns that would never have lived are now, with extraordinary intervention, being brought to survival. No one would question these medical miracles if the resulting children were fully normal, and many are, but many are not and all are "at risk" of brain damage and developmental disabilities. As noted above, there are strong reasons for regarding the birthed infant as entitled to protection, but its personhood is not one, and as ever younger infants are enabled to survive, the lack of personhood will become more compelling.

Although birth involves dramatic physiological and environmental changes, it does not cause an abrupt change in the nervous system that one could regard as conferring personhood. Whatever metaphors there are in our language, being born is not a sudden awakening to consciousness.

To summarize what neuroscience tells us is relevant to the question of abortion: The brain is the seat of personhood. Its development is gradual, but it only approaches the complexity of a child's or adult's brain in the seventh month of gestation; the neural equipment for personhood is not present prior to this time. Personhood develops well after birth in a gradual process and requires changes in this neural equipment, mainly in the connections between neurons. The changes are by no means understood in detail, but many examples are known. The beneficial effects on an infant's development of treating it as a person are well established. The beneficial effects on society of treating infants as endowed with personhood can also be adduced, but this is not a neuroscientific position. The existence of personhood in a fetus is unsupported and should not be an issue in considering abortion.

The Birth Ceremony As A Rite of Passage Into Infant Personhood

Leigh Minturn

ONE CHARACTERISTIC unique to the human species is the elaboration of culture. All humans live in organized social groups whose members share a common language, beliefs, values, and customs, that are as a totality known as culture. Since the family is the oldest human group, kinship is the oldest method regulating human social groups. Kinship networks and rules regulating the interactions of relatives are one of the culture traits shared by all known human societies. These kinship rules regulate marriage, paternity, the rights, duties, and status of relatives *vis a vis* each other, and the authority of senior relatives over junior relatives, particularly children.

Because all humans are organized into social groups, the birth of a human infant is always a social event. When human mothers give birth, they bring a new relative into their kin group, a new citizen into their country, and a new soul into their religion. The acceptance of an infant into its social group is an event that usually involves the infant's relatives, family friends (e.g., godparents), and religious practitioners (e.g., priest, minister).

This "social birth" is celebrated in virtually all societies by birth ceremonies. The birth ceremony is one of several life cycle ceremonies that mark significant changes in the status of societal members. In his classic study *Rites of Passage*, van Gennep identifies and analyzes these life cycle ceremonies (van Gennep, 1960). He identifies the most frequent rites of passage as: 1. pregnancy rites that separate a woman from her social group at the onset of pregnancy, 2. post-partum purification rites that signify the social return of the mother to her group, 3. birth ceremonies that celebrate the social arrival of the newborn, 4. initiation rites to celebrate social puberty, 5. betrothal and marriage, signifying the change in kinship ties and residence for one or both partners, and 6. funerals marking the separation of the deceased from the social world of the living and the transition of the soul into the world of the dead.

According to van Gennep, rites of passage may be divided into three stages: separation, transition, and incorporation. The separation rites sever the person's ties to the previous world or status. The transition periods mark a period of probation or trial during which the success of the separation rites may be assessed. If the individual passes through this transition period successfully, incorporation rites are performed that mark the completion of an individual's change of status and celebrate the new status.

At birth, this rite of passage begins by separating the infant from the mother's body by the birth itself and the cutting of the umbilicus. In many societies the umbilical cord is considered to be part of the infant and is saved or safely buried or burned in rituals believed to protect the newborn. In tribal societies these rites are usually performed by women attending the birth, (e.g. mothers, midwives, female relatives). The transition phase for a newborn is the time between the separation rites of birth to the time of the incorporation ceremony. This transition period may coincide with the mother's period of confinement, or be a separately defined time period as short as a few minutes or as long as a few years. During this time the infant's health, appearance and social position are evaluated, usually by the mother and midwife, who decide whether the infant is a viable candidate for the final, incorporation ceremony. The incorporation stage involves a ceremony held at the end of this transition period that accepts the infant into its new status as a member of the social community, subject to, and protected by, its laws and mores. These ceremonies are usually performed by male relatives and religious practitioners.

A variety of evidence can be cited indicating that infants are not considered to be persons in the social and legal sense until after they have completed the incorporation stage of the birth ceremony. Morgan's paper, presented in this session, describes differences in funeral customs as indicators of personhood. In this paper I present three types of evidence: analysis of birth ceremony symbolism, evidence that infanticide is performed during the transitional status period, and identification of beliefs and laws in Christian societies that avoid defining infanticide as murder.

The results of the birth ceremony and infanticide analysis are based on ethnographic reports about 57 tribal societies drawn from the Human Relations Area Files (HRAF). Information concerning birth ceremonies and infanticide was read by students and coded into categories derived from an overview of the material. Details of the procedure are presented in a previous article (Minturn and Stashak,1982). Information about Christian beliefs and laws comes from secondary sources, i.e. articles on the history of infanticide in Christian countries.

Birth Ceremonies

When describing birth ceremonies ethnographers typically refer to the incorporation ceremony, as this is usually the most elaborate celebration. Descriptions of the separation and transition phases of social birth are included in descriptions of birth practices, maternal confinement and status of the newborn. These rites are usually performed by the midwife or female relatives who attend the birth. Eighty-six percent of the societies in the HRAF sample had descriptions of birth ceremonies. The absence of descriptions in the other 14% of societies may be due to absence of reporting, rather than absence of the ceremony.

The timing of the incorporation ceremony varies; 29% are done within a few hours of birth, 39% from one day to one month after birth, and the remaining

21% within the first two years. The descriptions of incorporation ceremonies indicates that they involve doing something uniquely human to the infant, that is, something that no other species does for their infants. Humans celebrate the social birth of infants by human social and ceremonial events, that typically include purification, blessing, and naming.

The most common aspect of birth ceremonies, appearing in 29% of the HRAF societies, is naming. Kinship ties are identified by names and titles in all societies, therefore giving an infant a name clearly identifies it as a member of the social group. The registration of a birth and the issuing of a birth certificate is a secular addition to the naming ceremony.

The second most common practice, present in 24% of the societies, involves some type of purification or cleansing, independent of the cleaning of the newborn from amniotic fluid, etc. The Christian baptismal ceremony falls into this category. Often this purification ceremony is performed in conjunction with the naming ceremony.

Deities are invoked to bless and protect the infant in 15% of the societies. This may be done at the time of the purification ritual. Christening is a rite in which the infant is named, purified and blessed in one ceremony.

Ritual haircutting marks the birth ceremony in 12% of the sample societies. Purification and naming ceremonies are usually performed within a few hours or days after birth, but haircutting ceremonies may be performed as late as 18 months or two years of age, when the child has a full head of hair. Haircutting may symbolize purification and the hair may be offered to a deity, who is then expected to protect the child. Therefore, haircutting usually involves purification and blessing.

In societies where boys are more highly valued than girls, the birth ceremonies of boys are often more elaborate, involve more people, and are more expensive than the birth ceremonies of girls. Wealthy, noble, or socially prominent families may hold more elaborate ceremonies than poor families. These distinctions incorporate the infant into a status that befits its future standing in society.

The choice of persons who typically perform the birth ceremony symbolizes the social birth of the infant into the kin group. Mothers are frequently not present at birth ceremonies, which are often held during the mother's period of confinement. The absence of mothers from these ceremonies may be one indication that the ceremonies are designed to signify the separation of infants from the maternal womb.

Birth ceremonies are usually performed by adult men, the father in 24%, and a male other than the father in 37% of the sample societies. If the male officiator is not the father, he may be an elder male relative (grandfather, clan leader), or a religious practitioner (minister, priest, shaman). Thus, whereas women usually perform the separation ceremonies, it is men who usually perform the incorporation ceremonies. The combination involves both female and male relatives in the infant's social birth.

Abortion, Infanticide, Indirect Infanticide

Abortion, infanticide, and indirect infanticide caused by neglect of children, occurs with varying frequency in virtually all societies, and is not usually regarded as murder. (Devereux, 1976; Williamson, 1978).

A comprehensive study of abortion in primitive societies has been done by Devereux (1976). He found that women reportedly attempt to abort throughout the full course of the pregnancy. Some societies believe that abortions should take place or are possible only during early pregnancy, while other societies permit abortion until the time of birth. Like infanticide, abortion is usually considered to be a lesser crime than murder.

The most frequent reasons for abortion are that the child is illegitimate, the family has too many children, or that the mother does not want a child, for a variety of reasons. These are also the most frequent reasons reported for infanticide. In addition to these reasons, infanticide is frequently practiced when the newborn is found to be defective. All of these reasons, as well as other, less common, reasons for these practices essentially benefit mothers, and it is mothers or midwives who carry out abortions or infanticide in most societies.

Infanticide is defined by Langer (1974) as "the willful destruction of newborn babies through exposure, starvation, strangulation, smothering, poisoning, or through the use of some lethal weapon." Isolated cases of infanticide (e.g., the killing of deformed or illegitimate children) occur in virtually all societies, and the practice is an accepted method of disposing of unwanted children in a number of societies. These practices may be routine, if the population usually outstrips its food supply, or temporary, if the shortages come from periodic famine or war (Denham 1974). Infanticide is seldom regarded as murder and the penalties, if any, are less than the penalties for murder.

The killing of children, usually by exposure, was common in ancient Greece and Rome. Some Greek and Roman authors explicitly recognized infanticide as a desirable method of stabilizing the population. In Hellenistic Greece, infanticide, particularly female infanticide, was practiced so frequently that families were usually small and there was an abnormal discrepancy in the sex ratio. Aristotle was concerned with the poverty caused by excess population and suggested that abortion might be better than exposure as a method of birth control (Langer, 1974).

When infanticide is used for population control, the killing of female babies is the most effective practice, since a shortage of males can be corrected through polygamy (Ember 1974). Female infanticide has received much attention in anthropology. The practice has been widespread in China and northern India, and is still practiced in these countries. Miller has documented the practice of female infanticide in contemporary India (Miller 1981). In contemporary China, where the governmental one-child program has increased the traditional desire for boys, female infanticide is increasing. Births are not registered for three days, and infants may be killed during that time without the death being recorded. This delay in registration of births seems to be a bureaucratic definition of transitional period. Female infanticide has also been documented in some tribal groups, e.g., the Eskimo, Yanoama of Brazil, and Australian aborigines (Divale 1972; Williamson 1978). However, this practice is not common in tribal societies, and was reported in only 8.7% of our sample.

Neither the willful killing of animals, nor the accidental killing of humans is defined as murder in most societies. The legal and ethical definition for murder depends upon the willful intent of the killer and the personhood status of the victim.

If our assumption that infants are not considered to be persons until after they have been accepted into their group via the incorporation phase of a birth ceremony is correct, then it follows that, in societies where deliberate infanticide is an acceptable means of eliminating unwanted children, it should take place during the infant's transitional status, but not after the completion of the birth ceremony.

We published an investigation of the hypothesis in a paper entitled "Infanticide as a terminal abortion procedure" (Minturn and Stashak 1982). We assumed that infanticide occurs when abortion efforts have failed or when undesirable traits of the infant which can only be determined after birth have been identified (e.g., congenital deformities, sex). We argue that newborns are still considered to be fetal in nature at the time that they are killed, so that infanticide may be considered to be an extra-uterine abortion, just as abortion is an intra-uterine infanticide.

We tested this hypothesis with the same sample of 57 societies on which we obtained birth ceremony information. The testing of the infanticide hypothesis necessitated identifying the time of both the infanticide and the birth ceremony. Our sample contained only 30 societies for which both types of information were available. Infanticide takes place before the birth ceremony in all 30 societies. Therefore, the hypothesis is confirmed with no known negative cases (Minturn and Stashak, 1982).

The second part of our reasoning predicts that children who are killed after the incorporation ceremony should be killed by methods that can be considered accidental, so that the killer cannot be accused of willful intent. These practices are called indirect, passive, or deferred infanticide (Scrimshaw, 1984; Johansson, 1984). Indirect infanticide practices include various forms of death as a result of child neglect (e.g., accident, excessive punishment, malnutrition, exposure). Female infanticide through such indirect means has been documented in tribal societies (Williamson 1978), medieval England (Kellum 1984), nineteenth century Europe (Johansson 1984), twentieth century India (McKee 1984), and 140 twentieth century national populations (Preston 1976). Usually such deaths are viewed as accidental and parents are seldom prosecuted for them.

Infanticide in Christian Countries

The early Christian church, influenced by Judean law, regarded infanticide as a form of murder; however, the penalties for infanticide, while often harsh, were generally less severe than the penalties for other forms of murder. During the Middle Ages, when women were sometimes executed for infanticide, a number of beliefs and legal practices can be identified that functioned to evade the consequences of this strict prohibition. Some of these beliefs and laws extend into later times, with diminishing frequency.

The beliefs in question served to classify newborns as inhuman or not fully persons. The transitional status of the unbaptized infant was explicitly utilized to avoid equating infanticide with murder.

The transitional state of the post-partum mother was such that she was regarded as "no longer a real Christian until she is churched, for she has despoiled her Christianity *by the child* in the act of birth"' (Kellum 1974). The mother was despoiled because her child, the unbaptized infant, still steeped in original sin, was thought to be in the devil's power. Unbaptized infants could not be buried in the churchyard, and were sometimes buried with stakes through their hearts, so that they would not rise from the dead and injure the living.

Unbaptized infants were also thought to be in danger of being traded by fairies for their own children. These fairy children were known as "changelings" and were believed to be thin and sickly. One method of identifying a suspected changeling was to put it over a fire. Changelings were expected to scream, while human children were expected to remain silent! Since a changeling was a soulless demon it could be executed with impunity. Thus a mother faced with a sickly fussy baby could kill it and justify the act by identifying the infant as a changeling. This belief may account for the suspiciously high number of infant deaths through burning in the Middle Ages (Kellum 1974).

In nineteenth century Europe, at the onset of the population explosion, infanticide had become so common that Langer (1974:360) writes:

> The parish officers were helpless in the face of the problem. A law of 1803 specified that charges of infanticide must be tried according to the same rules of evidence as applied to murder, while yet another law required that 'it must be proved that the entire body of the child had actually been born into the world in a living state, and the fact of its having breathed is not conclusive proof thereof. There must be independent circulation in the child before it can be counted alive.'"

Langer interprets this law to mean that an infant might be killed with impunity as long as its body was still inside the mother. One might also presume that the phrase "independent circulation" refers to circulation of the blood after the cutting of the umbilical cord. A similar definition is used by the Iban, who perform birth ceremonies after the stump of the umbilicus has fallen off. Devereux reports that a Hopi woman killed her child by squeezing it between her legs during the birth (Devereux 1976).

When older children, who could not be classified as non-persons were killed, the law was lenient in defining the deaths as accidental. During some periods of history, exposure was not punished by law; overlaying, or smothering an infant in bed, was considered to be a relatively minor crime. In Medieval England, mothers frequently avoided prosecution for killing older children by pleading insanity, or describing the death as accidental (Kellum 1974).

Overlaying became so common that, in Medieval England, mothers were warned not to sleep with infants, and a three year penance was instituted as the standard punishment, with a reduction to two years if the death was judged to be accidental (Kellum 1974). The Malleus maleficarum held that witches often killed children and placed their bodies in the parental bed in such a position that it appeared that the mother had overlaid her child. Some also believed that witches caused mothers to overlay (Kellum 1974). The prevalence of overlaying as a cause of infant death in Europe and the formalization of this type of death in law is suspicious, since mothers routinely sleep with infants in many societies without smothering them, and accidental death by overlaying is not recognized in legal systems of other societies. Overlaying seems to have been a legal device that enabled clerics and courts to regard such deaths as accidental.

Exposure of infants became a common practice that eventually led to the creation of foundling hospitals. Foundling hospitals appeared as early as the eighth century in Italian cities and became common throughout Europe in the eighteenth century. In London 14,934 infants were admitted to the foundling hospital from 1756-1760, a number that caused Parliament to close the hospital to indiscriminate admissions. The problem of foundlings increased greatly with the nineteenth century population explosion. In 1833, 164,319 babies were left in French foundling hospitals. Since there were not enough wet nurses to care for these foundlings, they died with such frequency that the hospitals themselves became institutions for infanticide. In nineteenth century England wet nurses were known as "killer nurses" and "angel makers" (Langer 1974).

The court records of cases where mothers were convicted of infanticide show that poverty and illegitimacy were the most frequent causes of infanticide, and that convictions usually fell upon the poor, the destitute and the desperate. Since the church's prohibition on abortion was particularly severe when it was used to cover sin, conviction fell heavily on unwed mothers. For instance, in Nurmberg, 83 to 87 women executed for infanticide from 1513-1777 were unmarried girls who had killed their babies by violent means (Langer 1974).

Conclusion

What is the relevance of this information to the contemporary debate about abortion?

First, in most societies, including Christian societies, personhood is conferred on infants via birth ceremonies. Human infants do not become legal entities or social beings until some adult or group of adults (e.g., parents, godparents, kinsmen, religious practitioners) have named, purified and/or blessed them in a rite that says "This child belongs to us." By this ceremony the adults admit infants into their group and assume the responsibility of supporting and raising the babies they claim as their own. In modern nation states, the birth certificate or its equivalent confers citizenship upon native born infants and is a means by which the state claims newborns and confers upon them a civic identity.

Second, until the development of maternity hospitals and modern medicine, infants were not incorporated into their group unless they were capable of becoming acceptable and productive members of their society. Weak, deformed, illegitimate, excess and unwanted children were disposed of via abortion or infanticide before their birth ceremony. Since such infants were not considered to be members of their social group and protected by its laws, killing them was not considered to be murder. The time of this transition period varies from a few hours to as late as two years. During this transitional period, parents, particularly mothers, had the right to decide whether to keep the baby or dispose of it.

Only when babies are born in hospitals does the state registration of their birth precede the judgement of their parents concerning their eligibility for social personhood. When babies are born at home, their death at birth frequently is not a matter of official record. The contemporary Chinese custom of waiting three days to register births allows infanticide to take place during this interim period. In the United States, citizenship is conferred on infants at birth and births are registered immediately in hospital records.

Since abortion procedures are now safe, effective, and legal, unwanted pregnancies are terminated in the first trimester for most American mothers. Infanticide is not an issue in our society except for very low birth weight or seriously deformed infants. For these infants the extraordinary measures now available in modern hospitals further deprive parents of their traditional right to decide whether or not they want to accept defective infants and assume the responsibility and expense of raising them. The crippling expense and family tragedy incurred by parents of "Baby Doe" infants results from the absence of a legal and socially acceptable transition period even for infants who would not be viable without extraordinary medical intervention.

Three, when the legal system attempts to oppose abortion and infanticide, the historical record shows that the state does not become an effective agent to protect the lives of the unborn and the newborn. Instead, the courts are faced with the choice of either prosecuting poor, usually unmarried women, who cannot pay enough to successfully conceal their crime, or developing legal fictions that serve to define the dead infant as abnormal, stillborn, or inhuman, or the killing as accidental. The current attempts to define abortion as murder will predictably do more to deprive poor and unwed mothers of adequate medical care and increase the number of illegal and unsafe abortions than they will to protect the rights of the unborn.

References

Denham, W. W. (1974). Population structure, infant transport and infanticide among Pleistocene and Modern Hunter-Gatherers. *Journal of Anthropological Research, 30,* 191-198.

Devereux, George (1976). A Study of Abortion in Primitive Societies. New York: International University Press.

Divale, W. T. (1972). Systematic population growth in the middle and upper paleolithic: Inferences based on contemporary hunter-gatherers. *World Archaeology & Anthropology, 4,* 65-68.

Ember, M. (1974). Warfare, sex ratio and polygny. *Ethnology, 13,* 197-206.

Johansson, S. R. (1984). Deferred infanticide: Excess female mortality during childhood. In Glenn Hausfater and Sarah Blaffer Hrdy (Eds.) *Infanticide: Comparative and Evolutionary Perspectives.* New York: Aldine.

Kellum, B. A. (1974). Infanticide in England in the later Middle Ages. *History of Childhood Quarterly: The Journal of Psychohistory, 1,* 367-388.

Langer, W. L. (1974). Infanticide: A Historical Survey. *History of Childhood Quarterly: The Journal of Psychohistory.*

McKee, L. (1984). Child survival and sex differences in the treatment of children. *Journal of Medical Anthropology* (Guest Editor), Spring 1984, Vol. 8, No. 2.

Miller, B. D. (1981). *The Endangered Sex.* Cornell University Press.

Minturn, L. M., & Stashak, J. (1982). Infanticide as a terminal abortion procedure. *Behavior Science Research*, Vol. 17, No. 2, 70-90.

Minturn, L. (1984). Changes in the Differential treatment of Rajput girls in Khalapur: 1955-1975. In Lauris McKee (Guest Editor), Child survival and sex differences in the treatment of children. *Journal of Medical Anthropology*, Spring 1984, Vol. 8, No. 2.

Preston, S. H. (1976). *Mortality Patterns in National Populations.* New York: Academic Press.

Scrimshaw, S. C.M. (1984). Infanticide in human populations: Societal and individual concerns. In Glenn Hausfater and Sarah Blaffer Hrdy (Eds.) *Infanticide: Comparative and Evolutionary Perspectives.* New York: Aldine.

van Gennep, A. (1960). *The Rites of Passage.* Chicago, Ill: University of Chicago Press.

Williamson, L. (1978). Infanticide: An anthropological analysis. In *Infanticide and the value of life*, Marvin Kohl (Ed.) Pp. 61-75. Buffalo: Prometheus Books.

When Does Life Begin?

A Cross-Cultural Perspective on the Personhood of Fetuses and Young Children

Lynn M. Morgan

PARTICIPANTS IN THE U.S. abortion debate have argued about life and personhood from philosophical, religious, moral, biological, and political points of view, yet very few have examined the cultural dimensions of when life begins. Because they have overlooked the relevance of comparative cultural information, it has been difficult for participants in the debate to acknowledge the extent to which human life and personhood are culturally constructed. Perhaps a reflexive, cross-cultural perspective on personhood is an unaffordable luxury now, with the 1973 landmark *Roe v. Wade* Supreme Court decision legalizing abortion under fire from anti-abortion groups. Because the legality of abortion is seriously threatened, the subtleties and ambiguities about abortion are rarely acknowledged for fear of muddying the central policy issue.[1] In spite of the political stakes, however, I will argue that the discourse on personhood should be expanded to include perspectives from other cultures, thus encouraging Americans to confront and challenge the myriad culture-bound assumptions which permeate the U.S. debate over reproductive health policy.

The social recognition of fetuses, newborns, and young children is embedded within a wider social context. This observation is not new: a burgeoning literature illuminates the links between abortion, childrearing, women's status, social stratification, child welfare, ethnic and gender discrimination, and changing relations between the sexes. The process through which young human lives come to be valued is derived in part from these factors, but personhood is also a function of cultural divisions of the life cycle, attitudes toward death, the social organization of descent and inheritance, and social systems of authority and achievement. Anthropologists such as Mauss, Fortes, and LaFontaine[2] have documented a

---

1 Daniel Callahan, "How Technology is Reframing the Abortion Debate," Hastings Center Report (February 1986): 33-42, esp. 41.
2 Marcel Mauss, "A Category of the Human Mind: The Notion of Person, The Notion of Self," in *The Category of the Person*, ed. M. Carrithers, S. Collins, and S. Luke (Cambridge: Cambridge University Press, 1985), 1-25; Meyer Fortes, "On the Concept of the Person among the Tallensi," in *La*

rich and remarkable range of variation showing the relationship among notions of self, body imagery, social organization, and ideational features such as consciousness and individuality. The cross-cultural evidence shows that the early thresholds of human life and personhood are just one issue in the larger question of whom society allows to become a person, under what circumstances, and why.

Every human being is potentially at risk of being aborted, miscarried, stillborn, or killed by natural causes or human agency before being accepted into a social community and labelled a person, yet there has been no recent systematic attempt to examine when other cultures come to value human life. To address this question I reviewed the ethnographic literature, beginning with the Human Relations Area Files and continuing with other anthropological accounts, both early and contemporary. Although few of the accounts I found deal explicitly with the value of early life, notions of the moral and social value of young children may be inferred by analyzing burial customs, naming practices, birth ceremonies and taboos, and linguistic and historical evidence pertaining to fetuses and young children. Most of the accounts are inadequate to fully answer the questions posed here; some are of questionable reliability, and others are so old that it would be nearly impossible to verify them today.[3] Nonetheless, in the absence of contemporary empirical research, these accounts comprise the most complete account of cross-cultural variability regarding the valuation of young human life by diverse cultural groups.

Viewing the issue of personhood from a cross-cultural perspective helps to illustrate inconsistent and contradictory features of reproductive ethics debates in the United States. The ethnographic data show that the parameters of the U.S. abortion debate as presently constituted do not exhaust the realm of possibilities found among the earth's inhabitants. A close reading of the ethnographic evidence shows that killing neonates is often not regarded as murder, especially when the killing occurs before an infant is recognized as a human or person. Infanticide, then, with all the moral repugnance it evokes in the West, is a cultural construct rather than a universal moral edict. Apart from Tooley's influential *Abortion and Infanticide*,[4] few theorists have seriously considered the moral justifications for infanticide, yet the comparative cultural data indicate that this question deserves far more attention than it receives.

Notion de la Personne en Afrique Noire, ed. G. Dieterlen (Paris: Editions du Centre National de la Recherche Scientifique, 1973); J.S. LaFontaine, "Person and Individual: Some Anthropological Reflections," in *The Category of the Person*, ed. M. Carrithers, S. Collins, and S. Luke (Cambridge: Cambridge University Press, 1985), 123-140.

3 Mead and Newton have cautioned about using the ethnographic present to refer to customs described in early anthropological literature:

"Although the present tense is used in reporting the customs of some primitive peoples, it should be noted that such customs often change radically within a short period of time under the impact of contact with industrial culture. The customs referred to existed at the time of observation and recording but do not necessarily exist at present."

Margaret Mead and Niles Newton, "Cultural Patterning of Perinatal Behavior," in *Childbearing: Its Social and Psychological Aspects*, ed. S.A. Richardson and A.F. Guttmacher (New York: Williams & Wilkins Co., 1967), p. 153. For the reason cited by Mead and Newton, I have avoided using the ethnographic present except in very recent accounts. The only way to assess the representativeness and current state of beliefs about the value of young human life would be to conduct comparative research in several cultures among a wide sample of informants.

4 Michael Tooley, "Abortion and Infanticide," *Philosophy and Public Affairs 2* (1972): 37-65.

The cross-cultural evidence reveals two culturally-constructed concepts used widely to divide the human life cycle continuum at its earliest stages: human-ness and personhood. In order to be granted status as a person, a fetus or neonate must first be recognized as a member of the human species. In some societies the decision to call a fetus "human" is not made until biological birth when the new-born's physical attributes can be assessed. Personhood, in contrast, is a socially-recognized moral status. Neonates may not be labeled as persons until social birth rites are performed, often several days or months after biological birth. Social birth gives the neonate a moral status and binds it securely to a social community. Biological and social birth are not recognized as separate events in Western societies, even though they structure the onset of personhood in many non-Western societies. The U.S. abortion debate thus replicates Western divisions of the life cycle, overlooking the fact that even the human developmental cycle is socially patterned.

The attribution of personhood is a collective social decision, for the legal and ethical boundaries of personhood can only be negotiated within social settings. The limits of personhood are not decided by individuals, but by the entire society acting on shared cultural beliefs and values. For this reason, personhood -- the value placed on human life -- is not a concept which will be altered by religious mandate, nor by radical legislation by either the Right or the Left. Yet consensus is obviously eluding us, and seems destined to elude us as long as North Americans feel personal ambivalence and the compulsion to engage in increasingly polarized struggles over the issues surrounding abortion. Perhaps by reflecting on the social context of personhood and the value of fetuses and young children in other cultural contexts, we will be better able to understand how they are valued in our own.

'Human' Versus 'Person'

The furor over abortion in the United States has been waged in part through the manipulation of highly emotional symbols, resulting in a great deal of semantic confusion (a fetus may be called a "baby," an "unborn child," or "the product of conception"[5]). I will make only one semantic distinction while examining the cross-cultural evidence: between the concepts of "human" and "person." The difference between these terms is sometimes confused in the U.S. abortion debate. For example, in 1981 a U.S. Senate Subcommittee, headed by John P. East, held hearings to muster evidence in support of a proposed "Human Life Amendment" which, if passed, would have granted the rights of persons to every human being from the moment of conception. The Subcommittee's report stated:

> The Subcommittee rejects as misleading semantic efforts to manipulate the English language and the redefine "human being" according to particular value preferences; instead we adhere to the customary mean-

---

5 Leonard Kovit, "Babies as Social Products: The Social Determinants of Classification," *Social Science & Medicine 12* (1978): 347-351.

ing of "human being" as including every living member of the human species...the life of a human being begins at conception.[6]

The Subcommittee agreed, by extending their reasoning, that human life should also begin to be valued at conception; in my terms they would have said that personhood begins at conception. Yet in several non-Western societies the concepts "human" and "person" refer to distinct, non-interchangeable linguistic and cognitive categories. The term "human" applies to a categorization based on cultural perceptions of biology: a "human" is a member of a specific class of objects which we call the species *Homo Sapiens*. To be labelled and recognized as "human" does not imply any corresponding social, moral, or judicial status. In contrast, a "person" is a being who occupies a moral status which supercedes biology. Infants are sometimes treated differently from adults by rationalizing that they are not human, other times because they are not classed as persons. Some societies confer human-ness and person concurrently, while others see these as separate categories. Once in a while, the ethnographer's own linguistic and cognitive confusion makes it impossible for us to tell whether there is a difference between these two categories. In either case, killing is taking a life (human or not) while the crime of murder applies only to humans who are also recognized as persons.

Although "human" generally refers to a biological designation, the term is still subject to cultural influence and negotiation. In the United States, most people assume that the product of a human pregnancy will be human, yet the cross-cultural evidence shows greater variety. Among the Arunta of Central Australia, "[if] a child is born at a very premature stage, nothing will persuade the natives that it is an undeveloped human being, for it is nothing like a *Kuruna* [spirit] or a *ratappa* [newborn]; 'they are perfectly convinced that it is the young of some other animal, such as a kangaroo, which has by mistake got inside the woman'".[7] In Bang Chan, Thailand, women related episodes of "giving birth to 'gold,' 'jewels,' 'a monkey,' 'a fish's stomach,' and a mouse-like 'Golden Child'".[8] In aboriginal Australia and Thailand, the products of conception are not assumed *a priori* to be human, for human status must be empirically verified.

In societies where humanity and personhood are defined separately, the determination of humanity always precedes the determination of personhood. On the island of Truk, for example, people waited until biological birth to see whether the newborn could be categorized as human. They did not take for granted the anthropomorphic character of the creature which would emerge from the womb. Abnormal or deformed infants were labelled as ghosts and burned or thrown into the sea: "Culturally this is not defined as infanticide and the suggestion of infanticide horrified the Trukese; a ghost is not a person and

---

6 United States Senate Subcommittee on Separation of Powers. *Report to the Committee on the Judiciary.* The Human Life Bill -- S. 158. 97th Congress (1981). Washington, D.C. U.S. Government Printing Office, p. 12.

7 Ashley Montagu, *Coming Into Being Among the Australian Aborgines* (London: Routledge & Kegan Paul, 1974), p. 31.

8 Jane Richardson Hanks, *Maternity and its Rituals in Bang Chan* (Ithaca: Cornell Thailand Project, 1963), esp. 34-35.

cannot be killed in any case".[9] This case, in which humanity itself was denied, is characteristic of the justification given for killing twins in some societies. Among the Tallensi in Africa, Fortes reports that twins were regarded suspiciously, because they may have been "malicious bush spirits" in human guise. After the first month of birth, a twin would be treated as any other child, but "only when it reaches the age of about four, and is placed under the spiritual guardianship of an ancestor spirit, is a twin definitely regarded as a complete social being".[10] A turn-of-the-century account of childhood in southern Africa noted that twins were regarded as more animal than human, and thus dangerously unpredictable: "No woman would care to marry a twin, for she would say that he was not a proper human being, and might turn wild like an animal, and kill her".[11] In these societies the neonate is not assumed to be born human, but is "anthropomorphized" after birth on the basis of physical characteristics which may or may not subsequently be endowed with moral significance. The criteria used to anthropomorphize newborns in different cultural contexts vary with caretakers' perceptions of the status of neonates.

Defining Personhood

Personhood is contingent on social recognition, and a person is recognized using established sociocultural conventions. Persons possess a special moral stature within their societies, yet in specific historical circumstances this status has been denied to certain groups, including women, children, slaves, prisoners of war, lepers, countless subordinate ethnic groups, and the insane. In all cultures, persons are living human entities whose killing is classed as murder, that is, the killing invokes some degree of moral condemnation and social retribution. The social construction of personhood varies according to the environmental, cosmological, and historical circumstances of different societies. What this means, in sum, is that "people are defined by people".[12] There can be no absolute definition of personhood isolated from a sociocultural context.

Burial customs may provide one source of data on cultural definitions of personhood, since only "persons" are buried. The data show a range of variation sufficient to highlight some of the contradictions in current U.S. policy. For example, on one extreme, a Chippewa Amerindian woman:

"knew her baby was two or three months along when she lost it... You could tell that it was just beginning to form. They cleaned it just like a child that is born and wrapped it. They gave a feast for it just like for a dead person and buried it in the same way. They believe that a child is human when it is conceived."[13]

---

9 Thomas Gladwin and Seymour B. Sarason, *Truk: A Man in Paradise* (New York: Wenner-Gren Foundation, 1953), p. 133; quoted in George Devereux, *A Study of Abortion in Primitive Societies* (New York: International University Press, 1955), p. 344.

10 Meyer Fortes, *The Web of Kinship Among the Tallensi: The Second Part of an Analysis of the Social Structure of a Trans-Volta Tribe* (London: Oxford University Press, 1949), p. 271.

11 Dudley Kidd, Savage *Childhood: A Study of Kafir Children* (London: Adam and Charles Black, 1906), p. 45.

12 Andie L. Knutson, "The Definition and Value of a New Human Life," *Social Science & Medicine 1* (1967): 7-29.

13 Devereux 1955, p. 207-208.

Such behavior contrasts strikingly with burial practices in the United States, where fetuses weighing less than 500 grams are not buried, even in Roman Catholic hospitals where stated policy professes to respect human life from the time of conception.[14] On the other extreme, Ashanti children of Ghana who died before adolescence were reportedly thrown on the village midden heap,[15] indicating that burial rites and the full status of personhood were adult perquisites. In the U.S., "fetuses ex utero over 500 grams are considered premature newborns, and therefore birth certificates must be issued for them and they must be buried",[16] yet U.S. burial customs for children depend on more than the weight or size of the body. In New York City, a study revealed that many indigent children under one year of age were buried in unmarked graves in Potter's Field, where parents were not permitted to visit the gravesites.[17] Apparently child burial customs and the parents' right to graveside grieving are at least in part a function of social class in the U.S., suggesting that the lives of poor children are valued less than those from wealthier families.

Social Birth

In Western industrialized societies, people generally believe that biological birth marks the entrance of a new being into the social community. The tenacity of this belief results from the cultural conviction that biological events have social significance. Unconsciously but relentlessly, Westerners have imbued that biological act of birth with profound importance, to the extent that legal and civil institutions confer personhood instantly when an infant is born alive. The social status of personhood is thus granted concurrently with a biological act: emerging from the womb. In several non-Western societies, however, members observe a period of transitional, liminal time between biological birth -- when the infant can be seen, inspected, and evaluated -- and social birth, when the infant is formally accepted into its social community. This is a stage of the life cycle which acknowledges and reinforces the cultural and cognitive divisions between the marginal, uncertain status of the fetus and the secure, protected status of a person. As a clearly bounded life cycle division, this period between biological and social birth so characteristic of many non-Western societies is unknown in 20th century Western societies.

Until abortion became such a contentious issue, most people in the United States rarely stopped to question whether the social status of an infant could be separated from its biological status. It would be thought inappropriate to refer to the unborn fetus as a person complete with social identity (in part because the sex of the individual is essential to the construction of an individual's social identity). At birth the healthy child was automatically endowed with a social identity:

---

14 Caroline Whitbeck, "The Moral Implications of Regarding Women as People: New Perspectives on Pregnancy and Personhood," in *Abortion and the Status of the Fetus*, ed. William B. Bondeson et al. (Dordrecht, Holland: D. Reidel Publishing Company, 1983), 247-272, esp. 258.
15 Robert S. Rattray, *Religion and Art Among the Ashanti* (Oxford: Clarendon Press, 1927).
16 Whitbeck, p. 258.
17 Peter Kerr, "Groups Faults City Policy on Burial of Poor Infants," *New York Times* (May 25, 1986), p. 30.

as soon as the umbilical cord was cut, the neonate became a person. Biological birth was the major moral dividing line along the life cycle continuum: every individual who had passed the line was granted the rights and social status of persons,[18] while every individual shy of the line was not. Biological and social birth were inextricably intertwined in legal and medical institutions as well as in popular consciousness. This has changed only recently. In 1973, for example, *Roe v. Wade* established "viability" as the moral dividing line between fetuses which could be legally aborted and those which merited the protection of the State. Amniocentesis and other advances in medical technology have also altered the idea that persons could be distinguished from non-persons only at birth.

Many non-industrial societies, on the other hand, do not endow biological facts with the same degree of social importance. They separate the purely physiological act of birth from the social acceptance of the newborn. Social birth is marked by a ritual held sometime after biological birth, during which the newborn is granted a place in the social world. Social birth rituals often introduce the newborn formally for the first time to significant members of the community such as parents, siblings, godparents, other relatives, and community elders. The infant may also be presented to non-human entities considered important by the community, for example, sacred animals, natural entities, or supernatural beings. Social birth may be the occasion for some symbolically important event such as naming, hair cutting, depilation,[19] ear piercing,[20] removing incisor teeth[21] or circumcision. Social birth may take place anywhere from a few days to several years after biological birth. It can be a one-time occurrence or it may be a gradual process involving a number of socially significant events: crying, suckling, or weaning for the first time, or learning -- as a small child -- to perform certain chores.[22] Long, gradual transitions to personhood, sometimes lasting an entire lifetime, are common in non-Western societies,[23] yet a crucial induction into personhood often occurs early in life, with social birth. In a society where social birth rites are essential to personhood, an infant who dies before social birth has died before it was born.

Dividing the Life Cycle

Models of an individual life cycle, from the moment of conception to death and afterlife, are constructed differently from one society to the next. Societies divide the developmental cycle into segments, and mark transitions from one stage to the next by birthdays, marriage, parenthood, and religious rites of pas-

---

18 H. Tristram Engelhardt, Jr., "Viability and the Use of the Fetus," in *Abortion and the Status of the Fetus*, ed. William B. Bondeson et al. (Dordrecht, Holland: D. Reidel Publishing Company, 1983), 183-208, esp. 191.
19 Among the Siriono of eastern Bolivia, see Allan R. Holmberg, *Nomads of the Long Bow* (New York: Natural History Press, 1969).
20 Among the Argentine Araucanians, see M. Inez Hilger, Araucanian Child Life and Its Cultural Background (Washington: Smithsonian Miscellaneous Collections, Volume 133, 1957).
21 Performed among the Nuer when a child reached seven or eight years of age, see E.E. Evans-Pritchard, *Nuer Religion* (Oxford: Clarendon Press, 1956).
22 See Mead and Newton, p. 154, for examples.
23 LaFontaine, p. 132.

sage. Life cycle divisions are one way in which societies categorize their members. Life stages allow status to be monitored and evaluated by other members of society who look for age- and status-related cues to determine their attitudes and behavior toward those around them. Stages of life which North Americans take for granted, such as childhood, adolescence, and middle age, are in fact cultural constructions which have evolved in response to demographic, economic and social factors. Anthropologists have been acutely aware of the social nature of the life cycle since Margaret Mead wrote about the nature of adolescence in Samoa. In the twentieth century United States, she said, adolescence had become known "as the period in which idealism flowered and rebellion against authority was strong, a period during which difficulties and conflicts were absolutely inevitable".[24] In Samoa, however, teenagers did not pass through an analogous period of turmoil. Mead used the ethnographic evidence to show that adolescence was a phase of life unique to Western culture, specifically to the United States.

Childhood is another stage of life with a discernable social history, as Aries demonstrates for Western Europe. By analyzing European literature and iconography, Aries shows that children were not accorded the unique status they now occupy in the West until well after the advent of institutionalized schooling in the 16th and 17th centuries. Around that time, moralists began to argue that children needed to be trained, reformed, and subjected to "a kind of quarantine" before they would be fit company for adults.[25] The concept of infancy did not arise in western Europe until much later. British vital statistics did not distinguish among miscarried, stillborn, or infant deaths until late in the 19th century.[26] Until the mid-19th century, the French had no word for "baby".[27] During the first few months of life, when an infant could not interact with or respond to adult stimuli, it "simply 'did not count'".[28] As the concept of childhood evolved in modern Europe, so did parents' ideals of the number and quality of children they desired, and society's expectations of the appropriate behaviors characterizing ideal adults and children.

Middle-age, in addition to adolescence and childhood, is also a socially constructed life stage category. Brandes has shown that the American mid-life crisis (often associated with the fortieth birthday) is not a biological or developmental phenomenon, but cultural.[29] The turmoil and anxiety one feels on approaching the fortieth year is a reflection of our society's success in continuing the process of socialization through the adult years. Adults as well as children internalize society's popular wisdom and myths, one of which is that mid-life crisis is inevitable, natural, and almost genetically programmed. This relentlessly repeated message is deeply encoded in many realms of social life, including Western number symbolism. As a result, the American mid-life crisis has become a self-ful-

---

24 Margaret Mead, *Coming of Age in Samoa* (New York: American Museum of Natural History, 1928).
25 Philippe Aries, *Centuries of Childhood* (New York: Vintage Books, 1962), p. 412.
26 David Armstrong, "The Invention of Infant Mortality," *Sociology of Health and Illness 8* (1986): 211-232, p. 214.
27 Aries, p. 29.
28 Aries, p. 128.
29 Stanley H. Brandes, *Forty: The Age and the Symbol* (Knoxville: University of Tennessee Press, 1985).

filling prophecy: "the expectation of change at certain key times along the life course -- especially if such expectation is elevated to the position of a shared, transmitted cultural norm -- is likely actually to produce a change that might not otherwise occur".[30]

If the ethnographic evidence shows that the human developmental cycle is divided differently according to cultural and historical contingencies, then non-Western cultures can be expected to have divisions of the life cycle unfamiliar to Westerners. One well-known example is the clearly marked transition from childhood and adulthood celebrated by adolescent initiation rites in parts of Africa and Melanesia. Another such stage occurs early in life, during the period between biological birth and social birth.

Personhood, A Cross-Cultural View

When viewed in cross-cultural perspective, the criteria for personhood are widely divergent: in one society personhood may be an ascribed status, conferred automatically when an infant is born alive or given a name; in another society the status may be achieved only through a very long, gradual process of socialization. In Java "the people quite flatly say, 'To be human [i.e., a 'a person' in my terms] is to be Javanese.' Small children, boors, simpletons, the insane, the flagrantly immoral, are said to be *ndurung kjawa*, 'not yet Javanese'" and hence, not yet persons.[31] Evans-Pritchard reported that among the Nuer of the Nilotic Sudan, the death of a small child was not considered the death of a person:

> People do not mourn for a small child, for "a small child is not a person (*ran*). When he tethers the cattle and herds the goats he is a person. When he cleans the byres and spreads the dung out to dry and collects it and carries it to the fire he is a person. A man will not say he has a son till the child is about six years of age.[32]

A 1950s ethnographic account of Korea reported that the death of a new-born would receive "scarcely more deference than any other animal. If it lives, only through a long course of learning and ceremonies will it obtain the position of a recognized personality".[33] Personhood is not a "natural" category or a universal right of human beings, but a culturally and historically constructed assemblage of behaviors, knowledge, and practices. For societies which observe social birth rites, biological birth and the recognition of humanity are only early indications of what an individual may become. Biological birth acknowledges potential, but carries no guarantee of eventual acceptance into the social community.

Rites of Passage and Social Birth

Van Gennep's classic analysis of rites of passage divides each rite into three stages: separation, transition, and incorporation. He noted that many societies require an infant to pass through specified rites and time periods after birth and

---

30 Brandes, p. 126.
31 Clifford Geertz, *The Interpretation of Cultures* (New York: Basic, 1973), p. 52.
32 Evans-Pritchard, p. 146.
33 Cornelius Osgood, *The Koreans and their Culture* (New York: Ronald Press, 1951).

before being incorporated into a family.[34] The child must first be separated from its previous environment, either by removing the child from its mother's presence, by literally cutting something (umbilical cord, hair, foreskin), or by purifying the infant through bathing or rubbing.[35] Van Gennep did not mention the most obvious act of separation: biological birth itself. Separation is biologically inevitable, but is nonetheless assisted by elaborate social rituals designed to help the fetus be safely and expeditiously freed from its mother's body. Midwives, healers, and relatives try hard to exert their power over the birth by whatever means are preferred in their social milieu. Society, as well as biology, favors the separation of infant from mother.

If biological birth is the principal act of separation, then all rites which follow are transitional until social birth rites are performed to incorporate the infant into the community. Using this interpretation instead of Van Gennep's, transitional rites include cutting the umbilical cord, disposing of the placenta, hair cutting, ear piercing, purification, and seclusion of the mother and child. The time between biological birth and social birth is a liminal period fraught with uncertainty, ambiguity, and danger, during which the infant "passes through a realm which has few or none of the attributes of the past or coming state".[36] During this period the infant's corporeal existence is threatened as natural and supernatural forces struggle for control over its vulnerable life. The danger inherent in liminality can be minimized if the culture's customs are observed, for example, dietary taboos and careful disposal of the placenta or umbilical cord. An infant who passes safely through the liminal period is granted social birth rites, called "rites of incorporation" in Van Gennep's schema, which transform the neonate into a person.

Liminality, Danger, and the Fate of the Neonate

In many societies, the period between biological and social birth is treated socially and symbolically as an extension of being in the womb. The newborn is kept in seclusion, sheltered indoors away from the view of all save its mother (and perhaps a midwife or other female caretaker). Danger is minimized by recreating and maintaining a womb-like environment in which the infant resides until social birth. In the rural Philippines, for example, the newborn must be kept in strict seclusion for two weeks after biological birth, behind closed windows and above a well-sealed floor.[37] An ethnographer reporting on the Yavapai Amerindians of central Arizona wrote that mother and newborn stayed isolated and immobile for six days after parturition, resting on a bed of warm coals

---

34 Arnold Van Gennep, *The Rites of Passage* (Chicago: University of Chicago Press, 1960 [1908]), esp. 50-64.
35 Van Gennep, p. 52.
36 Victor Turner, "Betwixt and Between: The Liminal Period in Rites of Passage," in *Symposium on New Approaches to the Study of Religion*, ed. J. Helm (Seattle: American Ethnological Society, 1964), p. 5.
37 J. Landa Jocando, *Growing Up in a Philippine Barrio* (New York: Holt, Rinehart and Winston, 1969).

and earth and covered with grass.[38]   In society's terms none of these children have yet been born. They have emerged from their mother's uterus to a womb-like waiting room for pre-persons; their liminal status is perhaps analogous to a transitory phase at the other end of the life cycle known to Christians as purgatory.

Seclusion of infants is sometimes justified by citing the many perceived threats to their existence. Peoples of the Ghanaian Northern Territories told ethnographers that the infant may be reclaimed by spirits during the first seven days after biological birth:

> [A] newborn baby may in fact be a spirit-child, and not a human child at all.
> If it is a spirit, it will return to the world of spirits before a week is out, so for the first seven days after the birth the mother and child are confined to the room in which the birth took place, or at any rate to the house. If the child dies during that time, it is assumed that it was in fact a spirit-child. The body is mutilated and buried in a pot, to prevent its return in similar circumstances. The parents are not allowed to mourn its loss, but should show signs of joy at being rid of such an unwelcome guest.[39]

If the infant survives its first seven days outside the biological womb, it will be allowed to emerge from the symbolic social womb as well. At that point, "it is considered that the child is human, and it is 'out-doored', or brought into the open for the first time".[40] Supernatural threats to the newborn also justify an eight day hiatus between biological and social birth among the Ashanti of western Africa. Ashanti beliefs about conception and early infancy are known to anthropologists because of the *ntoro* concept, a spiritual bond passed from father to child in a society structured around matrilineal descent. At biological birth, the Ashanti question whether the newborn is meant to stay in the human world or whether it is a wandering ghost who will soon return to the spirit world. For eight days the mother and child remain indoors, with no special efforts made to bind the child to the human world: "It is given any kind of old mat or old rag to lie upon; it is not addressed in any endearing terms; water or pap, if given to it, is administered out of an old banana skin or ground-nut husk. It is true it is permitted to feed at the mother's breast, but it is hardly encouraged".[41] If the child is still alive after eight days, a *Nteatea* rite is performed, "when the child is named by its senior *ntoro* relative, and it is then for the first time regarded as a member of the human family".[42]

Similar "out-dooring" ceremonies have been recorded in other parts of the world. In the Nilgiri hills in south India, the Toda keep the newborn indoors for three months after biological birth. The sun is not allowed to touch the child's face. One morning after three months have passed, a "face opening" ceremony is held at dawn. The infant is brought outdoors with its face covered, and unveiled

---

38 E.W. Gifford, "Northeastern and Western Yavapai," *University of California Publications in American Archaeology and Ethnology 34* (1937): 247-354, esp. 300.
39 Barrington Kaye, *Bringing Up Children in Ghana* (London: George Allen & Unwin Ltd., 1962), pp. 56-57.
40 Kaye, p. 57.
41 Rattray, p. 59.
42 Edith Clarke, "The Sociological Significance of Ancestor Worship in Ashanti," *Africa 3* (1930): 431-470, esp. 431.

when the first bird sings. During this social birth rite the infant is introduced to the temple, to nature, to buffaloes, and to its clansmen. The infant is not considered a person until the ceremony has been performed.[43] Greeting the sun was also a feature of social birth ceremonies among the Hopi Amerindians a century ago. On the twentieth day after birth, a ceremony was held to purify the new mother, name the baby, and present the child to the sun. Great care was taken by the father to announce the precise moment the sun rose above the horizon. At that instant, the "godmother throws the blanket from the face of the baby" and presents a cornmeal offering to the sun.[44] All those present, including the newborn, then ate a ritual breakfast marking the entrance of a new person into the community.[45]

The above are quintessential examples of social birth rites: the newborn is kept indoors and out of sight for a specified period of time while the larger society remains symbolically unaware of its presence. This is a period of trial. The infant must "prove" it is worthy of personhood; first by managing to survive, then by exhibiting the vigor, health, and affect of one destined to become a functioning member of the community. If it survives and thrives, it is ready to pass through the social birth canal, to be ceremoniously welcomed as a person into the community. Completion of social birth rites ties the individual to the kin group and to the mortal world, granting it a moral status designed to protect it from harm by placing it under the protection of the group. If any of these criteria are not satisfied, the infant is classed as a non-person (and may in fact be labelled as non-human and hence not eligible for personhood, as with witches, ghosts and spirit-children). If it does not die of its own accord, it may be neglected until it does die, or it may be killed.

Infanticide is murder by definition, but most societies punish only the killing of human persons. It is problematic, then, to apply the label of infanticide to killing neonates before they are recognized as human or granted personhood. We might rather think of this as post-partum abortion, an image more applicable to the American experience. Induced abortion in the U.S. is rationalized (in part) by regarding the fetus as a pre-person, not yet accorded the same sanctity of life applied to "babies." Societies without safe and effective means of inducing abortion at early gestational stages may delay valuing the infant until well after biological birth. During this interim between biological and social birth the unwanted fetus (and it *is* still regarded as a fetus by that society) can be killed while its caretakers remain immune from punishment. Infanticide is condemned in most societies, but only after the newborn has been accorded human status or recognized as a person:

> [I]nfanticide is most readily condoned if it occurs before the infant is named and has been accepted as a bona fide member of its society. It seems that the primary and fundamental restriction in most societies is

---

43 David G. Mandelbaum, Department of Antrhopology, University of California, Berkeley, personal communication.

44 J.G. Owens, "Natal Ceremonies of the Hopi Indians," *Journal of American Ethnology and Archaeology 2* (1892): 163-75, esp. 170-73.

45 See Tilly E. Stevenson, "The Religious Life of a Zuni Child," *Fifth Annual Report of the Bureau of Ethnology* (1883-84): 539-555, esp. 546, for an account of a similar social birth rite which took place among the Zuni of western New Mexico.

the taboo on murder, i.e., killing a member of the ingroup. The less eligible a child is for membership in the group, the less seriously the act of killing the child is viewed.[46]

Thus the Bariba of Benin believe that some babies will be born witches, who may endanger their mothers' health and bring misfortune to the entire community. Witch babies can be identified at biological birth and should ideally be killed at that time to prevent future havoc.[47] In many societies the decision to expose or kill a neonate is made immediately at biological birth or within a few hours afterward. Among the Mohave Amerindians, if a newborn "was permitted to live long enough to be put to the breast, it was no longer subject to being killed".[48]

Post-partum abortion becomes infanticide if it is practiced after social birth rites are performed: "Thus in Athens the child could be exposed before the Amphidromia, a family ceremony at which the child was carried by its nurse around the hearth and thus received the religious consecration and its name".[49] In England during the 17th and 18th centuries, infanticide was practiced even though newborns were socially recognized as persons.[50] In those cases, however, personhood was granted incrementally, and infants were considered to be less significant persons than older children and adults. Under civil and religious law, killing a baby was a sin and a crime, but as practiced by the populace infanticide was less heinous than murdering an adult.

Becoming a person sometimes involves a long period of nurturing and socialization by the mother. This makes the infant's right to personhood in some societies contingent on the mother's survival and well-being. For example, an ethnographer reported that, among the Toba Amerindians of the Bolivian Gran Chaco, if a woman died in childbirth the newborn would be buried alive with her body. If both lived, personhood was granted only when the infant gained physical autonomy from the mother after weaning. Before that time, neither abortion nor infanticide was considered immoral: "A new-born child is no personality and has not an independent existence; its parents, and particularly the mother, have full right to decide over its life".[51] Yanomamo infants, also living in lowland South America, were considered appendages of their mothers until weaned at the end of their third year. When nursing ended, "the child, which hitherto belonged to the flesh and blood of the mother, has become an independent human be-

46 Clelland S. Ford, "Control of Contraception in Cross-Cultural Perspective," *Annals of the New York Academy of Sciences 54* (1952): 763-768; cited in Mildred Dickeman, "Demographic Consequences of Infanticide in Man," *Annual Review of Ecology and Systematics 6* (1975): 107-137, esp. 115.
47 Carolyn Fishel Sargent, *The Cultural Context of Therapeutic Choice* (Dordrecht, Holland: D. Reidel Publishing Company, 1982), esp. 89-91.
48 George Devereux, "Mohave Indian Infanticide," *The Psychoanalytic Review 35* (2, 1948): 126-139, esp. 127.
49 Glanville Williams, *The Sanctity of Life and Criminal Law* (New York: Knopf, 1957), p. 14.
50 Peter C. Hoffer and N.E.H. Hull, *Murdering Mothers: Infanticide in England and New England 1558-1803* (New York: New York University Press, 1981).
51 Rafael Karsten, *The Toba Indians of the Bolivian Gran Chaco* (Oosterhout N.B., The Netherlands: Anthropological Publications, 1967 [1923]), p. 24-25; thanks to Beth Ann Conklin for providing me with this reference.

ing".[52] The personhood of the newborn in these two societies was predicated, at least in part, on attaining physical independence from the mother.

Ethnographic accounts cite a wide range of socially significant events which mark the end of liminality and the beginning of personhood. Weaning is one example, but naming is by far the most common. A nameless infant, in many cases, is not considered a person. The social function of naming is discussed in Ford's cross-cultural study of reproductive behavior:

> Naming probably has derived its extremely widespread acceptance from the manifest advantages which result from the practice. A name facilitates social intercourse... Naming a child helps to pull him into the framework of his society as an accepted member of the group. By virtue of being named the infant becomes a person like everyone else in the society; he is no longer a nameless outsider.[53]

Killing a child prior to naming was acceptable among certain societies, while killing a child after it was named would be tantamount to murder.[54] This was apparently the case among the Atayal aborigines of Formosa, where an early ethnographer reported "there is no punishment for the killing of an as yet nameless -- i.e., less than two-or-three-year-old -- child".[55] Among Arctic coast peoples, an ethnographer noted that infants were named after the deceased, thereupon reincarnating their ghosts: "naming may have restrained infanticide...because killing a named child could offend the reincarnated ghost".[56] Countless similar cases are found in the literature, where the name is a symbol of having become a person, and where a child who died prior to receiving a name was not regarded as a person.[57] Cherokee Amerindian babies were generally named a few days after birth. If the birth were prolonged or difficult, however, the child would be named during birth "so as to have something 'material' by which to exercise an influence upon it".[58] In the contemporary United States, where biological and social birth occur simultaneously, most newborns have names already chosen for them, which allows them to move directly from the womb into a permanent social identity.

Not everywhere, however, is a name the dominant symbol of the value placed on a newborn's life. Naming is delayed in many societies, but this behavior can have completely different meanings according to the social and environmental context. In northeast Brazil, where infant mortality is high, delayed naming is one of the emotional defenses which poor mothers use to shield themselves from

52 Hans Becher, *Die Surara und Pakidai, swei Yanonami Stamme in Nordwestbrasilien* (Hamburg: Mirseum fur Voklerkinde, Mitteilunger 26, 1960).

53 Clelland S. Ford, *A Comparative Study of Human Reproduction* (New Haven: Human Relations Area Files Press, 1964), p. 77.

54 Clelland S. Ford, *Field Guide to the Study of Human Reproduction* (New Haven: Human Relations Area Files Press, 1964).

55 O. Wiedfeldt, "Wirtschaftliche, rechtliche, und soziale Grandtatsachen und Grandformen der Atayalen auf Formosa," *Deutsche Geselschaft fur Natur - und Volkerkunde Ostasiens*, Witteilungen 15 (Teil C, 1914): 1-55, esp. 23.

56 Asen Balicki, "Female Infanticide on the Arctic Coast," *Man* 2 (1967): 615-25, esp. 619.

57 Devereux 1955, p. 232; Mead and Newton, p. 154; and Gerald T. Perkoff, "Toward a Normative Definition of Personhood," in *Abortion and the Status of the Fetus,* ed. William B. Bondeson et al. (Dordrecht, Holland: D. Reidel Publishing Company, 1983), 159-166, esp. 162.

58 James Mooney and Frans M. Olbrechts, "The Swimmer Manuscript: Cherokee Sacred Formulas and Medicinal Prescriptions," *Smithsonian Institution Bureau of American Ethnology* 99 (1932): 127.

the devastating psychological impact of frequent infant death. These Brazilian women view their children "as human, but [as] significantly less human than the grown child or adult".[59] Extreme poverty, widespread hunger, and high infant mortality rates affect the mother's emotional investment in her children: emotional deprivation is, in this context, a product of material scarcity.[60] Conversely in the Himalayas, where infant mortality is also high, children are not called by their names precisely because their vulnerable young lives are highly valued. There Hindu children are named by a Brahmin priest on the tenth day after birth, but no one calls a child by this name for fear of making the child susceptible to the perils of "evil eye." Although not calling a child by its name may correspond with a denial of personhood in some societies, among the Hindus it is a "strong expression of the value and vulnerability placed on early lives, already begun but somehow requiring more protection".[61]

Discussion

The ethnographic literature offers no universal consensus about who or what constitutes a person, for personhood is evaluated and bestowed on the basis of moral criteria which vary tremendously among and within different sociocultural contexts. The value placed on the lives of fetuses, neonates, and young children is determined according to a complex constellation of cultural factors, and cannot be determined simply by asking, "When does life begin?" Without a more general understanding of what it means to be a person in a given society, the beginnings of personhood can never be fully understood. An awareness of beginnings affords us only rudimentary insights into the social construction of personhood, which depends on the social relevance of gender, age, and material conditions and is in many contexts a gradual process. An example from West Africa will illustrate the point.

The Ashanti were mentioned earlier in connection with social birth rites which occur eight days after birth, but apparently these rites did not complete the transition to personhood. According to Rattray personhood was sometimes not solidified until adolescence: "In times not so very remote, persons dying before they reached adolescence were in no case accorded the ordinary funeral rites, and were often merely buried on the village midden heap. They were classed with the 'ghost children' who had not even survived eight days".[62] Not until passing through adolescent initiation rites did an Ashanti youngster become a complete person. As reflected in burial rites, children were not as highly valued as adults. This can be understood by examining the context and significance of personhood within Ashanti society. Among the Ashanti, differentiation between the sexes was an essential feature of adulthood, but sexual differentiation was insignificant until a child reached puberty and acquired the capacity to reproduce. Because

59 Nancy Scheper-Hughes, "Culture, Scarcity, and Maternal Thinking: Maternal Detachment and Infant Survival in a Brazilian Shantytown," *Ethos 13* (1985): 291-317, esp. 312.
60 Scheper-Hughes, p. 292.
61 Lois McCloskey, School of Public Health, University of California, Los Angeles, personal communication.
62 Rattray, p. 61.

reproduction was crucial to the perpetuation of the socio-political order, adolescent initiation rites symbolized the growth not only of the individual physical body but of the collective social body as well. Adolescents embodied society's hopes for its future. This point is made in Comaroff's discussion of healing among the Tshidi; there adolescent initiation rites "linked the natural maturation of the physical body to the reproduction of the socio-political system".[63] The importance of continuing the social formation is underscored by rites which grant personhood to adolescents: in La Fontaine's terms, "The concept [of person] serves to fuse the finite span of a human life with the unlimited continuity of social forms, by identifying personhood with self reproduction".[64] For the Ashanti child, to be a person meant to enjoy bodily autonomy with few corresponding social obligations, but to be an adult person meant that one's social responsibilities were multiplied, intensified, and enmeshed more tightly within the body politic.

So far we have been concerned with the valuation of fetuses and children cross-culturally, yet societal norms affect the personhood of the mother as well as the fetus, newborn, and young child. The mother's status as a person depends in most societies on her reproductive condition, the reproductive choices she makes, and her society's attitudes toward childbearing and childrearing. Feminist scholars writing in the United States argue that the abortion debate has focused too exclusively on fetal rights, virtually ignoring the role of women in society.[65] Recent attempts to reverse this trend include books by Luker, who demonstrates that U.S. women's opinions about abortion are conditioned by their life circumstances and perceived career options,[66] and Petchesky, who argues that the reproductive choices available to women must be understood within the broad socio-economic and political framework affecting the role of women.[67] Certainly these insights are applicable cross-culturally as well. Throughout the world women are primarily responsible for decisions affecting the lives and well-being of fetuses, neonates, and young children, and the choices women make in this regard are contingent on their own assessments of available options. The options change with the social tides, alternately restricting and expanding womens' responsibilities for their born and unborn offspring. Such changes can be seen in a California lawsuit where a woman was charged with the wrongful death of her newborn child because she took illicit drugs and had sexual relations late in pregnancy, disregarding her doctor's orders. If this trend continues, American women will be increasingly held responsible for prenatal child abuse and neglect, even though fetuses have not been been granted the rights of persons under the U.S. constitution.

The ethnographic and historical literature is filled with accounts illustrating that a woman's status -- even her claim to personhood and life itself -- is contingent on her reproductive choices. In 15th century England, for example, moth-

63 Jean Comaroff, "Medicine: Symbol and Ideology," in *The Problem of Medical Knowledge*, ed. P. Wright and A. Treacher (Edinburgh: Edinburgh University Press, 1982), 49-68, esp. 52.
64 LaFontaine, p. 132.
65 See Whitbeck, 1983.
66 Kristin Luker, *Abortion and the Politics of Motherhood* (Berkeley: University of California Press, 1984).
67 Petchesky, Rosalind P. *Abortion and Women's Choice: The State, Sexuality, and Reproductive Freedom* (Boston: Northeastern University Press, 1985).

ers known to have destroyed their newborn children were punished by death, while wet nurses guilty of the same crime were not punished.[68] Piers argues that the reason for differential treatment was class bias, since wealthy women could afford to hire wet nurses for their children while poor women could not. Wet nurses were not executed for infanticide because breast milk was a rare and valuable commodity and wet nurses were scarce: "society simply could not have afforded to kill her".[69] Indigent natural mothers, in contrast, were relatively expendable, and these were the women most often found guilty of murdering their babies. The 15th century criminal sentence for murdering an infant depended not on the value of the infant's life, but on the social class of the accused. The hierarchy of values ranked the lives of wet nurses above the lives of "natural" mothers, obscuring the fact that wet nurses were themselves natural mothers. While Christian moralists railed against child murder, society's response reflected how certain classes of women were so devalued and oppressed that their execution was condoned. Their crime was in reality the inability to afford a wet nurse.

A woman's status within society can be heightened, undermined or made ambiguous by pregnancy. Generally if the pregnancy results in a healthy newborn (in some patrilineal societies only a healthy newborn boy is satisfactory) her status will be enhanced but, if the pregnancy outcome is viewed as negative, she may suffer irreparable damage or even death. Devereux cites at least two societies where women could reportedly be killed with impunity for inducing an abortion.[70] The mother's status in such cases was rendered ambiguous by the liminal status of the fetus. Whereas before the pregnancy her murder would have been a punishable crime, in pregnancy her life was valued less than that of the fetus she carried.

Most often the woman making reproductive decisions is held directly responsible for her own actions, as interpreted through societal mores and prejudices. In some cases, though, the lives of several people may be affected by a woman's decision. The Azande of central Africa have a polygamous, patriolocal social structure which allowed a woman's reproductive decisions to have far-reaching repercussions:

> If the husband learns that his wife has used an abortifacient plant, he considers this tantamount to the assassination of his child. He therefore asks his father-in-law for a second wife, or else, in vengeance, he kills the wife of his father-in-law or one of his father-in-law's children.[71]

In this case, the woman's relatives paid the consequences of her actions, demonstrating the links between fetal status, female status, and the status of other members of society. A similar issue can be seen in the United States abortion debates: should the decision to induce abortion be made in private between a woman and her physician, or should the permission of the father also be required? To what extent is the personhood of the woman contingent on her relationship to others in her sphere of social relations? Anthropologists have shown that in some societies one's social identity and personhood is completely, inextri-

---

68 Maria W. Piers, *Infanticide* (New York: W.W. Norton & Company, 1978).
69 Piers, p. 51.
70 Devereux 1955, pp. 58, 248.
71 Devereux 1955, p. 188.

cably embedded in the social structure, to the point where individuals cannot envision having relationships not dictated by social structural roles and statuses.[72] The very essence of personhood is negotiated, manipulated, bestowed, and denied in accordance with the tacit or considered approval of society's members.

In the United States, the abortion debate has been foreshortened by a culture-bound discourse on personhood. The discussion of fetal personhood and abortion legislation has been limited almost exclusively to the period between conception and biological birth, largely as a result of a shared, cultural belief that biological birth is the event which distinguishes persons from non-persons. Consequently, the only space left to negotiate the boundaries of personhood is prior to biological birth. We have framed the debate over abortion in such a way that we argue whether it would be defensible to push the dividing line earlier, toward conception, but not later, toward early childhood. In the process of limiting debate to this realm, we have largely ignored the expansive, multiple meanings of personhood in American society, including the implications for adult women and men of the social context which determines our life decisions.

How can the range of cultural variability discussed here affect the U.S. abortion policy debates? In spite of the relativist stance presented here, I will not argue that Americans should weigh the merits of post-partum abortion -- that would be ignoring a fundamental U.S. cultural reality which gave us the term "infanticide." Nonetheless Americans have felt forced to construct convoluted philosophical justifications for their positions on these issues, even when contorted logic theoretically could be avoided by admitting the existence and relevance of cultural variation. Debates over fetal personhood would be more honest, although undoubtedly more agonizing, if it were easier to admit that the moral dividing of life between persons and non-persons at biological birth or "viability" is a cultural construction. The question is whether we can tolerate knowing that our beliefs and values are remarkably malleable, arbitrary products of our cultural milieu.

---

72 LaFontaine 1985: 129.

Acknowledgements

The ideas presented here developed over a period of years, stimulated by discussion with many people, some of whom are undoubtedly unaware of their influence. For example, in 1980 Dr. Marvin Harris casually mentioned that he thought someone should do a cross-cultural study of when life begins; the idea has been with me since then. Dr. Michele Shedlin introduced me to the cross-cultural literature on reproductive health. Dr. Virginia Ernster provided the opportunity and encouragement for me to do the first systematic investigation of this topic. The late Dr. David Mandelbaum kindly shared data from his own field work among the Toda; he, Dr. Pauline Kolenda, and Dr. Stanley Brandes commented on earlier versions of this paper. Dr. Nancy Scheper-Hughes, Lesley Sharp, and Nicholas Townsend provided theoretical insights and editorial advice. The ideas presented here have also benefitted from lengthy conversations with Beth Ann Conklin, Anita Garey, and Frank Zimmerman. My warmest thanks go to James Trostle and Lois McCloskey, who have always shared in and supported this project.

Personality Profiles of 'Pro-Choice' and 'Anti-Choice' Individuals and Cultures

James W. Prescott

I WOULD LIKE to briefly summarize some fifteen years of cross-cultural studies that I have conducted on the social behavioral characteristics of "pro-choice' and "anti-choice cultures' and individuals.

We have been told by the anti-choice movement that their position, namely, that the fetus is a person from conception and, thus, its termination of live is equivalent to murder - is one that "respects life;" and that this "right to life" position is derived from what Cardinal Bernardin has called a "seamless garment" of respect for life. These assumptions of the benevolent personality character structure of the "anti-choice" person and culture have been questioned and invalidated by my research over the past fifteen years. Contrary to their claim, the "anti-choice" personality or culture has a consistent profile of tolerance of and even support for human violence and pain with authoritarian control over personal liberties.

Specifically, I found from my studies of both primitive cultures and contemporary legislative actions in North America (Canadian Parliament; U.S. Congress; Pennsylvania House and Senate) that the "anti-choice" person or culture has the following statistically significant characteristics: support for slavery (primitive cultures); support for killing, torturing, and mutilation of enemies captured in warfare (primitive cultures); exploitation of women and children (primitive cultures); punish and/or reject pre-marital and extra-marital sexual activity (primitive and contemporary cultures); kin group is patrilineal (primitive cultures); support capital punishment (legislators); support for Vietnam War and aid to the Nicaraguan "Contras" (legislators); support "no-knock" laws (legislators); oppose hand-gun controls (legislators); oppose use of medical heroin for dying cancer patients (legislators); support outlawing of fornication and adultery (legislators); have approximately 50% lower family and child nurturance scores than "pro-choice" (legislators); support societal punishment of prostitution; and believe that sexual pleasure weakens moral character (psychometric studies).

In summary, "anti-choice" persons and cultures are characterized by: (a) an intolerance for the dignity, integrity, and life of the human body; (b) a high tolerance for and/or indifference toward human pain and suffering; (c) a lower value on nurturance of children and families; and (d) an anti-sexual pleasure ethic.

On the basis of my research, I concluded that the "anti-choice" personality and/or culture is motivated primarily by a moral concept of "sexual sin" where "illicit" sexual pleasures of the body must be denied, controlled or punished. Tolerance of choice on abortion represents a *de facto* recognition of a "sexuality for pleasure ethic" that is disassociated from procreation. This moral view of human sexuality is unacceptable to the patristic, authoritarian moral fundamentalists who believe in "sexual sin," favor the subordination of women to men, and fear full sexual equality for women. (The above scientific findings and conclusions are more fully presented in the article reprinted as Appendix C.)

It is of more than passing interest to note the parallels between the co-existence of "torture, mutilation and killing of enemy captured in warfare" with punishment of abortion and pre-marital and extra-marital sexuality in the primitive cultures with that of the Roman Catholic church and its history of "torture, mutilation and killing of heretics," (burning at the stake and the torture chambers of the Papal and Spanish Inquisitions) with the Vatican's opposition to abortion and pre-marital and extra-marital sexuality. (It is a matter of historical fact that Pope Innocent IV first authorized torture in the Papal Inquisition in the Papal Bull: *Ad Extirpanda* in 1252.)

The above findings and historical events further invalidate the claim that the psychology or motivation underlying "opposition to abortion" reflects a "Seemless Garment" of "Respect for Life."

Summing Up the Linchpin Question: When Does A Human Become A Person, and Why?

Robert T. Francoeur

THE EMOTIONS of the abortion debate have promoted some fuzzy and dangerous thinking. Medical, scientific, and philosophical terms are exploited for emotional impact without regard for their clearly defined and accepted usages. Terms like "baby," "fetus," "human," "person," and "murder" are politicized and redefined in order to convert them from instruments of enlightenment in the quest for truth into crusaders' clubs with which to beat the enemy into submission.

This is as it has always been when people in power and the powerless struggle for life, liberty and the pursuit of happiness. Long before the Magna Carta or American Constitution, the term "person" carried with it certain rights and moral responsibilities. The Sumerian creation myth of Gilgamesh, the earliest extant human document, describes King Gilgamesh, his friend Enkidu, and other males as real "persons" with unique identities and individuality. Women, ordinary citizens, and slaves were ignored. Their human status might be acknowledged, but not their status as individuals endowed by nature or the gods with certain rights. In ancient Greece, women and slaves were recognized as human, but not as persons on a par with free men.

In the Middle Ages and Renaissance, men claimed that studies of aborted fetuses clearly showed that male fetuses attained human form, and therefore a human should and personhood, about forty days after conception. Since female fetuses did not develop their sexual form, they did not receive their soul until some eighty days after conception and so could not be on a par with men. This philosophical conclusion used the science of the day to reinforce women's subordinate status as persons as defined by the Bible. It also allowed both Protestant and Catholic leaders, including several Popes, to accept abortion in the first trimester, before quickening which indicated the presence of an immortal human soul and the status of personhood.[1]

1 Doncell, J.F. 1970. "Animation and hominization." *Theological Studies*. 31(1):76-105. Francoeur, R.T. 1985. "From then to now: The evolution of bioethical decision making in prenatal intensive care." In C.C. Harris & F. Snowden, eds. *Bioethical Frontiers in Prenatal Intensive Care*. Natchitoches, LA: Northwestern State University Press. pp. 22-24.

Few today would question the *human status* of the zygote, embryo, or fetus that results from the union of a human sperm and human egg. Status as a *human* is not dependent on heterosexual coitus followed by fertilization of the ovum in the woman's fallopian tubes, and by implantation and gestation in her uterus. In this age of artificial insemination, *in vitro* fertilization, embryo transplants, and surrogate mothers, the status and rights of a "test tube" baby as a human and as a person with inalienable rights is not dependent on how it was conceived or gestated. We need not call on modern genetics and chromosome studies to witness to the human status of an egg, sperm, zygote, embryo, fetus, newborn, adult or comatose individual like Karen Ann Quinlan. *Personhood*, however, is another issue.

The central issue in the modern debate over abortion is *personhood*. Hence the precise focus of this anthology. Since we attribute certain inalienable, God-given rights to persons, society's decision about who is recognized as a person, when they achieve that status, and when they cease to have status as a person becomes crucial. It is central in our debates about the end of life on this earth, in controversies over life-support systems for comatose patients, the right to die with dignity, and euthanasia. It is equally pivotal in our debates about abortion.

Running through all the chapters in this volume is the basic question of how we define personhood today and what criteria we can use as characteristic of personhood. The perspective adopted by all these experts is one in which personhood is viewed as a process, an emerging phenomenon. Early in the 1960s debate among Catholics about contraception, Louis Dupre warned that "to talk about human nature [and personhood] as if it were an immutable entity, given in its entirety [at fertilization or any other time] is to ignore the most essential characteristic of *human* nature."[2] This process view is exactly the perspective used by the Justices of the U.S. Supreme Court in the *Roe v. Wade* decision. It is this perspective, however, which is totally rejected by those opposed to abortion. For them, the fullness of human nature and personhood is present from the moment of fertilization on without qualification.

Unfortunately, in discussing the emergence of fetal personhood, the Justices focused on the criteria of "viability." The rapid advances of perinatal medical care make "viability" as unstable as quicksand, especially if one considers the probable development of a functional artificial placentation system or "artificial womb" in the near future.

But the Justices also gave weight to the issue of maternal versus fetal rights, forcing us to discuss the many dimensions of personhood within a *process* view. Drawing on modern embryology and medicine, the Justices based their decision about the constitutional legality of abortion on the personal rights of a woman to privacy and control of her own body. They also relied on our understanding that the nine months of pregnancy is a process in which a one-celled fertilized egg slowly develops its genetic potential to become a person with inalienable rights. Something essential comes into existence that was not present at the beginning of the nine-month process. A fertilized human egg or zygote develops through a blastocyst stage of many undifferentiated cells to an embryo which at the end of

---

2 Dupre, L. 1964. *Contraception and Catholics*. Baltimore: Helicon Press, p. 45.

the second month of gestation has not yet attained the status of person despite its development of all basic organ systems. Because the fetus has not yet achieved the neurological substrate that allows intrapersonal and intrapersonal experiences in its first six months of gestation, the Supreme Court decided fetal inchoative rights do not outweigh established maternal rights.

In 1973, a six month fetus, weighing about two pounds or 1000 grams, might survive outside the womb with medical care. Today, a fetus weighing only one pound or 500 grams might survive with the latest perinatal intensive care, although the small number of such infants that leave the hospital to lead a normal life raises serious questions about the moral justification of treating aggressively premature infants that weight less than 700 to 800 grams.[3]

As the threshold of viability changes, the emphasis of the Justices in *Roe v. Wade* on fetal "personhood" increasingly takes center stage in the on-going abortion debate. Speaking from a dual perspective, as a developmental biologist and amateur theologian, I would like to draw together some of the key insights provided by the theologians, lawyers, neurobiologists, and anthropologists in this volume.

As an embryologist interested in human evolution and trained in Roman Catholic theology, I am intrigued by the vagaries of theological pronouncements on abortion. Early in the *Roe v. Wade* debates, ethicist Joseph Fletcher warned about the dangers of prolepsis. Webster defines prolepsis as "an anticipating; especially, the describing of an event as taking place before it could have done so, the treating of a future event as if it had already happened." Anti-choice, anti-abortion forces today are constantly engaging in prolepsis when they try to redefine critical terms like person, fetus, and murder to support their crusade.[4]

As a classic example, let me cite church authorities in my own Roman Catholic tradition. The Vatican frequently reminds Catholics that, while its pronouncements "find support in the more secure findings of the natural sciences," the Church's teaching authorities can also confidently "*transcend* the horizons of science."[5] Medical scientists universally speak about fertilization - the union of sperm and egg as distinct from conception - the implantation of the blastocyst in the uterus five to six days after fertilization. We also talk about the embryo in weeks two through eight and a fetal period in the last seven months of pregnancy. Yet, speaking for the Vatican, Father Joseph Fox informs us that the term "fetus" now includes all human life from the moment of fertilization until birth.[6] Anti-abortionists say that abortion is murder because "babies" exist at fertilization.

3 Mitchell, C. 1984. "Care of severely impaired infants raises ethical issues." *American Nurse.* 16(3):9-10. Schenchner, S. 1980. "For the 1980s: How small is to small?" *Clinics in Perinatology.* 7:143. Strong, C. 1983. "The tiniest newborns." *Hastings Center Report.* 13(1):14-19. Weir, R.F. 1984. *Selective Nontreatment of Handicapped Newborns.* New York: Oxford University Press.
4 "What is called in logic the 'error of potentiality' is to confuse what is yet to be or could be, with what is. It supposes that because a fetus [looks human and] cold possibly or probably become a person, it is therefore a person *now*. This 'prolepsis' falsifies reality; in its eagerness it slips into thinking that what we want is already possessed, when if fact we are only hoping for it. In fact, a fetus is precisely and only a fetus." J. Fletcher. 1979. *Humanhood: Essays in Biomedical Ethics.* Buffalo: Prometheus Press, p. 97.
5 Congregation for the Doctrine of the Faith. 1986. Letter to the Bishops of the Catholic Church on the pastoral care of homosexual persons. In J. Gramich & Pat Furey, eds. *The Vatican and Homosexuality.* New York: Crossroad, p. 1.
6 *National Catholic Reporter.* 1988 (December 9). "Church officials clarify definition of abortion." p. 2.

Monsignor Caffarra, the Pope's own theologian, completes this redefinition effort by urging a return to the condemnation of contraception as "homicide" found in canon law before its 1917 codification. Even if not taken literally, contraception is said to be "homicide in the heart."[7]

Where does this prolepsis take those who claim a person is present at fertilization and thus denounce all abortion as murder? If every human egg fertilized is immediately a "fetus," "baby" and "person," then God and nature play a mean trick on us. Scientists estimate that in the five-six days following union of egg and sperm, between one-third and one-half of all "persons" spontaneously degenerate and are reabsorbed or expelled. In the second week, 42 percent of the implanted "persons" abort. In the third and fourth week, 15 percent of the remaining "persons" abort. In the fetal period, one-third of the remaining fetuses spontaneously miscarry.[8] Thus, out of every 1000 "persons" "conceived," only 120 to 160 survive to be born! How do the anti-abortionists and theologians who denounce abortion as murder account for this prodigious waste of human life in the divine plan?

The practical consequences of this attempt to redefine person, fetus and murder has already led us into the quagmire of forced Caesarean sections described by Janet Benshoof and Judith C. Rosen in the legal section of this volume. The courts have begun intervening in cases where pregnant women were using drugs. Medical and lay fetal-protection advocates, who are also anti-abortion, have sought to enlist the support of the courts to protect the unborn against "fetal abuse." In rejecting one such suit, the Illinois Supreme Court noted that such cases could subject a pregnant mother's "every waking and sleeping moment" to second guessing.[9] In February 1989, in in a Mineola, N.Y. case, one anti-abortion advocate asked the court to appoint him legal guardian for 32-year-old Nancy Klein who was pregnant and comatose. In a parallel action, a second anti-abortion advocate asked the court to appoint him legal guardian for Mrs. Klein's fetus. The purpose of both requests was to prevent the husband and family of Mrs. Klein from authorizing an abortion which, in the medical opinion of their physicians, would improve her chances of recovery. The court denied the fetal guardian appointment because the fetus was "nonviable" at eighteen weeks and thus not subject to a legal guardian. If the embryo were legally a "person" at fertilization rather than when it achieved "viability," the court logically might have appointed a fetal guardian in this and similar cases where anti-abortion advocates try to set themselves up as "pregnancy police" and "fetal guardians."

Before we accept the theological or philosophical redefinitions of key concepts in the abortion debate, we need to consider seriously the many draconian consequences raised by declaring that a true person with inalienable rights "in fact" exists from the moment of conception. It is not inconceivable that theological and legal pronouncements about fetal personhood from the moment of conception could be translated into a Brave New World with pregnancy police on

7 Habblethwaite. P. 1988 (December 16). "Meetings celebrate 20 years of *Humanae Vitae*." *National Catholic Reporter*.
8 Moore, K.L. 1988. *The Developing Human: Clinically Oriented Embryology*. 4th ed. Philadelphia: W.B. Saunders Company, pp. 46-47.
9 Gest, T. 1989 (February 6). "The pregnancy police, on patrol." *U.S. World & News Report*. p. 50.

patrol to make certain all fertile women have their monthly pregnancy test and all pregnancies are monitored to assure the constitutional, God-given, inalienable rights of every fertilized human egg to life, liberty and the pursuit of happiness!

In this on-going debate, the perspectives and historical insights offered by Catholic theologian Marjorie Reiley Maguire and Paul Simmons, professor of Christian Ethics at the Southern Baptists Theological Seminary, provide a needed balance to the polemic attempts to redefine the process of human reproduction and the pervasive denial of the vagaries and contradictions of past theological judgments on abortion.

The cross-cultural and historical perspectives offered by James W. Prescott, Leight Minturn, and Lynn M. Morgan clearly show that personhood is both a relationship and a social construct. Definitions of who is a person, when someone becomes a person, and when they cease to be a person with inalienable human rights are both socially and culturally determined. Inevitably, these definitions vary and change depending on social conditions, political agendas, and the new, inescapable insights into the nature of human nature uncovered by psychologists and developmental biologists.

I hope the reader will not charge me with being biased when I admit that, although I greatly value the anthropological, legal and theological insights offered in this volume and find them most provocative, I find the developmental neurobiological perspectives to be the keystone against which all arguments about abortion must be tested. If personhood exists from the time a human sperm fertilizes the egg, then we have a moral responsibility to protect its rights. Freedom of speech allows anyone to state anything they want about personhood, but those who denounce all abortion because they claim a fertilized egg is a person must be ready and able to document and support their claim with scientific evidence. Without evidence, such a claim is, to use the Biblical phase, "tinkling brass and sounding cymbals, signifying nothing."

From a neurophysiological perspective, personhood and the consciousness which is characteristic of it, is an emergent property whose emergence depends on the growing differentiation and interconnection of neurons in the brain. While all the cells of the neocortex appear to be in place by the 20th or 21st week of gestation, the "mature wiring" of neurons in the conscious areas of the brain begins in earnest in the 28th to 32nd week. This is a keystone fact which must be considered in all abortion debates. It means that 99.99 percent of all abortions in the United States occur before fetal personhood can develop.

The findings of modern developmental neuropsychology, outlined by Michael Bennett and Michael J. Flower, clearly support the early theological theory of ensoulment and mediate animation outlined by theologians Maguire and Simmons and in the cultural perspective by Minturn and Morgan. Yet, antiabortionists of all religious persuasions conveniently ignore this concurrence of evidence in their dogmatic claims that abortion is and has always been against the laws of nature and God.

Sixteen years after the U.S. Supreme Court rendered its decision in *Roe v. Wade*, we are at a turning point. A very vocal minority, about 18 percent of Americans, want all abortion declared illegal. About 24 percent want abortion available with no limitations. And a solid majority of about 57 percent want abortion legal under certain circumstances.[10] Hopefully the essays in this volume, coming as they do from experts in the law, theology, developmental neurobiology, and anthropology, will help clarify the real issues in this on-going debate.

10 Lewin, T. 1989 (January 22). "Views on abortion are sharply split 16 years after Supreme Court ruling." *New York Times*, p. 21.

Appendix A

Roe et al. v. Wade, District Attorney of Dallas County

Appeal from the United States District Court For The Northern District of Texas

No. 70-18. Argued December 13, 1971 - Reargued October 11, 1972 - Decided January 22, 1973

Mr. Justice Blackmun delivered the opinion of the Court.

This Texas federal appeal and its Georgia companion, Doe v. Bolton, post, p. 179, present constitutional challenges to state criminal abortion legislation. The Texas statutes under attack here are typical of those that have been in effect in many states for approximately a century. The Georgia statutes, in contrast, have a modern cast and are a legislative product that, to an extent at least, obviously reflects the influences of recent attitudinal change, of advancing medical knowledge an techniques, and of new thinking about an old issue.

We forthwith achnowledge our awareness of the sensitive and emotional nature of the abortion controversy, of the vigorous opposing views, even among physicians, and of the deep and seemingly absolte convictions that the subject inspires. One's philosophy, one's experiences, one's exposure to the raw edges of human existence, one's religious training, one's attitues toward life and family and their values, and the moral standards one establishes and seeks to observe, are all likely to influence and to color one's thinking and conclusions about abortion.

In addition, population growth, pollution, poverty, and racial overtones tend to complicate and not to simplify the problem.

Our task, of course, is to resolve the issue by constitutional, measurement, free of emotion and of predilection. We seek earnestly to do this, and, because we do, we have inquired into, and in this opinion place some emphasis upon, medical and medical-legal history and what that history reveals about man's attitudes toward the abortion procedure over the centuries. We bear in mind, too, Mr. Justice Holmes' admonition in his now vindicated dissent in Lochner v. New York:

"[The Constitution] is made for people of fundamentally differing views, and the accident of our finding certain opinions natural and familiar or novel and even shocking ought not to conclude our judgment upon the question whether statutes embodying them conflict with the Constitution of the United States."

I

The Texas statutes that concern us here are Arts. 1191-1194 and 1196 of the State's Penal Code. These make it a crime to "procure an abortion," as therein defined, or to attempt one, except with respect to "an abortion procured or attempted by medical advice for the purpose of saving the life of the mother." Similar statutes are in existence in a majority of the States.

Texas first enacted a criminal abortion statute in 1854. This was soon modified into language that has remained substantially unchanged to the present time. The final article in each of these compilations provided the same exception, as does the present Article 1196, for an abortion by "medical advice for the purpose of saving the life of the mother."

II

Jane Roe, a single woman who was residing in Dallas County, Texas, instituted this federal action in March 1970 against the District Attorney of the county. She sought a declaratory judgment that the Texas criminal abortion statutes were unconstitutional on their face, and an injunction restraining the defendant from enforcing the statutes.

Roe alleged that she was unmarried and pregnant; that she wished to terminate her pregnancy by an abortion "performed by a competent, licensed physician, under safe, clinical conditions"; that she was unable to get a "legal" abortion in Texas because her life did not appear to be threatened by the continuation of her pregnancy; and that she could not afford to travel to another jurisdiction in order to secure a legal abortion under safe conditions. She claimed that the Texas statutes were unconstitutionally vague and that they abridged her right of personal privacy, protected by the First, Fourth, Fifth, Ninth, and Fourteenth Amendments. By an amendment to her complaint Roe purported to sue "on behalf of herself and all other women" similarly situated.

James Hubert Hallford, a licensed physician, sought and was granted leave to intervene in Roe's action. In his complaint he alleged that he had been arrested previously for violations of the Texas abortion statutes and that two such prosecutions were pending against him. He described conditions of patients who came to him seeking abortions, and he claimed that for many cases he, as a physician, was unable to determine whether they fell within or outside the exception recognized by Article 1196. He alleged that, as a consequence, the statutes were vague and uncertain, in violation of the Fourteenth Amendment, and that they violated his own and his patients' rights to privacy in the doctor-patient rlationship and his own right to practice medicine, rights he claimed were guaranteed by the First, Fourth, Fifth, Ninth, and Fourteenth Amendments.

John and Mary Doe, a married couple, filed a companion complaint to that of Roe. They also named the District Attorney as defendant, claimed like constitutuional deprivations, and sought declaratory and

---

In the interest of making the text more readable, we have omitted the footnotes and case citations.

injunctive relief. The Does alleged that they were a childless couple; that Mrs. Doe was suffering from a "neuralchemical" disorder; that her physician had " advised her to avoid pregnancy until such time as her condition has materially improved" (although a pregnancy at the present time would not present "a serious risk" to her life); that, pursuant to medical advice, she had discontinued use of birth control pills; and that if she should become pregnant, she would want to terminate the pregnancy by an abortion performed by a competent, licensed physician under safe, clinical conditions. By an amendment to their complaint, the Does purported to sue "on behalf of themselves and all couples similarly situated."

The two actions were consolidated and heard together by a duly convened three-judge district court. The suits thus presented the situations of the pregnant single woman, the childless couple, with the wife not pregnant, and the licensed practicing physician, all joining in the attack on the Texas criminal abortion statutes. Upon the filing of affidavits, motions were made for dismissal and for summary judgment. The court held that Roe and members of her class, and Dr. Hallford, had standing to sue and presented justiciable controversies, but that the Does had failed to allege facts sufficient to state a present controversy and did not have standing. It concluded that, with respect to the requests for a declaratory judgment, abstention was not warranted. On the merits, the District Court held that the "fundamental rights of single women and married persons to choose whether to have children is protected by the Ninth Amendment, through the Fourteenth Amendment," and that the Texas criminal abortion statutes were void on their face because they were both unconstituuionally vague and constituted an overbroad infringement of the plaintiffs' Ninth Amendment rights. The court then held that abstention was warranted with respect to the requests for an injunction. It therefore dismissed the Does' complaint, declared the abortion statutes void, and dismissed the application for injunctive relief.

The plaintiffs Roe and Doe and the intervenor Hallford, pursuant to 28 U. S. C. § 1253, have appealed to this Court from that part of the District Court's judgment denying the injunction. The defendant District Attorney has purprted to cross-appeal, pursuant to the same statute, from the court's grant of declaratory relief to Roe and Hallford. Both sides also have taken protective appeals to the United States Court of Appeals for the Fifth Circuit. That court ordered the appeals held in abeyance pending decision here. We postponed decision on jurisdiction to the hearing on the merits.

III

It might have been preferable if the defendant, pursuant to our Rule 20, had presented to us a petition for certiorari before judgment in the Court of Appeals with respect to the granting of the plaintiffs' prayer for declaratory relief. Our decisions in Mitchell v. Donovan, are to the effect that § 1253 does not authorize an appeal to this Court from the grant or denial of declaratory relief alone. We conclude, nevertheless, that those decisions do not foreclose our review of both the injunctive and the declaratory aspects of a case of this kind under § 1253 from specific denial of injunctive relief, and the arguments as to both aspects are necessarily identical. It would be destructive of time and energy for all concerned were we to rule otherwise.

IV

We are next confronted with issues of justiciability, standing, and abstention. Have Roe and the Does established that "personal stake in the outcome of the controversy," that insures that " the dispute sought to be adjudicated will be presented in an adversary context and in a form historically viewed as capable of judicial resolution," ? And what effect did the pendency of criminal abortion chages against Dr. Hallford in state court have upon the propriety of the federal court's granting relief to him as a plaintiff-intervenor?

A. Jane Roe. Despite the use of the pseudonym, no suggestion is made that Roe is a fictitious person. For purposes of her case, we accept as true, and as established, her existence; her pregnant state, as of the inception of her suit in March 1970 and as late as May 21 of that year when she filed an alias affidavit with the District Court; and her inability to obtain a legal abortion in Texas.

Viewing Roe's case as of the time of its filing and therafter until as late as May, there can be little dispute that it then presented a case or controversy and that, wholly apart from the class aspects, she, as a pregnant single woman thwarted by the Texas criminal abortion laws, had standing to challenge those statutes. Indeed, we do not read the appellee's brief as really asserting anything to the contrary. The "logical nexus between the status asserted and the claim sought to be adjudicated," and the necessary degree of contentiousness, are both present.

The appellee notes, however, that the record does not disclose that Roe was pregnant at the time of the District Court hearing on May 22, 1970, or on the following June 17 when the court's opinion and judgment were filed. And he suggests that Roe's case must now be moot because she and all other members of her class are no longer subject to any 1970 pregnancy.

The usual rule in federal cases is that an actual controversy must exist at stages of appellate or certiorari review, and not simply at the date the action is initiated.

But when, as here, pregnancy is a significant fact in the litigation, the normal 266-day human gestation period is so short that the pregnancy will come to term before the usual appellate process is complete. If that termination makes a case moot, pregnancy litigation seldom will survive much beyond the trial stage, and appellate review will be effectively denied. Our law should not be that rigid. Pregnancy often comes more than once to the same woman, and in the general population, if man is to survive, it will always be with us. Pregnancy provides a classic justification for a conclusion of nonmootness. It truly could be "capable of repetition, yet evading review."

We therefore, agree with the District Court that Jane Roe had standing to undertake this litigation, that she presented a justiciable controversy, and that the termination of her 1970 pergnancy has not rendered her case moot.

B. Dr. Hallford. The doctor's position is different. He entered Roe's litigation as a plaintiff-intervenor, alleging in his complaint that he:

"[I]n the past has been arrested for violating the Texas Abortion Laws and at the present time stands charged by indictment with violating said laws in the Criminal District Court of Dallas laws in the Criminal District Court of Dallas County, Texas to-wit: (1) The State of Texas vs.James H. Hallford, and (2) The State of Texas vs. James H. Hallford. In both cases the defendant is charged with abortion...."

In his application for leave to intervene, the doctor made like representations as to the abortion charges pending in th state court. These representations wre also repeated in the affidavit he executed and filed in support of his motion for summary judgment.

Dr. Hallford is, therefore, in the position of seeking, in a federal court, declaratory and injunctive relief with respect to the same statutes under which he stands charged in criminal prosecutions simultaneously pending in state court. Although he stated that he has been arrested in the past for violating the State's abortion laws, he makes no allegation of any substantial and immediate threat to any federally protected right that cannot be asserted in his defense against the state prosecutions. Neither is there any allegation of harassment or bad-faith prosecution. In order to excape the rule articulated in the cases cited in the next paragraph of this opinion that, absent harassment and bad faith, a defendant in a pending state criminal case cannot affirmatively challenge in federal court the statutes under which the State is prosecuting him, Dr. Hallford seeks to distinguish his status as a present state defendant from his status as a "potential future defendant" and to assert only the latter for standing purposes here.

We see no merit in that distinction. Our decision in Samuels v. Mackell compels the conclusion that the District Court erred when it granted declaratory relief to Dr. Hallford instead of refraining from so doing. The court, of course, was correct in refusing to grant injunctive relief to the doctor. The reasons supportive of that action, however, are those expressed in Samuels v. Mackell, and in Younger v. Harris; Boyle v. Landry; Perez v. Ledesma. We note, in passing, that Younger and its companion cases were decided after the three-judge District Court decision in this case.

Dr. Hallford's complaint in intervention, therefore, is to be dismissed. He is remitted to his defenses in the state criminal proceedings against him. We reverse the judgment of the District Court insofar as it granted Dr. Hallford relief and failed to dismiss his complaint in intervention.

C. The Does. In view of our ruling as to Roe's standing in her case, the issue of the Does' standing in their case has little significance. The claims they assert are essentially the same as those of Roe, and they attack the same statutes. Nevertheless, we briefly note the Does' posture.

Their pleadings present them as a childless married couple, the woman not being pregnant, who have no desire to have children at this time because of their having received medical advice that Mrs. Doe should avoid pregnancy, and for "other highly personal reasons. But they "fear... they may face the prospect of becoming parents." And if prgnancy insues, they "would want to terminate" it by abortion. They assert an inability to obtain an abortion legally in Texas and, consequently, the prospect of obtaining an illegal abortion there or of going outside Texas to some place where the procedure could be obtained legally and competently.

We thus have as plaintiffs a married couple who have, as their asserted immediate and present injury, only an alleged "detrimental effect upon [their] marital happiness" because they are forced to "the choice of refraining form normal sexual relations or of endangering Mary Doe's health through a possible pregnancy." Their claim is that sometime in the future Mrs. Doe might become pregnant because of possible failure of contraceptive measures, and at that time in the future she might want an abortion that might then be illegal under the Texas statutes.

This very phrasing of the Does' position reveals its speculative character. Their alleged injury rests on possible future contraceptive failure, possible future pregnancy, possible future unpreparedness for parenthood, and possible future impairment of health. Any one or more of these several possibilities might have some real or imagined impact upon their marital happiness. But we are not prepared to say that the bare allegation of so indirect an injury is sufficient to present an actual case or controversy. The Does' claim falls far short of those resolved otherwise in the cases that the Does urge upon us.

The Does therefore are not appropriate plaintiffs in this litigation. Their complaint was properly dismissed by the District Court, and we affirm that dismissal.

V

The principal thrust of appellant's attack on the Texas statutes is that they improperly invade a right, said to be possessed by the pregnant woman, to choose to terminate her pregnancy. Appellant would discover this right in the concept of personal "liberty" embodied in the Fourteenth Amendment's Due Process Clause; or in personal, marital, familial, and sexual privacy said to be protected by the Bill of Rights or its penumbras, see Griswald v. Connecticut; or among those rights reserved to the people by the Ninth Amendment. Before addressing this claim, we feel it desirable briefly to survey, in several aspects, the history of abortion, for such insight as that history may afford us, and then to examine the state purposes and interests behind the criminal abortion laws.

VI

It perhaps is not generally appreciated that the restrictive criminal abortion laws in effect in a majority of States today are of relatively recent vintage. Those laws, generally proscribing abortion or its attempt at any time during pregnancy except when necessary to preserve the pregnant woman's life, are not of ancient or even common-law origin. Instead, they derive from statutory changes effected, for the most part, in the latter half of the 19th century.

1. Ancient attitudes. These are not capable of precise determination. We are told that at the time of the Persian Empire abortifacients were known and that criminal abortions were severly punished. We are also told, however, that abortion was practiced in Greek times as well as in the Roman Era, and that "it was resorted to without scruple." The Ephesian, Soranos, often described as the greatest of the ancient gynecologists, appears to have been generally opposed to Rome's prevailing free-abortion practices. He found it necessary to think first of the life of the mother, and he resorted to abortion when, upon this standard,

125

he felt the procedure advisable. Greek and Roman law afforded little protection to the unborn. If abortion was prosecuted in some places, it seems to have been based on a concept of a violation of the father's right to his offspring. Ancient religion did not bar abortion.

2. The Hippocratic Oath. What then of the famous Oath that has stood so long as the ethical guide of the medical profession and that bears the name of the great Greek (460(?)-377(?) B. C.), who has been described as the Father of Medicine, the "wisest and the greatest practitioner of his art," and the "most important and most complete medical personality of antiquity," who dominated the medical schools of his time, and who typified the sum of the medical knowledge of the past? The Oath varis somewhat according to the particular translation, but in any translation the content is clear: "I will give no deadly medicine to anyone if asked, nor suggest any such counsel; and in like manner I will not give to a woman a pessary to produce abortion," or "I will neither give a deadly drug to anybody if asked for it, nor will I make a suggestion to this effect. Similarly, I will not give to a woman an abortive remedy."

Although the Oath is not mentioned in any of the principal briefs in this case or in Doe v. Bolton, it represents the apex of the development of strict ethical concepts in medicine, and its influence endures to this day. Why did not the authority of Hippocrates dissuade abortion practice in his time and that of Rome? The late Dr. Edelstein provides us with a theory: The Oath was not uncontested even in Hippocrates' day; only the Pythagorean school of philosophers frowned upon the related act of suicide. Most Greek thinkers, on the other hand, commended abortion, at least prior to viability. See Plato, Republic, V, 461; Aristotle, Politics, VII, 1335b 25. For the Pythagoreans, however, it was a matter of dogma. For them the embryo was animate from the moment of conception, and abortion meant destruction of a living being. The abortion clause of the Oath, therefore, "echoes Pythagorean doctrines," and "[i]n no other stratum of Greek opinion were such views held or proposed in the same spirit of uncompromising austerity."

Dr. Edelstein then concludes that the Oath originated in a group representing only a small segment of Greek opinion and that it certainly was not accepted by all ancient physicians. He points out that medical writings down to Galen (A. D. 130-200) "give evidence of the violation of almost every one of its injunctions." But with the end of antiquity a decided change took place. Resistance against suicide and against abortion became common. The Oath came to be popular. The emerging teachings of Christianity were in agreement with the Pythagorean ethnic. The Oath "became the nucleus of all medical ethics" and "was applauded as the embodiment of truth." Thus, suggests Dr. Edelstein, it is "a Pythagorean manifesto and not the expression of an absolute standard of medical conduct."

This, it seems to us, is a satisfactory and acceptable explanation of the Hippocratic Oath's apparent rigidity. It enables us to understand, in historical context. a long-accepted and revered statement of medical ethics.

3. The common law. It is undisputed that at common law, abortion performed before "quickening"- the first recognizable movement of the fetus in utero, appearing usually from the 16th to the 18th week of pregnancy -was not an indictable offense. The absence of a common-law crime for pre-quickening abortion appears to have developed from a confluence of earlier philosophical, theological, and civil and canon law concepts of when life begins. These disciplines variously approached the question in terms of the point at which the embryo or fetus became "formed" or recognizably human, or in terms of when a "person" came into being, that is, infused with a "soul" or "animated." A loose consensus evolved in early English law that these events occurred at some point between conception and live birth. This was "mediate animation." Although Christian theology and the canon law came to fix the point of animation at 40 days for a male and 80 days for a female, a view that persisted until the 19th century, there was otherwise little agreement about the precise time of formation or animation. There was agreement, however, that prior to this point the fetus was to be regarded as part of the mother, and its destruction, therefore, was not homicide. Due to continued uncertainty about the precise time when animation occurred, to the lack of any empirical basis for the 40-80- day view, and perhaps to Aquinas' definition of movement as one of the two first principles of life, Bracton focused upon quickening as the critical point. The significance of quickening was echoed by later common-law scholars and found its way into the received common law in this country.

Whether abortion of a quick fetus was a felony at common law, or even a lesser crime, is still disputed. Bracton, writing early in the 13th century, thought it homicide. But the later and predominant view, following the great common-law scholars, has been that it was, at most, a lesser offense. In a frequently cited passage, Coke took the position that abortion of a woman "quick with childe" is "a great misprision, and no murder." Blackstone followed, saying that while abortion after quickening had once been considered manslaughter (though not murder), "modern law" took a less severe view. A recent review of the common-law precedents argues, however, that those precedents contradict Coke and that even post-quickening abortion was never established as a common-law crime. This is of some importance because while most American courts ruled, in holding or dictum, that abortion of an unquickened fetus was not criminal under their received common law, others followed Coke in stating that abortion of a quick fetus was a "misprision," a term they translated to mean "misdemeanor." That their reliance on Coke on this aspect of the law was uncritical and, apparently in all the reported cases, dictum (due probably to the paucity of common-law prosecutions for post-quickening abortion), makes it now appear doubtful that abortion was every firmly established as a common-law crime even with respect to the destruction of a quick fetus.

4. The English statutory law. England's first criminal abortion statute, Lord Ellenborough's Act came in 1803. It made abortion of a quick fetus, § 1, a capital crime, but in § 2 it provided lesser penalties for the felony of abortion before quickening, and thus preserved the "quickening" distinction. This contrast was continued in the general revision of 1828. It disappeared, however, together with the death penalty in 1837 and did not reappear in the Offenses Against the Person Act of 1861 that formed the core of English anti-abortion law until the liberalizing reforms of 1967. In 1929, the Infant Life (Preservation) Act came into being. Its emphasis was upon the destruction of "the life of a child capable of being born alive." It made a willful act performed with the necessary intent a felony. It contained a proviso that one was not to be found guilty of the offense "unless it is proved that the act which caused the death of the child was not done in good faith for the purpose only of preserving the life of the mother."

A seemingly notable development in the English law was the case of Rex v. Bourne, [1963]. This case apparently answered in the affirmative the question whether an abortion necessary to preserve the life of the pregnant woman was excepted from the criminal penalties of the 1861 Act. In his instructions to the jury, Judge Macnaghten referred to the 1929 Act, and observed that that Act related to "the case where a child is killed by a wilful act at the time when it is being delivered in the ordinary course of nature." He concluded that the 1861 Act's use of the word "unlawfully," imported the same meaning expressed by the specific proviso in the 1929 Act, even though there was no mention of preserving the mother's life in the 1861 Act. He then construed the phrase "preserving the life of the mother" broadly, that is, "in a reasonable sense," to include a serious and permanent threat to the mother's health, and instructed the jury to acquit Dr. Bourne if it found he had acted in a good-faith belief that the abortion was necessary for this purpose. The jury did acquit.

Recently, Parliament enacted a new abortion law. This is the Abortion Act of 1967. The Act permits a licensed physician to perform an abortion where two other licensed physicians agree (a) "that the continuance of the pregnancy would involve risk to the life of the pregnant woman, or of injury to the physical or mental health of the pregnant woman or any existing children of her family, greater than if the pregnancy were terminated," or (b) "that there is a substantial risk that if the child were born it would suffer from such physical or mental abnormalities as to be seriously handicapped." The Act also provides that, in making this determination, "account may be taken of the pregnant woman's actual or reasonably foreseeable environment." It also permits a physician, without the concurrence of others, to terminate a pregnancy where he is of the good-faith opinion that the abortion "is immediately necessary to save the life or to prevent grave permanent injury to the physical or mental health of the pregnant woman."

5. The American Law. In this country, the law in effect in all but a few States until mid-19th century was the pre-existing English common law. Connecticut, the first State to enact abortion legislation, adopted in 1821 that part of Lord Ellenborough's Act that related to a woman "quick with child." The death penalty was not imposed. Abortion before quickening was made a crime in that State only in 1860. In 1828, New York enacted legislation that, in two respects, was to serve as a model for early anti-abortion statutes. First, while barring destruction of an unquickened fetus as well as a quick fetus, it made the former only a misdemeanor, but the latter second-degree manslaughter. Second, it incorporated a concept of therapeutic abortion by providing that an abortion was excused if it "shall have been necessary to preserve the life of such mother, or shall have been advised by two physicians to be necessary for such purpose." By 1840, when Texas had received the common law, only eight American States had statutes dealing with abortion. It was not until after the War Between the States that legislation began generally to rplace the common law. Most of these initial statutes dealt severely with abortion after quickening but were lenient with it before quickening. Most punished attempts equally with completed abortions. While many statutes included the exception for an abortion thought by one or more physicians to be necessary to save the mother's life, that provision soon disappeared and the typical law required that the procedure actually be necessary for that purpose.

Gradually, in the middle and late 19th century the quickening distinction disappeared from the statutory law of most States and the degree of the offense and the penalties were increased. By the end of the 1950's, a large majority of the jurisdictions banned abortion, however and whenever performed, unless done to save or preserve the life of the mother. The exceptions, Alabama and the District of Columbia, permitted abortion to preserve the mother's health. Three States permitted abortions that were not "unlawfully" performed or that were not "without lawful justification," leaving interpretation of those standards to the courts. In the past several years, however, a trend toward liberalization of abortion statutes has resulted in adoption, by about one-third of the States, of less stringesnt laws, most of them patterned after the ALI Model Penal Code.

It is thus apparent that at common law, at the time of the adoption of our Constitution, and throughout the major portion of the 19th century, abortion was viewed with less disfavor than under most American statutes currently in effect. Phrasing it another way, a woman enjoyed a substantially broader right to terminate a pregnancy than she does in most States today. At least with respect to the early stage of pregnancy and very possibly without such a limitation, the opportunity to make this choice was present in this country well into the 19th century. Even later, the law continued for some time to treat less punitively an abortion procured in early pregnancy.

6. The position of the American Medical Association. The anti-abortion mood prevalent in this country in the late 19th century was shared by the medical profession. Indeed, the attitude of the profession may have played a significant role in the enactment of stringent criminal abortion legislation during that period.

An AMA Committee on Criminal Abortion was appointed in May 1857. It presented its report to the Twelfth Annual Meeting. That report observed that the Committee had been appointed to investigate criminal abortion "with a view to its general suppression." It deplored abortion and its frequency and it listed three causes of "this general demoralization":

"The first of these causes is a wide-spread popular ignorance of the true character of the crime- a belief, even among mothers themselves, that the fetus is not alive till after the period of quickening.

"The second of the agents alluded to is the fact that the profession themselves are frequently supposed careless of fetal life....

"The third reason of the frightful extent of this crime is found in the grave defects of our laws, both common and statute, as regards the independent and actual existence of the child before birth, as a living being. These errors, which are sufficient in most instances to prevent conviction, are based, and only based, upon mistaken and exploded medical dogmas. With strange inconsistency, the law fully acknowledges the foetus in utero and its inherent rights, for civil purposes; while personally and as criminally affected, it fails to recognize it, and to its life as yet denies all protection."

The Committee then offered, and the Association adopted, resolutions protesting "against such unwarrantable destruction of human life," calling upon state legislatures to revise their abortion laws, and requiesting the cooperation of state medical societies "in pressing the subject."

In 1871 a long and vivid report was submitted by the Committee on Criminal Abortion. It ended with the observation, "We had to deal with human life. In a matter of less importance we could entertain no compromise. An honest judge on the bench would call things by their proper names. We could do no less." It proffered resolutions, adopted by the Association, id., at 38-39, recommending, among other things, that it "be unlawful and unprofessional for any physician to induce abortion or premature labor, without the concurrent opinion of at least one respectable consulting physician, and then always with a view to the safety of the child-- if that be possible," and calling "the attention of the clergy of all denominations to the perverted views of morality entertained by a large class of females--aye, and men also, on this important question."

Except for periodic condemnation of the criminal abortionist, no further formal AMA action took place until 1967. In that year, the Committee on Human Reproduction urged the adoption of a stated policy of opposition to induced abortion, except when there is "documented medical evidence" of a threat to the health or life of the mother, or that the child "may be born with incapacitating physical deformity or mental deficiency," or that a pregnancy "resulting from legally established statutory or forcible rape or incest may constitute a threat to the mental or physical health of the patient," two other physicians "chosen because of their recognized professional competence have examined the patient and have concurred in writing," and the procedure "is performed in a hospital accredited by the Joint Commission an Accreditation of Hospitals." The providing of medical information by physicians to state legislatures in their consideration of legislation regarding therapeutic abortion was "to be considered consistent with the principles of ethics of the American Medical Association." This recommendation was adopted by the House of Delegates.

In 1970, after the introduction of a variety of proposed resolutions, and of a report from its Board of Trustees, a reference committee noted "polarization of the medical profession on this controversial issue"; division among those who had testified; a difference of opinion among AMA councils and committees; "the remarkable shift in testimony" in six months, felt to be influenced "by the rapid changes in state laws and by the judicial decisions which tend to make abortion more freely available;" and a feeling "that this trend will continue." On June 25, 1970, the House of Delegates adopted preambles and most of the resolutions proposed by the reference committee. The preambles emphasized "the best interests of the patient," "sound clinical judgment," and informed patient consent," in contrast to "mere acquiescence to the patient's demand." The resolutions asserted that abortion is a medical procedure that should be performed by a licensed physician in an accredited hospital only after consultation with two other physicians and in conformity with state law, and that no party to the procedure should be required to violate personally held moral principles. Proceedings of the AMA House of Delegates 220 (June 1970). The AMA Judicial Council rendered a complementary opinion.

7. The position of the American Public Health Association. In October 1970, the Exective Board of the APHA adopted Standards for Abortion Services. These were five in number :

"a. Rapid and simple abortion referral must be readily available through state and local public health departments, medical societies, or other nonprofit organizations.

"b. An important function of counseling should be to simplify and expedite the provision of abortion services; it should not delay the obtaining of these services.

"c. Psychiatric consultation should not be mandatory. As in the case of other specialized medical services, psychiatric consultation should be sought for definite indications and not on a routine basis.

"d. A wide range of individuals from appropriately trained, sympathetic volunteers to highly skilled physicians may qualify as abortion counselors.

"e. Contraception and/or sterilization should be discussed with each abortion patient."

Among factors pertinent to life and health risks associated with abortion were three that "are recognized as important":

"a. the skill of the physician,

"b. the environment in which the abortion is performed, and above all

"c. the duration of pregnancy, as determined by uterine size and confirmed by menstrual history."

It was said that "a well-equipped hospital" offers more protection "to cope with unforeseen difficulties than an office or clinic without such resources... The factor of gestational age is of overriding importance." Thus, it was recommended that abortions in the second trimester and early abortions in the presence of existing medical complications be performed in hospitals as inpatient procedures. For pregnancies in the first trimester, abortion in the hospital with or without overnight stay "is probably the safest practice." An abortion in an extramural facility, however, is an acceptable alternative "provided arrangements exist in advance to admit patients promptly if unforeseen complications develop." Standards for an abortion facility were listed. It was said that at present abortions should be performed by physicians or osteopaths who are licensed to practice and who have "adequat training." Id., at 398.

8. The position of the American Bar Association. At its meeting in February 1972 the ABA House of Delegates approved, with 17 opposing votes, the Uniform Abortion Act that had been drafted and approved the preceding August by the Conference of Commissioners on Uniform State Laws.

VII

Three reasons have been advanced to explain historically the enactment of criminal abortion laws in the 19th century and to justify their continued existence.

It has been argued occasionally that these laws were the product of a Victorian social concern to discourage illicit sexual conduct. Texas, however, does not advance this justification in the present case, and it appears that no court or commentator has taken the argument seriously. The appellants and amici contend, moreover, that this is not a proper state purpose at all and suggest that, if it were, the Texas statutes are overbroad in protecting it since the law fails to distinguish between married and unwed mothers.

A second reason is concerned with abortion as a medical procedure. When most criminal abortion laws were first enacted, the procedure was a hazardous one for the woman. This was particularly true prior to the development of antisepsis. Antiseptic techniques, of course, were based on discoveries by Lister, Pasteur, and others first announced in 1867, but were not generally accepted and employed until about the turn of the century. Abortion mortality was high. Even after 1900, and perhaps until as late as the development of antibiotics in the 1940's, standard modern techniques such as dilation and curettage were not nearly so safe as they are today. Thus, it has been argued that a State's real concern in enacting a criminal abortion law was to protect the pregnant woman, that is, to restrain her from submitting to a procedure that placed her life in serious jeopardy.

Modern medical techniques have altered this situation. Appellants and various amici refer to medical data indicating that abortion in early pregnancy, that is, prior to the end of the first trimester, although not without its risk, is now relatively safe. Mortality rates for women undergoing early abortions, where the procedure is legal, appear to be as low as or lower than the rates for normal childbirth. Consequently, any interest of the State in protecting the woman from an inherently hazardous procedure, except when it would be equally dangerous for her to forgo it, has largely disappeared. Of course, important state interests in the areas of health and medical standards do remain. The State has a legitimate interest in seeing to it that abortion, like any other medical procedure, is performed under circumstances that insure maximum safety for the patient. This interest obviously extends at least to the performing physician and his staff, to the facilities involved, to the availability of after-care, and to adequate provision for any complication or emergency that might arise. The prevalence of high mortality rates at illegal "abortion mills" strengthens, rather than weakens, the State's interest in regulating the conditions under which abortions are performed. Moreover, the risk to the woman increases as her pregnancy continues. Thus, the State retains a definite interest in protecting the woman's own health and safety when an abortion is proposed at a late stage of pregnancy.

The third reason is the State's interest--some phrase it in terms of duty--in protecting prenatal life. Some of the argument for this justification rests on the theory that a new human life is present from the moment of conception. The State's interest and general obligation to protect life then extends, it is argued, to prenatal life. Only when the life of the pregnant mother herself is at stake, balanced against the life she carries within her, should the interest of the embryo or fetus not prevail. Logically, of course, a legitimate state interest in this area need not stand or fall on acceptance of the belief that life begins at conception or at some other point prior to live birth. In assessing the State's interest, recognition may be given to the less rigid claim that as long as at least potential life is involved, the State may assert interests beyond the protection of the pregnant woman alone.

Parties challenging state abortion laws have sharply disputed in some courts the contention that a purpose of these laws, when enacted, was to protect prenatal life. Pointing to the absence of legislative history to support the contention, they claim that most state laws were designed solely to protect the woman. Because medical advances have lessened this concern, at least with respect to abortion in early pregnancy, they argue that with respect to such abortions the laws can no longer be justified by any state interest. There is some scholarly support for this view of original purpose. The few state courts called upon to interpret their laws in the late 19th and early 20th centuries did focus on the State's interest in protecting the woman's health rather than in preserving the embryo and fetus. Proponents of this view point out that in many States, including Texas, by statute or judicial interpretation, the pregnant woman herself could not be prosecuted for self-abortion or for cooperating in an abortion performed upon her by another. They claim that adoption of the "quickening" distinction through received common law and state statutes tacitly recognizes the greater health hazards inherent in late abortion and impliedly repudiates the theory that life begins at conception.

It is with these interests, and the weight to be attacked to them, that this case is concerned.

VIII

The Constitution does not explicitly mention any right of privacy. In a line of decisions, however, going back perhaps as far as Union Pacific R. Co. v. Botsford, the Court has recognized that a right of personal privacy, or a guarantee of certain areas or zones of privacy, does exist under the Constitution. In varying contexts, the Court or individual Justices have, indeed, found at least the roots of that right in the First Amendment; in the Fourth and Fifth Amendments; in the penumbras of the Bill of Rights; in the Ninth Amendment; or in the concept of liberty guaranteed by the first section of the Fourteenth Amendment. These decisions make it clear that only personal rights that can be deemed "fundamental" or "implicit in the concept of ordered liberty," are included in this guarantee of personal privacy. They also make it clear that the right has some extension to activities relating to marriage; procreation; contraception; family relationships; and child rearing and education.

This right of privacy, whether it be founded in the Fourteenth Amendment's concept of personal liberty and restrictions upon state action, as we feel it is, or, as the District Court determined, in the Ninth Amendment's reservation of rights to the people, is broad enough to encompass a woman's decision whether or not to terminate her pregnancy. The detriment that the State would impose upon the pregnant woman by denying this choice altogether is apparent. Specific and direct harm medically diagnosable even in early pregnancy may be involved. Maternity, or additional offspring, may force upon the woman a distressful life and future. Psychological harm may be imminent. Mental and physical health may be taxed by child care. There is also the distress, for all concerned, associated with the unwanted child, and there is the problem of bringing a child into a family already unable, psychologically and otherwise, to care for it. In other cases, as in this one, the additional difficulties and continuing stigma of unwed motherhood may be involved. All these are factors the woman and her responsible physician necessarily will consider consultation.

On the basis of elements such as these, appellant and some amici argue that the woman's right is absolute and that she entitled to terminate her pregnancy at whatever time, in whatever way, and for whatever reason she alone chooses. With this we do not agree. Appellant's arguments that Texas either has no valid interest at all in regulating the abortion decision, or no interest strong enough to support any limitation upon the woman's sole determination, are unpersuasive. The Court's decisions recognizing a right of privacy also acknowledge that some state regulation in areas protected by that right is appropriate. As noted above, a State may properly assert important interests in safeguarding health, in maintaining medical standards, and in protecting potential life. At some point in pregnancy, these respective interests become sufficiently compelling to sustain regulation of the factors that govern the abortion decision. The privacy right involved, therefore, cannot be said to be absolute. In fact, it is not clear to us that the claim asserted by some amici that one has an unlimited right to do with one's body as one pleases bears a close relationship to the right of privacy previously articulated in the Court's decisions. The Court has refused to recognized an unlimited right of this kind in the past.

We, therefore, conclude that the right of personal privacy includes the abortion decision, but that this right is not unqualified and must be considered against important state interests in regulation.

We note that those federal and state courts that have recently considered abortion law challenges have reached the same conclusion. A majority, in addition to the District Court in the present case, have held state laws unconstitutional, at least in part, because of vagueness or because of overbreadth and abridgment of rights.

Others have sustained stat statutes. Although the results are divided, most of these courts have agreed that the right of privacy, however based, is broad enough to cover the abortion decision; that the right, nonetheless, is not absolute and is subject to some limitations; and that at some point the state interests as to protection of health, medical standards, and prenatal life, become dominant. We agree with this approach.

Where certain "fundamental rights" are involved, the Court has held that regulation limiting these rights may be justified only by a "compelling state interest," and that legislative enactments must be narrowly drawn to exxpress only the legitimate state interests at stake.

In the recent abortion cases, cited above, courts have recognized these principles. Those striking down state laws have generally scrutinized the State's interests in protecting health and potential life, and have concluded that neither interest justified broad limitations on the reasons for which a physician and his pregnant patient might decide that she should have an abortion in the early stages of pregnancy. Courts sustaining state laws have held that the State's determinations to protect health or prenatal life are dominant and constitutionally justifiable.

IX

The District Court held that the appellee failed to meet his burden of demonstrating that the Texas statute's infringement upon Roe's rights was necessary to support a compelling state interest, and that, although the appellee presented "several compelling justifications for state presence in the area of abortons," the statutes outstripped these justifications and swept "far beyond any areas of compelling state interest." Appellant and appellee both contest that holding. Appellant, as has been indicated, claims an absolute right that bars any state imposition of criminal penalties in the area. Appellee argues that the State's determination to recognize and protect prenatal life from and after conception constitutes a compelling state interest. As noted above, we do not agree fully with either formulation.

A. The appellee and certain amici argue that the fetus is a "person" within the language and meaning of the Fourteenth Amendment. In support of this, they outline at length and in detail the well-known facts of fetal development. If this suggestion of personhood is established, the appellant's case, of course, collapses, for the fetus' right to life would then be guaranteed specifically by the Amendment. The appellant conceded as much on reargument. On the other hand, the appellee conceded on reargument that no case could be cited that holds that a fetus is a person within the meaning of the Fourteenth Amendment.

The Constitution does not define "person" in so many words. Section 1 of the Fourteenth Amendment contains three references to "person." The first, in defining "citizens," speaks of "persons born or naturalized in the United States." The word also appears both in the Due Process Clause and in the Equal Protection Clause. "Person" is used in other places in the Constitution: in the listing of qualifications for Representatives and Senators; in the Apportionment Clause; in the Emolument Clause; in the Electors provisions; in the provision outlining qualifications for the office of President; in the Extradition provisions and the superseded Fugitive Slave Clause; and in the Fifth, Twelfth, and Twenty-second Amendments, as well as in § § 2 and 3 of the Fourteenth Amendment. But in nearly all these instances, the use of the word is such that it has application only postnatally. None indicates, with any assurance, that it has any possible pre-natal application.

All this, together with our observation, suprs, that throughout the major portion of the 19th century prevailing legal abortion practices were far freer than they are today, persuades us that the word "person," as used in the Fourteenth Amendment, does not include the unborn. This is in accord with the results reached in those few cases where the issue has been squarely presented. Indeed, our decision in United States v. Vuitch, inferentially is to the same effect, for we there would not have indulged in statutory interpretation favorable to abortion in specified circumstances if the necessary consequence was the termination of lfie entitled to Fourteenth Amendment protection.

This conclusion, however, does not of itself fully answer the contentions raised by Texas, and we pass on to other considerations.

B. The pregnant woman cannot be isolated in her privacy. She carries an embryo and, later, a fetus, if one accepts the medical definitions of the developing young in the human uterus. The situation therefore is inherently different from marital intimacy, or bedroom possession of obscene material, or marriage, or procreation, or education, with which Eisenstadt and Griswold, Stanley, Loving, Skinner, and Pierce and Meyer were respectively concerned. As we have intimated above, it is reasonable and appropriate for a State to decide that at some point in time another interest, that of health of the mother or that of potential human life, becomes significantly involved. The woman's privacy is no longer sole and any right of privacy she possesses must be measured accordingly.

Texas urges that, apart from the Fourteenth Amendment, life begins at conception and is present throughout pregnancy, and that, therefore, the State has a compelling interest in protecting that life from and after conception. We need not resolve the difficult question of when life begins. When those trained in the respective disciplines of medicine, philosophy, and theology are unable to arrive at any consensus, the judiciary at this point in the development of man's knowledge, is not in a position to speculate as to the answer.

It should be sufficient to note briefly the wide divergence of thinking on this most sensitive and difficult question. There has always been strong support for the view that life does not begin until live birth. This was the belief of the Stoics. It appears to be the predominant, though not the unanimous, attitude of the Jewish faith. It may be taken to represent also the position of a large segment of the Protestant community, insofar as that can be ascertained; organized groups that have taken a formal postion on the abortion issue have generally regarded abortion as a matter for the conscience of the individual and her family. As we have noted, the common law found greater significance in quickening. Physicians and their scientific colleagues have regarded that event with less interest and have tended to focus either upon conception, upon live birth, or upon the interim point at which the fetus becomes "viable," that is, potentially able to live outside the mother's womb, albeit with artificial aid. Viability is usually placed at about seven months (28 weeks) but may occur earlier, even at 24 weeks. The Aristotelian theory of "mediate animation," that held sway throughout the Middle Ages and the Renaissance in Europe, continued to be official Roman Catholic dogma until the 19th century, despite opposition to this "ensoulment" theory from those in the Church who would recognize the existence of life from the moment of conception. The latter is now, of course, the official belief of the Catholic Church. As one brief amicus discloses, this is a view strongly held by many non-Catholics as well, and by many physicians. Substantial problems for precise definition of this view are posed, however, by new embryological data that purport to indicate that conception is a "process" over time, rather than an event, and by new medical techniques such as menstrual extraction, the "morning-after" pill, implantation of embryos, artificial insemination, and even artificial wombs.

In areas other than criminal abortion, the law has been reluctant to endorse any theory that life, as we recognize it, begins before live birth or to accord legal rights to the unborn except in narrowly defined situations and except when the rights are contigent upon live birth. For example, the traditional rule of tort law denied recovery for prenatal injuries even though the child was born alive. That rule has been changed in almost every jurisdiction. In most States, recovery is said to be permitted only if the fetus was viable, or at least quick, when the injuries were sustained, though few courts have squarely so held. In a recent development, generally opposed by the commentators, some States permit the parents of a stillborn child to maintain an action for wrongful death because of prenatal injuries. Such an action, however, would appear to be to vindicate the parents' interest and is thus consistent with the view that the fetus, at most, represents only the potentiality of life. Similarly, unborn children have been recognized as acquiring rights or interests by way of inheritance or other devolution of property, and have been represented by guardians ad litem. Perfection of the interests involved, again, has generally been contingent upon live birth. In short, the unborn have never been recognized in the law as persons in the whole sense.

X

In view of all this, we do not agree that, by adopting one theory of lfie, Texas may override the rights of the pregnant woman that are at stake. We repeat, however, that the State does have an important and legitimate interest in preserving and protecting the health of the pregnant woman, whether she be a resident of the State or a nonresident who seeks medical consultation and treatment there, and that it has still another important and legitimate interest in protecting the potentiality of human life. These interests are separate and distinct. Each grows in substantiality as the woman approaches term and, at a point during pregnancy, each becomes "compelling."

With respect to the State's important and legitimate interest in the health of the mother, the "compelling" point, in the light of present medical knowledge, is at approximately the end of the first trimester. This is so because of the now-established medical fact that until the end of the first trimester mortality in abortion may be less than mortality in normal childbirth. It follows that, from and after this point, a State may regulate the abortion procedure to the extent that the regulation reasonably relates to the preservation and protection of maternal health. Examples of permissible state regulation in this area are requirements as to the qualifications of the person who is to perform the abortion; as to the licensure of that person; as to the facility in which the procedure is to be performed, that is, whether it must be a hospital or may be a clinic or some other place of less-than-hospital status; as to the licensing of the facility; and the like.

This means, on the other hand, that, for the period of pregnancy prior to this "compelling" point, the attending physician, in consultation with his patient, is free to determine, without regulation by the State, that, in his medical judgment, the patient's pregnancy should be terminated. If that decision is reached, the judgment may be effectuated by an abortion free of interference by the State.

With respect to the State's important and legitimate interest in potential life, the "compelling" point is at viability. This is so because the fetus then presumably has the capability of meaningful life outside the mother's womb. State regulation protective of fetal life after viability thus has both logical and biological justifications. If the State is interested in protecting fetal life after viability, it may go so far as to proscribe abortion during that period, except when it is necessary to preserve the life or health of the mother.

Measured against these standards, Art. 1196 of the Texas Penal Code, in restricting legal abortions to those "procured or attempted by medical advice for the purpose of saving the life of the mother," sweeps too broadly. The statute makes no distinction between abortions performed early in pregnancy and those performed later, and it limits to a single reason, "saving" the mother's life, the legal justification for the procedure. The statute, therefore, cannot survive the constitutional attack made upon it here.

This conclusion makes it unnecessary for us to consider the additional challenge to the Texas statute asserted on grounds of vagueness.

XI

To summarize and to repeat:

1. A state criminal abortion statute of the current Texas type, that excepts from criminality only a lifesaving procedure on behalf of the mother, without regard to pregnancy stage and without recognition of the other interests involved, is violative of the Due Process Clause of the Fourteenth Amendment.

(a) For the stage prior to approximately the end of the first trimester, the abortion decision and its effectuation must be left to the medical judgment of the pregnant woman's attending physician.

(b) For the stage subsequent to approximately the end of the first trimester, the State, in promoting its interest in the health of the mother, may, if it chooses, regulate the abortion procedure in ways that are reasonably related to maternal health.

(c) For the stage subsequent to viability, the State in promoting its interest in the potentiality of human life may, if it chooses, regulate, and even proscribe, abortion except where it is necessary, in appropriate medical judgment, for the preservation of the life or health of the mother.

2. The State may define the term "physician," as it has been employed in the preceding paragraphs of this Part XI of this opinion, to mean only a physician currently licensed by the State, and may proscribe any abortion by a person who is not a physician as so defined.

In Doe v. Bolton procedural requirements contained in one of the modern abortion statutes are considered. That opinion and this one, of course, are to be read together.

This holding, we feel, is consistent with the relative weights of the respective interests involved, with the lessons and examples of medical and legal history, with the lenity of the common law, and with the demands of the profound problems of the present day. The decision leaves the State free to place increasing restrictions on abortion as the period of pregnancy lengthens, so long as those restrictions are tailored to the recognized state interests. The decision vindicates the right of the physician to administer medical treatment according to his professional judgment up to the points where important state interests provide compelling justifications for intervention. Up to those points, the abortion decision in all its aspects is inherently, and primarily, a medical decision, and basic responsibility for it must rest with the physician. If an individual practitioner abuses the privilege of exercising proper medical judgment, the usual remedies, judicial and intra-professional, are available.

XII

Our conclusion that Art. 1196 is unconstitutional means, of course, that the Texas abortion statutes, as a unit, must fall. The exception of Art. 1196 cannot be struck down separately, for then the State would be left with a statute proscribing all abortion procedures no matter how medically urgent the case.

Although the District Court granted appellant Roe declaratory relief, it stopped short of issuing an injunction against enforcement of the Texas statutes. The Court has recognized that different considerations enter into a federal court's decision as to declaratory relief, on the one hand, and injunctive relief, on the other. We are not dealing with a statute that, on its face, appears to abridge free expression, an area of particular concern under Dombrowski and refined in Younger v. Harris.

We find it unnecessary to decide whether the District Court erred in withholding injunctive relief, for we assume the Texas prosecutorial authorities will give full credence to this decision that the present criminal abortion statutes of that State are unconstitutional.

The judgment of the District Court as to intervenor Hallford is reversed, and Dr. Hallford's complaint in intervention is dismissed. In all other respects, the judgment of the District Court is affirmed. Costs are allowed. It is so ordered.

MR. JUSTICE STEWART, concurring.

In 1963, this Court, in Ferguson v. Skrupa, purported to sound the death knell for the doctrine of substantive due process, a doctrine under which many state laws had in the past been held to violate the Fourteenth Amendment. As Mr. Justice Black's opinion for the Court in Skrupa put it: "We have returned to the original constitutional proposition that courts do not substitute their social and economic beliefs for the judgment of legislative bodies, who are elected to pass laws."

Barely two years later, in Griswold v. Connecticut, the Court held a Connecticut birth control law unconstitutional. In view of what had been so recently said in Skrupa, the Court's opinion in Griswold understandably did its best to avoid reliance on the Due Process Clause of the Fourteenth Amendment as the ground for decision. Yet, the Connecticut law did not violate any provision of the Bill of Rights, nor any other specific provision of the Constitution. So it was clear to me then, and it is equally clear to me now, that the Griswold decision can be rationally understood only as a holding that the Connecticut statute substantively invaded the "liberty" that is protected by the Due Process Clause of the Fourteenth Amendment. As so understood, Griswold stands as one in a long line of pre-Skrupa cases decided under the doctrine of substantive due process, and I now accept it as such.

"In a Constitution for a free people, there can be no doubt that the meaning of 'liberty' must be broad indeed." The Constitution nowhere mentions a specific right of personal choice in matters of marriage and family life, but the "liberty" protected by the Due Process Clause of the Fourteenth Amendment covers more than those freedoms explicitly named in the Bill of Rights.

As Mr. Justice Harlan once wrote : [T]he full scope of the liberty guaranteed by the Due Process Clause cannot be found in or limited by the precise terms of the specific guarantees elsewhere provided in the Constitution. This 'liberty' is not a series of isolated points pricked out in terms of the taking of property; the freedom of speech, press, and religion; the right to keep and bear arms; the freedom from unreasonable searches and seizures; and so on. It is a rational continuum which, broadly speaking, includes a freedom from all substantial arbitrary impositions and purposeless restraints...and which also recognizes, what a reasonable and sensitive judgment must, that certain interests require particularly careful scrutiny of the state needs asserted to justify their abridgment." In the words of Mr. Justice Frankfurter, "Great concepts like...'liberty' ...were purposely left to gather meaning from experience. For they relate to the whole domain of social and economic fact, and the statesmen who founded this Nation knew too well that only a stagnant society remains unchanged."

Several decisions of this Court make clear that freedom of personal choice in matters of marriage and family life is one of the liberties protected by the Due Process Clause of the Fourteenth Amendment. As recently as last Term, in Eisenstadt v. Baird, we recognized "the right of the individual, married or single, to be free from unwarranted governmental intrusion into matters so fundamentally affecting a person as the decision whether to bear or beget a child." That right necessarily includes the right of a woman to decide whether or not to terminate her pregnancy. "Certainly the interests of a woman in giving of her physical and emotional self during pregnancy and the interests that will be affected throughout her life by the birth and raising of a child are of a far greater degree of significance and personal intimacy than the right to send a child to private school protected in Pierce v. Society of Sisters, or the right to teach a foreign language protected in Meyer v. Nebraska." Abele v. Markle, 351 F. Supp. 224, 227 (Conn. 1972).

Clearly, therefore, the Court today is correct in holding that the right asserted by Jane Roe is embraced within the personal liberty protected by the Due Process Clause of the Fourteenth Amendment.

It is evident that the Texas abortion statute infringes that right directly. Indeed, it is difficult to imagine a more complete abridgment of a constitutional freedom than that worked by the inflexible criminal statute now in force in Texas. The question then becomes whether the state interests advanced to justify this abridgment can survive the "particularly careful scrutiny" that the Fourteenth Amendment here requires.

The asserted state interests are protection of the health and safety of the pregnant woman, and protection of the potential future human life within her. These are legitimate objectives, amply sufficient to permit a State to regulate abortions as it does other surgical procedures, and perhaps sufficient to permit a State to regulate abortions more stringently or even to prohibit them in the late stages of pregnancy. But such legislation is not before us, and I think the court today has thoroughly demonstrated that these state interests cannot constitutionally support the broad abridgment of personal liberty worked by the exisiting Texas law. Accordingly, I join the Court's opinion holding that that law is invalid under the Due Process Clause of the Fourteenth Amendment.

MR. JUSTICE REHNQUIST, dissenting.

The Court's opinion brings to the decision of this troubling question both extensive historical fact and a wealth of legal scholarship. While the opinion thus commands my respect, I find myself nonetheless in fundamental disagreement with those parts of it that invalidate the Texas statute in question, and therefore dissent.

I

The Court's opinion decides that a State may impose virtually no restriction on the performance of abortions during the first trimester of pregnancy. Our previous decisions indicate that a necessary predicate for such an opinion is a plaintiff who was in her first trimester of pregnancy at some time during the pendency of her lawsuit. While a party may vindicate his own constitutional rights, he may not seek vindication for the rights of others. The Court's statement of facts in this case makes clear, however, that the record in no way indicates the presence of such plaintiff. We know only that plaintiff Roe at the time of filing her complaint was a pregnant woman; for aught that appears in this record, she may have been in her last trimester of pregnancy as of the date the complaint was filed.

Nothing in the Court's opinion indicates that Texas might not constitutionally apply its proscription of abortion as written to a woman in that stage of pregnancy. Nonetheless, the Court uses her complaint against the Texas statute as a fulcrum for deciding that States may impose virtually no restrictions on medical abortions performed during the first trimester of pregnancy. In deciding such a hypothetical lawsuit, the Court departs from the longstanding admonition that it should never "formulate a rule of constitutional law broader than is required by the precise facts to which it is to be applied."

II

Even if there were a plaintiff in this case capable of litigating the issue which the Court decides, I would reach a conclusion opposite to that reaches by the Court. I have difficulty in concluding, as the Court does, that the right of "privacy" is involved in this case. Texas, by the statute here challenged, bars the performance of a medical abortion by a licensed physician on a plaintiff such as Roe. A transaction resulting in an operation such as this is not "private" in the ordinary usage of that word. Nor is the "privacy" that the Court finds here even a distant relative of the freedom from searches and seizures protected by the Fourth Amendment to the Constitution, which the Court has referred to as embodying a right to privacy.

If the Court means by the term "privacy" no more than that the claim of a person to be free from unwanted state regulation of consensual transactions may be a form of "liberty" protected by the Fourteenth Amendment, there is no doubt that similar claims have been upheld in our earlier decisions on the basis of that liberty. I agree with the statement of MR. JUSTICE STEWART in his concurring opinion that the "liberty," against deprivation of which without due process the Fourteenth Amendment protects, embraces more than the rights found in the Bill of Rights. But that liberty is not guaranteed absolutely against deprivation, only against deprivation without due process of law. The test traditionally applied in the area of social and economic legislation is whether or not a law such as that challenged has a rational relation to a valid state objective. The Due Process Clause of the Fourteenth Amendment undoubtedly does place a limit, albeit a broad one, on legislative power to enact laws such as this. If the Texas statute were to prohibit an abortion even where the mother's life is in jeopardy, I have little doubt that such a statute would lack a rational relation to a valid state objective under the test stated in Williamson. But the Court's sweeping invalidation of any restrictions on abortion during the first trimester is impossible to justify under that standard, and the conscious weighing of competing factors that the Court's opinion apparently substitutes for the established test is far more appropriate to a legislative judgment than to a judicial one.

The Court eschews the history of the Fourteenth Amendment in its reliance on the "compelling state interest" test. But the Court adds a new wrinkle to this test by transposing it from the legal considerations associated with the Equal Protection Clause of the Fourteenth Amendment to this case arising under the Due Process Clause of the Fourteenth Amendment. Unless I misapprehend the consequences of this transplanting of the "compelling state interest test," the Court's opinion will accomplish the seemingly impossible feat of leaving this area of the law more confused than it found it.

While the Court's opinion quotes from the dissent of Mr. Justice Holmes in Lockner v. New York, the result it reaches is more closely attuned to the majority opinion of Mr. Justice Peckham in that case. As in Lochner and similar cases applying substantive due process standards to economic and social welfare legislation, the adoption of the compelling state interest standard will inevitably require this Court to examine the legislative policies and pass on the wisdom of these policies in the very process of deciding whether a particular state interest put forward may or may not be "compelling." The decision here to break pregnancy into three distinct terms and to outline the permissible restrictions the State may impose in each one, for example, partakes more of judicial legislation than it does of a determination of the intent of the drafters of the Fourteenth Amendment.

The fact that a majority of the States reflecting, after all, the majority sentiment in those States, have had restrictions on abortions for at least a century is a strong indication, it seems to me, that the asserted right to an abortion is not "so rooted in the traditions and conscience of our people as to be ranked as fundamental. Even today, when society's views on abortion are changing, the very existence of the debate is evidence that the "right" to an abortion is not so universally accepted as the appellant would have us believe.

To reach its result, the Court necessarily has had to find within the scope of the Fourteenth Amendment a right that was apparently completely unknown to the drafters of the Amendment. As early as 1821, the first state law dealing directly with abortion was enacted by the Connecticut Legislature. By the time of the adoption of the Fourteenth Amendment in 1868, there were at least 36 laws enacted by state or territorial legislatures limiting abortion. While many States have amended or updated their laws, 21 of the laws on the books in 1868 remain in effect today. Indeed, the Texas statute struck down today was, as the majority notes, first enacted in 1857 and "has remained substantially unchanged to the present time."

There apparently was no question concerning the validity of this provision or of any of the other state statutes when the Fourteenth Amendment was adopted. The only conclusion possible from this history is that the drafters did not intend to have the Fourteenth Amendment withdraw from the States the power to legislate with respect to this matter.

III

Even if one were to agree that the case that the Court decides were here, and that the enunciation of the substantive constitutional law in the Court's opinion were proper, the actual disposition of the case by the Court is still difficult to justify. The Texas statute is struck down in toto, even though the Court apparently concedes that at later periods of pregnancy Texas might impose these selfsame statutory limitations on abortion. My understanding of past practice is that a statute found to be invalid as applied to a particular plaintiff, but not unconstitutional as a whole, is not simply "struck down" but is, instead, declared unconstitutional as applied to the fact situation before the Court.

For all of the foregoing reasons, I respectfully dissent.

Appendix B

Statements About Abortion Rights

by

National Religious Organizations

American Baptist Churches 1988

Genuine diversity of opinion threatens the integrity of our covenant community, but the nature of covenant demands mutual love and respect.

As American Baptists we oppose abortion
As a means of avoiding responsibility of conception;
As a primary means of birth control, without regard for the far-reaching consequences of the act.

We grieve with all who struggle with the difficult circumstances that lead them to consider abortion. Recognizing that each person is ultimately responsible to God, we encourage women and men in these circumstances to seek spiritual counsel as they prayerfully and conscientiously consider their decision.

We condemn violence and harassment directed against abortion clinics, their staff and clients, as well as sanctions and discrimination against medical professionals whose conscience prevents them from being involved in abortions.

We acknowledge the diversity of deeply held convictions within our fellowship even as we seek to interpret the Scriptures under the guidance of the Holy Spirit.

American Ethical Union 1965 (reaffirmed 1979)

Abridgement of individual civil and human liberties as guaranteed by the United States Constitution is a danger to all. Among those liberties that must continue free of threat is the right of every woman to self-determination insofar as continued pregnancy is concerned.

American Ethical Union, National Women's Conference 1976 (reaffirmed 1979)

We believe in the right of each individual to exercise his or her conscience; every woman has a civil and human right to determine whether or not to continue her pregnancy. We support the decision of the United States Supreme Court of January 22, 1973 regarding abortion.

We believe that no religious belief should be legislated into the legal structure of our country; the state must be neutral in all matters related to religious concepts. (1976)

The American Ethical Union wishes to express its disapproval of efforts to amend or circumvent the United States Constitution in such manner as would nullify or impede the decision of the United States Supreme Court regarding abortion. We further believe that denial of federal or state funds for abortion where they are provided for other medical services discriminates against poor women and abridges their freedom to act according to their conscience. (1979)

American Friends Service Committee 1970

On religious, moral, and humanitarian grounds, therefore, we arrived at the view that it is far better to end an unwanted pregnancy than to encourage the evils resulting from forced pregnancy and childbirth. At the center of our position is a profound respect and reverence for human life, not only that of the potential human being who should never have been conceived, but that of the parent, the other children and the community of man.

Believing that abortion should be subject to the same regulations and safeguards as those governing other medical and surgical procedures, we urge the repeal of all laws limiting either the circumstances under which a woman may have an abortion or the physicians' freedom to use his best professional judgment in performing it.

American Humanist Association, Annual Conference, 1977

We affirm the moral right of women to become pregnant by choice and to become mothers by choice. We affirm the moral right of women to freely choose a termination of unwanted pregnancies. We oppose actions by individuals, organizations and governmental bodies that attempt to restrict and limit the woman's moral right and obligation of responsible parenthood.

The American Jewish Committee 1988

The American Jewish Committee, a human relations organization founded in 1906, has long been committed to the advancement of civil, religious, and political rights for members of all ethnic and religious groups.

The issue of abortion is a difficult one for many of us. But our deep commitment to civil liberties has led the American Jewish Committee to support reproductive choice.

135

The American Jewish Committee strongly supports the U.S. Supreme Court's *Roe v. Wade* decision and has been active in efforts to prevent its erosion.

American Jewish Congress and Women's Division, American Jewish Congress, Biennial Convention, 1978

The American Jewish Congress respects the religious and conscientious scruples of those who reject the practice of abortion. However, to the extent that they would embody their religious scruples in laws binding on all, we oppose them. We believe such laws violate the constitutional principle of separation of church and state, to which we are deeply committed.

We affirm our position that all laws prohibiting or restricting abortion should be repealed. We believe that it is the right of a woman to choose whether to bear a child and that restrictive or prohibitive abortion laws violate woman's right of privacy and liberty in matters pertaining to marriage, family and sex.

American Lutheran Church, General Convention, 1974

The American Lutheran Church accepts the possibility that an induced abortion may be a necessary option in individual human situations. Each person needs to be free to make this choice in light of each individual situation. Such freedom to choose carries the obligation to weigh the options and to bear the consequences of the decision.

The position taken by the American Lutheran Church is a pro-life position. It looks in awe at the mystery of procreation and at the processes through which a human being develops, matures, and dies. It takes seriously the right of the developing life to be born. It takes into account the rights of the already born to their health, their individuality, and the wholeness of their lives. It allows the judgment that, all pertinent factors responsibly considered, the developing life may need to be terminated in order to defend the health and wholeness of persons already present and already participating in the relationships and responsibilities of life.

American Protestant Hospital Association, 1977

Voluntary abortion may be accepted as an option where all other possible alternatives may lead to greater distress of human life. Whenever pregnancy is interrupted by choice, there is a moral consequence because life is a gift. To this end, counseling resources should be available through medical centers to both individuals and families considering this alternative.

Circumstances which may lead to choosing to interrupt a pregnancy include medical indications of physical or mental deformity or disease, conception as a result of rape or incest, and a variety or social, psychological or economic conditions where the physical or mental health of either the mother or child would be seriously threatened. All reasonable efforts should be made to remove economic barriers which would prohibit the exercise of this option.

Baptist Joint Committee on Public Affairs, 1973

It was voted that the Baptist Joint Committee on Public Affairs go on record as opposed to the Buckley-Hatfield amendment and any like or similar constitutional amendments, and that the staff be authorized to take all available action to oppose them.

B'nai B'rith Women, Biennial Convention, 1976 (reaffirmed 1978)

Although we recognize there is a great diversity of opinion on the issue of abortion, we also underscore the fact that every woman should have the legal choice with respect to abortion consistent with sound medical practice and in accordance with her conscience.

We wholeheartedly support the concepts of individual freedom of conscience and choice in the matter of abortion. Any constitutional amendment prohibiting abortion would deny to the population at large their basic rights to follow their own teachings and attitudes on this subject which would threaten First Amendment rights. Additionally, legislation designed to ban federal funding for health facilities for abortions is discriminatory, since it would affect disadvantaged women, who have no access to expensive private institutions.

Catholics for a Free Choice, 1975

We affirm the religious liberty of Catholic women and men and those of other religions to make decisions regarding their own fertility free from church or governmental intervention in accordance with their own individual conscience.

Central Conference of American Rabbis, 1975

We believe that in any decision whether or not to terminate pregnancy, the individual family or woman must weigh the tradition as they struggle to formulate their own religious and moral criteria to reach their own personal decision...We believe that the proper locus for formulating these religious and moral criteria and for making this decision must be the individual family or woman and not the state or other external agency.

As we would not impose the historic position of Jewish teaching upon individuals nor legislate it as normative for society at large, so we would not wish the position of any other group imposed upon the Jewish community or the general population.

We affirm the legal right of a family or a woman to determine on the basis of their or her own religious and moral values whether or not to terminate a particular pregnancy. We reject all constitutional amendments which would abridge or circumscribe this right.

Christian Church (Disciples of Christ), General Assembly, 1975

Therefore be it resolved, that the General Assembly of the Christian Church (Disciples of Christ)
1. Affirm the principle of individual liberty, freedom of individual conscience, and sacredness of life for all persons.
2. Respect differences in religious beliefs concerning abortion and oppose, in accord with the principle of religious liberty, any attempt to legislate a specific religious opinion or belief concerning abortion upon all Americans.
3. Provide through ministry of the local congregation, pastoral concern, and nurture of persons faced with the responsibility and trauma surrounding undesired pregnancy.

Church of the Brethren, Annual Conference, 1972

Let it be clear that the Brethren ideal upholds the sacredness of human life and that abortion should be accepted as an option only where all other possible alternatives will lead to greater destruction of human life and spirit.

However...our position is not a condemnation of those persons who reject this position or of women who seek and undergo abortions. Rather, it is a call for Christlike compassion in seeking creative alternatives to abortion.

We support persons who, after prayer and counseling, believe abortion is the least destructive alternative available to them, that they may make their decision openly, honestly, without the suffering imposed by an uncompromising community.

Laws regarding abortion should embody protection of human life, protection of freedom of moral choice, and availability of good medical care.

The Episcopal Church, General Convention, 1988

Resolved: While we acknowledge that in this country it is the legal right of every woman to have a medically safe abortion, as Christians we believe strongly that if this right is exercised, it should be used only in extreme situations. We emphatically oppose abortion as a means of birth control, family planning, sex selection, or any reason of mere convenience.

In those cases where an abortion is being considered, members of this Church are urged to seek the dictates of their consciences in prayer, to seek the advice and counsel of members of the Christian community and where appropriate the sacramental life of this Church.

It is the responsibility of members of this Church, especially the clergy, to become aware of local agencies and resources which will assist those faced with problem pregnancies.

We believe that legislation concerning abortions will not address the root of the problem. We therefore express our deep conviction that any proposed legislation on the part of national or state governments regarding abortions must take special care to see that individual conscience is respected, and that the responsibility of individuals to reach informed decisions in this matter is acknowledged and honored.

Episcopal Women's Caucus, Annual Meeting, 1978

We are deeply disturbed over the increasingly bitter and divisive battle being waged in legislative bodies to force continuance of unwanted pregnancies and to limit an American woman's right to abortion.

We believe that all should be free to exercise their own consciences on this matter and that where widely differing views are held by substantial sections of the American religious community, the particular believe of one religious body should not be forced on those who believe otherwise.

To prohibit or severely limit the use of public funds to pay for abortions abridges and denies the right to an abortion and discriminates especially against low income, young and minority women.

Friends Committee on National Legislation, General Committee, 1975

Members of the Religious Society of Friends (Quakers) have a long tradition and witness of opposition to killing of human beings, whether in war or capital punishment or personal violence. On the basis of this tradition, some Friends believe that abortion is always wrong.

Friends also have a tradition of respect for the individual and a belief that all persons should be free to follow their own consciences and the leading of the Spirit. On this basis some Friends believe that the problem of whether or not to have an abortion at least in the early months of pregnancy is one primarily of the pregnant woman herself, and that it is an unwarranted denial of her moral freedom to forbid her to do so.

We do not advocate abortion. We recognize there are those who regard abortion as immoral while others do not. Since these disagreements exist in the country in general as well as with the Society of Friends, neither view should be imposed by law on those who hold the other.

Recognizing that differences among Friends exist, nevertheless we find general unity in opposing the effort to amend the United States Constitution to say that abortion shall be illegal.

Lutheran Church in America, Biennial Convention, 1970 (reaffirmed 1978)

Since the fetus is the organic beginning of human life, the termination of its development is always a serious matter. Nevertheless, a qualitative distinction must be made between its claims and the rights of a responsible person made in God's image who is in living relationships with God and other human beings. This understanding of responsible personhood is congruent with the historical Lutheran teaching and practice whereby only living persons are baptized.

On the basis of the evangelical ethic, a woman or couple may decide responsibly to seek an abortion. Earnest consideration should be given to the life and total health of the mother, her responsibilities to others in her family, the stage of development of the fetus, the economic and psychological stability of the home, the laws of the land, and the consequences for society as a whole.

National Council of Jewish Women, National Convention, 1969 (reaffirmed 1979)

The members of the National Council of Jewish Women reaffirm the firm commitment of "work to protect every woman's individual right to choose abortion and to eliminate any obstacles that would limit her reproductive freedom."

We believe that those who would legislate to deny freedom of choice compound the problems confronting women who are already condemned by poverty. It is therefor essential that federal and state funding be made available to women in need who choose abortion, just as such funding is available for other medical procedures.

We decry the fact that poor and young women must bear the major brunt of anti-abortion rights measures, and call upon all public officials to support and protect the right of *every* American woman to choose or reject the act of childbearing. (1979)

National Federation of Temple Sisterhoods, Biennial Assembly, 1975

The National Federation of Temple Sisterhoods affirms our strong support for the right of a woman to obtain a legal abortion, under conditions now outlined in the 1973 decision of the United States Supreme Court. The Court's position established that during the first two trimesters, the private and personal decision of whether or not to continue to term an unwanted pregnancy should remain a matter of choice for the woman; she alone can exercise her ethical and religious judgment in this decision. Only by vigorously supporting this individual right to choose can we also ensure that every woman may act according to the religious and ethical tenets to which she adheres.

Presbyterian Church in the U.S., General Assembly, 1970 (reaffirmed 1978)

The willful termination of pregnancy by medical means on the considered decision of a pregnant woman may on occasion be morally justifiable. Possible justifying circumstances would include medical indications of physical or mental deformity, conception as a result of rape or incest, conditions under which the physical or mental health of either mother or child wold be gravely threatened, or the socio-economic condition of the family...Medical intervention would be made available to all who desire and qualify for it, not just to those who can afford preferential treatment. (1970)

Because of the great diversity in the scientific and theological disciplines as to when life begins, no single religious position should claim universal opinion and become law. This seems to breach the basis for church and state separation. While laws may legislate behavior, they cannot legislate morality. If religious freedom of choice is to be maintained, then all acceptable alternatives must be available for competent, moral, and loving choices to be made. (1978)

Reformed Church in America, General Synod, 1975

To use, or not to use, legal abortions should be a carefully considered decision of all the persons involved, made prayerfully in the love of Jesus Christ.

Christians and the Christian community should play a supportive role for persons making a decision about or utilizing abortion.

Reorganized Church of Jesus Christ of Latter Day Saints, 1974

We affirm that parenthood is partnership with God in the creative processes of the universe.

We affirm the necessity for parents to make responsible decisions regarding the conception and nurture of their children.

We affirm a profound regard for the personhood of the woman in her emotional, mental and physical health; we also affirm a profound regard and concern for the potential of the unborn fetus.

We affirm the inadequacy of simplistic answers that regard all abortions as murder, or on the other hand, regard abortion only as a medical procedure without moral significance.

We affirm the right of the woman to make her own decision regarding the continuation or termination of problem pregnancies.

Union of American Hebrew Congregations, Biennial Convention, 1975

The UAHC reaffirms its strong support for the right of a woman to obtain a legal abortion on the constitutional grounds enunciated by the Supreme Court in its 1973 decision...This rule is a sound and enlightened position on this sensitive and difficult issue, and we express our confidence in the ability of the woman to exercise her ethical and religious judgment in making her decision.

The Supreme Court held that the question of when life begins is a matter of religious belief and not medical or legal fact. While recognizing the right of religious groups whose beliefs differ from ours to follow the dictates of their faith in this matter, we vigorously oppose the attempts to legislate the particular beliefs of those groups into the law which governs us all. This is a clear violation of the First Amendment. Furthermore, it may undermine the development of interfaith activities. Mutual respect and tolerance must remain the foundation of interreligious relation.

Unitarian Universalist Association, General Assembly, 1977, 1982

Whereas, attempts are now being made to deny Medicaid funds for abortion and to enact constitutional amendments that would limit abortions to life-endangering situations and thus remove this decision from the individual and her physician; and

Whereas, such legislation is an infringement of the principle of the separation of church and state as it tries to enact a position of private morality into public law; and

Whereas, we affirm the right of each woman to make the decisions concerning her own body and future and we stress the responsibilities and long-term commitment involved in the choice of parenthood.

Therefore, be it resolved: that the 1977 General Assembly of the Unitarian Universalist Association goes on record opposing the calling of a national constitutional convention for the purpose of amending the Constitution to prohibit abortion (1977).

Whereas, the constitutional principles of religious liberty and the separation of church and state that safeguards liberty, and the ideal of a pluralistic society are under increasing attack in the Congress of the United States, in state legislatures, and in some sectors of the communications media by a combination of sectarian and secular special interests;

Be it resolved: That the 1982 General Assembly of UUA reaffirms its support for these principles and urges the Board of Trustees and President of the Association, member societies and Unitarian Universalists in the United States to:...

Uphold the constitutional privacy right of every woman, acknowledged by the Supreme Court in 1973 in *Roe v. Wade* and other rulings, to plan the number and spacing of her children and to terminate a problem pregnancy in collaboration with her physician, opposing all efforts through legislation or constitutional amendment to restrict that right or to impose by law a "theology of fetal personhood."...(1982)

Unitarian Universalist Women's Federation, Biennial Convention, 1975

The Unitarian Universalist Women's Federation reaffirm[s] the right of any woman of any age or marital or economic status to have an abortion at her own request upon consultation with her physician and urges all Unitarian Universalists in the United States and all Unitarian Universalist societies in the United States to resist through their elected representatives the efforts now under way by some members of the Congress of the United States to curtail their right by means of a constitutional amendment or other means.

United Church of Christ, General Synod, 1971 (reaffirmed 1977)

The theological and scientific views on when human life begins are so numerous and varied that one particular view should not be forced on society through its legal system.

Present laws prohibiting abortion are neither just nor enforceable. They compel women either to bear unwanted children or to seek illegal abortions regardless of the medical hazards and suffering involved. By severely limiting access to safe abortions, these laws have the effect of discriminating against the poor.

United Methodist Church, General Conference, 1976

When an unacceptable pregnancy occurs, a family, and most of all the pregnant woman, is confronted with the need to make a difficult decision. We believe that continuance of a pregnancy which endangers the life or health of the mother, or poses other serious problems concerning the life, health, or mental capability of the child to be, is not a moral necessity. In such a case, we believe the path of mature Christian judgment may indicate the advisability of abortion. We support the legal right to abortion as established by the 1973 Supreme Court decisions. We encourage women in counsel with husbands, doctors, and pastors to make their own responsible decisions concerning the personal or moral questions surrounding the issue of abortion.

Our belief in the sanctity of unborn human life makes us reluctant to approve abortion. But we are equally bound to respect the sacredness of the life and well-being of the mother, for whom devastating damage may result from an unacceptable pregnancy. In continuity with past Christian teaching, we recognize tragic conflicts of life with life that may justify abortion.

United Methodist Church, Women's Division 1975

We believe deeply that all should be free to express and practice their own moral judgment on the matter of abortion. We also believe that on this matter, where there is no ethical or theological consensus, and where widely differing views are held by substantial sections of the religious community, the Constitution should not be used to enforce one particular religious belief on those who believe otherwise.

United Presbyterian Church in the U.S.A., General Assembly, 1972 (reaffirmed in 1978)

Whereas, God has given persons the responsibility of caring for creation as well as the ability to share in it, and has shown his concern for the quality and value of human life; and

Whereas, sometimes when the natural ability to create life and the moral and spiritual ability to sustain it are not in harmony, the decisions to be made must be understood as moral and ethical ones and not simply legal;

Therefore, in support of the concern for the value of human life and human wholeness...the 184the General Assembly:

b. Declares that women should have full freedom of personal choice concerning the completion or termination of their pregnancies and that artificial or induced termination of pregnancy, therefore, should not be restricted by law, except that it be performed under the direction and control of a properly licensed physician.

c. Continues to support the establishment of medically sound, easily available and low-cost abortion services.

United Synagogue of America, Biennial Convention, 1975

"In all cases 'the mother's life takes precedence over that of the fetus' up to the minute of its birth. This is to us unequivocal principle. A threat to her basic health is moreover equated with a threat to her life. To go a step further, a classical response places danger to one's psychological health, when well established, on an equal footing with a threat to one's physical health." (1967)

[A]bortions, "though serious even in the early stages of conception, are not to be equated with murder, hardly more than is the decision not to become pregnant."

The United Synagogue affirms once again its position that "abortions involve very serious psychological, religious, and moral problems, but the welfare of the mother must always be our primary concern" and urges its congregations to oppose any legislative attempts to weaken the force of the [1973] Supreme Court's decisions through constitutional amendments or through the deprivation of medicaid, family services and other current welfare services in cases relation to abortion.

Women of the Episcopal Church, Triennial Meeting, 1973

Whereas the Church stands for the exercise of freedom of conscience by all and is required to fight for the right of everyone to exercise that conscience, therefore, be it resolved that the decision of the U.S. Supreme Court allowing women to exercise their conscience in the matter of abortion be endorsed by the Church.

Women's League for Conservative Judaism, Biennial Convention, 1974

National Women's League believes that freedom of choice as to birth control and abortion is inherent in the civil rights of women.

Young Women's Christian Association of the U.S.A., National Convention, 1967 (reaffirmed 1979)

In line with our Christian purpose we, in the YWCA, affirm that a highly ethical stance is one that has concern for the quality of life of the living as well as for the potential life. We believe that a woman also has a fundamental, constitutional right to determine, along with her personal physician, the number and spacing of her children. Our decision does not mean we advocate abortion as the most desirable solution to the problem, but rather that a woman should have the right to make the decision. (1973)

Appendix C

The Abortion of *The Silent Scream*

James W. Prescott

The anti-abortion movement's members would have us believe that their concern for fetal life is derived from a broad base of respect for human life and a concern for human pain, suffering, and violence. The production of the film *The Silent Scream* is an attempt to dramatize those concerns by illustrating alleged fetal pain and suffering during an abortion procedure.

The perception of pain is a complex biological and psychological phenomenon that involves states of "consciousness" which can probably never be fully understood or known for certain stages of fetal development. Relevant to this inquiry are certain neurobiological and biobehavioral facts concerning states of "consciousness" and "pain" perception during fetal development that should be known by all concerned citizens.

Patricia A. Jaworski has produced an audio tape, "Thinking About the Silent Scream," in which she interviews several internationally renowned neuroscientists on fetal brain development, the alleged fetal perception of "pain," and alleged fetal "personhood." Some of the highlights of those interviews are summarized in the following paragraphs.

Dr. Michael Bennett, chairman of the neuroscience department of Albert Einstein Medical School, when asked whether a brain exists at conception and whether there can be a person without a brain, answered with an unequivocal "no!" to both questions. It was pointed out that the human brain has approximately *100 billion brain cells* and that there are an estimated *100 trillion* connections between neurons in the brain. This extraordinary neuronal "interconnectivity" provides the neurostructural foundation for complex perceptions and "personhood" and takes many months and often years to fully develop and function.

Dr. Patricia Goldman-Rakic, professor of neuroscience at Yale University Medical School, emphasizes that brain neurons do not exist prior to *four weeks in utero*, that the *peak period* for brain neuron development is from *two to five months in utero*, and that the existence of neurons, per se, does not indicate the existence of a developed, functioning brain. Once the brain cell is born, there is a long process of *migration* of brain cells that occurs mainly from *two to six months in utero* during which the brain cells move (migrate) to their final destination in the brain. An even longer process of development makes possible the "interconnectivity" of brain cells which is absolutely essential for sensation, perception, conscious experience, thought, and behavior. The formation of brain synapses that make possible brain cell communication does not begin until about the *third month in utero*, and most are formed after birth.

Dr. Clifford Grobstein, former chairman of the Department of Biology at Stanford University and now at the University of California at San Diego, highlights the complexity of brain development by noting that the brain does not develop uniformly. For example, certain parts of the brain develop earlier and some later. The cerebral neocortex that is responsible for complex perceptions is one of the last to develop.

Dr. Dominick Purpura, dean of Albert Einstein Medical School, has been studying human brain development since 1974 with his research on mental retardation. Dr. Purpura emphasizes that there are a minimum number of neurons and synaptic connections that are necessary before the qualities of "humanness" and "personhood" can be developed and that this capacity *begins to occur* in the middle of the last trimester. Thus, about *twenty-eight to thirty weeks in utero* is the *minimal time* for the beginning of this capacity - "It can't begin earlier," according to Dr. Purpura.

Dr. Purpura also emphasizes that critical changes are seen in the fetal brain wave pattern at thirty-one weeks when the brain waves become more organized and, thus, meaningful; the first signs of sleep and wakefulness are not observed until a few weeks later. It is emphasized that all cells have electrical potentials and that the mere presence of such signals, per se, does not mean that the capacity for complex perceptions or "personhood" exists. How these neuronal signals become *organized* and reflect underlying neuronal and structural *organization* is fundamental to understanding the basic neurobiological principle that *structure precedes function*.

Thus, it can be concluded that neither pain perception nor personhood exists *at conception* and that the *beginning* capacity for personhood may only begin at *twenty-eigth to thirty weeks in utero*. Why, then, the film *The Silent Scream*, with all its deliberate distortions and errors of fact? It is the intent of this socio-psychological study to address the producers and supporters of *The Silent Scream* - a film which has been offered as a manifestation of their compassion for human pain, suffering, and violence - to illustrate through a review of both previous and new data that their motivation for *The Silent Scream* was not fetal well-being. This study will show that the anti-abortion motivation behind the producers and supporters of *The Silent Scream* resides in an authoritarian control and denial of the fundamental human right of self-determination and the sexual expression of affection and love as a basic right of all persons.

In the production of *The Silent Scream* questions must be raised as to the elements of compassion and malevolence that made that film possible. Presumably, those who abhor abortion under any circumstances would not support any abortion, including participation in filming an abortion they consider to be a murder! Why did the anti-abortionists not stop the filming of the abortion and the

---

Reprinted by permission of *The Humanist*, September/October 1986.

abortion itself which made the film possible? Or is the fetus simply an object to be exploited for ulterior motives - like the children of the anti-abortion cultures?

Is it appropriate to compare from a *moral perspective* the production of *The Silent Scream* and the production of "snuff" films in which women are enticed into a sexual encounter and, unknown to them, are scheduled for sexual torture, mutilation, and murder? Assuming that abortion is murder and "snuff" is murder, do the producers and supporters of these two kinds of films share a *certain common morality*? If so, what would be the nature of that common morality?

When the Reverent R.L. Hymers, Jr., pastor of the Fundamentalist Baptist Tabernacle in Los Angeles, called Supreme Court Justice William J. Brennan, Jr., a "baby killer" and led his four-hundred member congregation in prayer to ask God to kill Brennan so that President Reagan could replace him with a judge who opposes abortion, does this not reinforce a common morality of violence in the anti-abortionist mentality as it is reflected in *The Silent Scream* and the fire-bombings of abortion clinics and personnel? (See, *The Washington Post*, June 2, 1986.)

Since the morality of pain and pleasure reside at the core of abortion controversy, it may be helpful to reflect upon the following data as these moral questions are addressed.

In an attempt to clarify the ideological and motivational structure of the anti-abortion personality and "sub-culture," this writer published a series of research articles that addressed these issues (Prescott, 1975; 1978; Prescott and Wallace, 1978). A summary of these findings would appear helpful as a background to the new studies reported herein which will shed further light on the lack of compassion for human pain, suffering, and violence that is a salient characteristic of the militant anti-abortion movement.

The question of whether abortion represents a "murderous" act or a "benevolent" act is addressed in the 1975 article in *The Humanist* by examining the social-behavioral characteristics of primitive cultures that permitted or punished abortion and by examining the relationship between voting patterns in the Canadian Federal Parliament on abortion and capital punishment legislation.

It was hypothesized that, if abortion reflected a "murderous" violent act, then the cultures which permitted abortion should be similarly characterized; conversely, if abortion reflected a benevolent act, then the cultures which permitted abortion should also be characterized as benevolent and peaceful. Similarly hypothesized was whether votes on abortion rights correlated positively or negatively with votes on capital punishment.

In brief, the following relationships were obtained from twenty-one primitive cultures where coded anthropological information was available on abortion and other behaviors:

1. 55% of cultures that punnish abortion practice slavery while 92% of cultures that permit abortion prohibit slavery.

2. 73% of cultures that punish abortion also torture, mutilate, and kill enemy captured in warfare while 80% of cultures that permit abortion do not torture, mutilate, and kill enemy captured in warfare.

3. 78% of cultures that punish abortion punish premarital coitus while 67% of cultures that permit abortion permit premarital coitus.

4. 88% of cultures that punish abortion punish extramarital coitus while 67% of cultures that permit abortion permit extramarital coitus.

5. 70% of cultures that punish abortion exploit children while 78% of cultures that permit abortion do not exploit children.

With respect to the voting patterns in the Canadian Parliament on abortion and capital punishment, the following relationships were established:

1. 59% voted for abortion rights and against capital punishment. 2. 21% voted against abortion rights and for capital punishment. 3. 80% supported a statistically valid relationship between anti-choice and anti-life voting patterns, and vice versa.

These voting patterns in the Canadian Parliament were consistent with the data obtained from primitive cultures that established a strong relationship between anti-choice and anti-life sentiments. It was concluded that the above data did not support the anti-abortion movement's claim to be a "Right to Life" movement and, in fact, supported the opposite.

In a further effort to validate the above relationships, this writer examined the voting patterns in the United States Senate on bills involving abortion, capital punishment, support of the Vietnam War, support of the "no-knock" law (police did not need a court order to break into a private home), and opposition to gun control legislation (Prescott, 1978).

In summary, the following statistically significant relationships were obtained between abortion and bills on human violence:

1. 71% valid relationship between anti-choice beliefs and support of capital punishment and its converse relationship. 2. 72% valid relationship between anti-choice beliefs and support of the Vietnam War and its converse relationship. 3. 65% valid relationship between anti-choice beliefs and support of the "no-knock" law and its converse relationship. 4. 71% valid relationship between anti-choice beliefs and and opposition to handgun control and the converse relationship.

The preceding data are fully consistent with and cross-validate the findings obtained from primitive cultures and from and Canadian Parliament that established a strong relationship between anti-abortion beliefs and support of human oppression and violence, and the converse relationship.

In a further examination of these relationships, this writer utilized the National Farmers Union ratings of U.S. senators on a scale from zero to one hundred to study the senators' support of legislation that helped families and their children - such as support of school lunch and milk programs. This rating was based upon the senators' voting records on fifteen different bills and was interpreted by this writer as a valid and reliable measure of family nurturance. It was found that the average Family Nurturance Score of senators who supported abortion rights of women and opposed capital punishment was *ninety-six out of one hundred*. The average family nurturance score of the senators who opposed abortion rights of women and supported capital punishment was *forty-four out of one hundred* - less than half of the family nurturance score of the pro-choice senators.

The Abortion of 'The Silent Scream'

It was concluded from the above data that the anti-abortion ideology did not reflect compassion and respect for human life but, rather, an ideology of authoritarian control over the personal lives of individuals that included violent means of human oppression.

In the final article on the abortion issue, which was coauthored by my associate, Dr. Douglas Wallace, the major motivating force underlying the anti-abortion ideology that was suggested from the primitive culture data was examined - namely, anti-sexual pleasure (Prescott and Wallace, 1978).

An analysis of the voting patterns of the Pennsylvania House on abortion and on a bill that made fornication and adultery a felony yielded the following results: 85% who supported abortion rights supported rights of self-determination of sexual expression; and 86% who opposed abortion rights opposed rights of self-determination of sexual expression.

Similarly, the voting patterns in the Pennsylvania Senate with respect to abortion and a bill that would prevent homosexuals from being hired by the state government were examined. These evaluations yielded the following results: 73% who supported abortion rights supported homosexual rights of employment; and 89% who opposed abortion opposed homosexual rights of employment.

In addition to the above findings, extensive questionnaire data were reported from 688 males and 1,178 females from various walks of life on abortion ideology and other life values. Based upon the fifty-six-item questionnaire, the following items were the most highly and statistically linked to the statement, "Abortion should be punished by society" (Prescott and Wallace, 1978):

1. Prostitution should be punished by society. 2. Unmarried persons having sex with their lovers is wrong. 3. Sexual pleasures help build a weak moral character. 4. Physical punishment and pain help build a strong moral character. 5. Society should interfere with private sexual behavior between adults. 6. Nudity within the family has a harmful influence upon children.

The above findings taken collectively from primitive cultures, modern cultures, and legislative bodies strongly support an "anti-sexual pleasure" ethic as a major driving force underlying the anti-abortion ideology.

Although the above data have been available over the past eight to eleven years, they have not been utilized in confronting the increasing virulence and violence of the anti-abortion movement - that is, the numerous fire bombings and violent attacks against medical clinics and personnel providing abortion services to women and the increasing legislative attacks on the fundamental right of women to be mothers by choice.

The production of *The Silent Scream* by the anti-abortion movement is another attempt to mislead the public and legislators into believing that the anti-abortion movement has a fundamental concern and compassion about human pain, suffering, and violence. Since the publication of the above studies, additional statistics on voting on bills before the U.S. Congress have become available, making possible the direct examination of the anti-abortion movement's claims of compassion for human pain, suffering, and violence, as purportedly reflected in *The Silent Scream*, and for the cross-validation in the U.S. House of Representatives of certain relationships that had been previously established in the U.S. Senate.

The following analyses of voting patterns evaluate the one hundred pro-choice congressmen and one hundred anti-choice congressmen identified by Catholics for a Free Choice as *totally supporting* or *totally opposing* abortion rights of women (Catholics for a Free Choice, 1985). I have characterized the three legislative bills evaluated for this study as: (1) Human Pain and Suffering Bill (H.R. 5290); (2) Jeopardizing Human Lives Bill (H.R. 4332); and (3) Promoting Human Violence Bill (H.J. Res. 540).

The Human Pain and Suffering Bill was the bill to permit the use of parenteral diacetylmorphine (heroin) for the relief of intractable pain due to terminal cancer (H.R. 5290: Compassionate Pain Relief Act). The vote analyzed was on the Hughes Amendment and other amendments to H.R. 5290 which specified circumstances when pain "may not be effectively treated with currently available analgesic medications." The Hughes Amendment was defeated 231 to 178, with 22 not voting on September 19, 1984. (See, *Congressional Record*, U.S. House of Representatives, Roll No. 400 Hughes Amendment to H.R. 5290: Compassionate Pain Relief Act; September 19, 1984; H9790-9791.)

The Jeopardizing Human Lives Bill was on gun control legislation, specifically the Federal Firearms Law Reform Act of 1986 (H.R. 4322). The vote analyzed was on the Hughes Amendment, which limited the serious weakening of the 1968 Gun Control Act under H.R. 4332. If H.R. 4332 was passed without the Hughes Amendment, it would have significantly increased the danger to lives of the public and law enforcement of officers. (Police organizations supported the Hughes Amendment.) The vote was taken on April 9, 1986, and the Hughes Amendment was defeated 242 to 177, with 15 not voting. (See, *Congressional Record*, U.S. House of Representatives, Roll. NO. 71 Hughes Amendment to H.R. 4332; Federal Firearms Law Reform Act of 1986; April 9, 1986; H1704.)

The promoting Human Violence Bill was the vote on "Contra Aid" (H.J. Res. 540) which "approves the additional authorities and assistance for the Nicaraguan democratic resistance that the President requested pursuant to the International Security and Development Cooperation Act of 1985, not withstanding section 10 of Public Law 91-672." The vote was taken on March 20, 1986, Roll No. 64, and was defeated 222 to 210, with 3 not voting. (See, *Congressional Record*, U.S. House of Representatives, Roll No. 64, H.J. Res. 540: Contra Aid; March 20, 1986; H1493.)

TABLES 1 through 4 present the roll call votes on the above three bills for the one hundred prochoice and one hundred anti-choice congressmen. The data have been organized into the following four basic groups:

TABLE 1: Pro-choice and Anti-pain (supports H.R. 5290)
TABLE 2: Anti-choice and Pro-pain (opposes H.R. 5290)
TABLE 3: Pro-choice and Pro-pain (opposes H.R. 5290)
TABLE 4: Anti-choice and anti-pain (supports H.R. 5290)

143

TABLE 1

U.S. House of Representatives Roll Call Vote of Pro-choice and Anti-pain Congressmen
(Average Pro-Child-Life Score equals 92)

Congressman	Party/State	Pro-Child Score	Gun Control	Contra Aid	Congressman	Party/State	Pro-Child Score	Gun Control	Contra Aid
Ackerman	D–NY	100	Y	N	Leven	D–MI	100	Y	N
Barnes	D–MD	100	Y	N	Levine	D–CA	100	Y	N
Bates	D–CA	100	Y	N	Lundine	D–NY	100	N	N
Bellenson	D–CA	100	Y	N	McKernan	R–ME	83	N	Y
Berman	D–CA	100	Y	N	Mikulski	D–MD	100	Y	N
Bosco	D–CA	83	N	N	Miller	D–CA	100	Y	N
Boxer	D–CA	100	Y	N	Mineta	D–CA	100	Y	N
Britt	D–NC	100	O	O	Moody	D–WI	100	Y	N
Burton	D–CA	100	Y	N	Neal	D–NC	100	N	N
Carr	D–MI	83	N	N	Obey	D–WI	100	N	N
Clay	D–MO	100	Y	N	Ottinger	D–NY	100	O	O
Coelho	D–CA	100	N	N	Pease	D–OH	100	Y	N
Coleman	D–TX	100	N	N	Pickle	D–TX	83	Y	N
Dellums	D–CA	100	Y	N	Pritchard	R–WA	33	O	O
Dicks	D–WA	100	Y	N	Richardson	D–NM	100	N	N
Downey	D–NY	100	Y	N	Roybal	D–CA	100	Y	N
Edgar	D–PA	100	Y	N	Sabo	D–MN	100	Y	N
Edwards	D–CA	100	Y	N	Savage	D–IL	67	Y	N
Evans	D–IL	100	Y	N	Scheuer	D–NY	100	Y	N
Fazio	D–CA	100	Y	N	Schroeder	D–CO	83	Y	N
Feighan	D–OH	83	Y	N	Schumer	D–NY	83	Y	N
Foley	D–WA	100	N	N	Seirberling	D–OH	100	Y	N
Ford	D–TN	100	Y	N	Smith	D–VA	100	O	O
Frank	D–MA	100	Y	N	Snowe	R–ME	83	N	N
Gejdenson	D–CT	100	Y	N	Solarz	D–NY	100	Y	N
Gekas	R–PA	33	N	Y	Stark	D–CA	100	Y	N
Green	R–NY	67	Y	N	Stokes	D–OH	67	A	N
Hall	D–IN	67	?	?	Waxman	D–CA	100	Y	N
Hoyer	D–MD	100	A	N	Weiss	D–NY	100	Y	N
Johnson	R–CT	83	Y	Y	Williams	D–MT	100	N	N
Kastenmeier	D–WI	100	Y	N	Wirth	D–CO	100	Y	N
Kennelly	D–CT	100	Y	N	Wise	D–WV	100	N	N
Lantos	D–CA	67	Y	N	Wolpe	D–MI	83	Y	N
Leland	D–TX	50	Y	N	Yates	D–IL	100	Y	N

Y=Yes; N=No; A=Abstain; O=Not a member of the 99th Congress

In addition to the above information, a "Pro-Child-Life Score" is listed for each congressman and ranges from zero to one hundred. This score was developed by Catholics for a Free Choice on six legislative bills that affected the health and well-being of children (Catholics for a Free Choice, 1985). The six legislative bills used to derive the score dealt with budget increase, child nutrition, Medicaid and Aid for Families with Dependent Children, Head Start and child care, budget reduction for the Department of Health and Human Services, and the food stamp program. This score is analogous to the National Farmers Union Family Nurturance Score utilized in my previous studies and is compared to it below.

The average Pro-Child-Life Score for the pro-choice and anti-pain congressmen is ninety-two; it is only forty-nine for the anti-choice and pro-pain congressmen. This finding is comparable to and cross-validates the NFU Family Nurturance Scores in the U.S. Senate study in which the pro-choice and anti-capital-punishment senators had an average score of ninety-six compared to forty-four for anti-choice and pro-capital-punishment senators.

TABLE 5 presents the basic analysis that compares the relationship between votes on abortion and human pain. In brief: 36% (68 of 187) of the total sample support pro-choice and human pain relief legislation; 47% (88 of 187) of the total sample oppose pro-choice and human pain relief legislation; 83% (156 of 187) of the total sample support the basic psychological relationship between abortion values and human pain which is statistically very significant.

More specifically: 72% (68 of 94) of pro-choice congressmen support human pain relief; 95% (88 of 93) of anti-choice congressmen oppose human pain relief in dying cancer patients!

Only three percent of the sample are anti-choice and anti-pain, which is interpreted as reflecting a "consistent life" position. The average Pro-Child-Life Score of this group is eighty, although the reliability of this score is limited given the small sample size and its variability.

TABLE 2

U.S. House of Representatives Roll Call Vote of Anti-choice and Pro-pain Congressmen
(Average Pro-Child-Life Score equals 49)

Congressman	Party/State	Pro-Child Score	Gun Control	Contra Aid	Congressman	Party/State	Pro-Child Score	Gun Control	Contra Aid
Nevil	D-AL	100	N	Y	Lowery	R-CA	17	N	Y
Bilirakis	R-FL	33	N	Y	McCain	R-AZ	33	N	Y
Boggs	D-LA	83	Y	N	McEwen	R-OH	17	N	Y
Borski	D-PA	100	Y	N	Martin	R-NY	50	A	Y
Broomfield	R-MI	50	Y	Y	Mavroules	D-MA	100	Y	N
Burton	R-IN	17	N	Y	Mazzoli	D-KY	100	Y	N
Byron	D-MD	50	N	Y	Michel	R-IL	17	N	Y
Clinger	R-PA	67	N	Y	Miller	R-OH	17	N	Y
Coats	R-IN	17	N	Y	Molinari	R-NY	33	Y	Y
Conte	R-MA	67	Y	N	Mollohan	D-WV	100	N	N
Crane	R-IL	0	N	Y	Montgomery	D-MA	50	N	Y
Dannemeyer	R-CA	0	N	Y	Murtha	D-PA	100	N	Y
Daub	R-NE	17	N	Y	Myers	D-KY	17	N	Y
Duncan	R-TN	33	N	Y	Natcher	D-KY	83	N	N
Durbin	D-IL	100	N	N	Nelson	D-FL	50	N	Y
Emerson	R-MO	33	N	Y	Nichols	D-AL	67	A	Y
Fields	R-TX	33	N	Y	Nielson	R-UT	17	N	Y
Gaydos	D-PA	67	N	Y	Oberstar	D-MN	100	N	N
Gerphardt	D-MO	100	A	N	Packard	R-CA	17	N	Y
Gibbons	D-FL	67	Y	Y	Petri	R-WI	50	N	Y
Gingrich	R-GA	0	N	Y	Quillen	R-TN	17	N	Y
Goodling	R-PA	33	Y	Y	Regula	R-OH	33	N	Y
Gradison	R-OH	17	Y	Y	Rinaldo	R-NH	67	Y	Y
Gregg	R-NH	17	N	Y	Ritter	R-PA	17	N	Y
Hall	D-TX	50	?	?	Roe	D-NJ	*100	Y	N
Hansen	R-UT	17	N	Y	Rogers	R-KY	33	N	Y
Hertel	D-MI	83	Y	N	Roth	R-WI	33	N	Y
Hiler	R-IN	17	N	Y	Rudd	R-AZ	17	N	Y
Holt	R-MD	33	N	Y	Russo	D-IL	100	Y	N
Hopkins	R-KY	33	N	N	St. Germain	D-RI	100	Y	N
Hunter	R-CA	0	N	Y	Schaefer	R-CO	17	N	Y
Hutto	D-FL	67	Y	Y	Sensenbrenner	R-WI	0	N	Y
Hyde	R-IL	50	N	Y	Shaw	R-FL	17	N	Y
Kemp	R-NY	17	N	Y	Sikorski	D-MN	100	N	N
Kildee	D-MI	100	Y	N	Skelton	D-MO	83	N	Y
Lagomarsino	R-CA	17	N	Y	Smith	R-NJ	50	Y	Y
Latta	R-OH	17	N	Y	Smith	R-OR	17	N	Y
Leath	D-TX	33	N	Y	Smith	R-NE	33	N	Y
Lipinski	D-IL	100	Y	Y	Whitten	D-MA	83	N	N
Livingston	R-LA	33	N	Y	Wolf	R-VA	33	Y	Y
Lloyd	D-TN	50	N	N	Yatron	D-PA	100	N	Y
Loeffler	R-TX	33	N	Y	Young	R-FL	33	Y	Y
Long	D-LA	100	N	N	Young	R-AK	67	N	Y
Lott	R-MS	33	N	Y	Young	D-MO	100	N	Y

Y = Yes; N = No; A = Abstain; O = Not a member of the 99th Congress

The most psychologically and politically complex group of voters is the pro-choice and pro-pain group, and it demonstrates the greatest variability in Pro-Child-Life Scores. Time and space does not permit a further discussion of this group of voters.

In summary, these data contravene the claims of members of the anti-abortion movement that they have a basic compassion for human pain and suffering, which they attempt to portray in *The Silent Scream*.

TABLE 6 presents the basic analysis that compares the pro-choice and anti-pain congressmen with the anti-choice and pro-pain congressmen on gun control. In brief: 32% (47 of 145) of the total sample who are pro-choice and anti-pain support gun control legislation; 43% (63 of 145) of the total sample who are anti-choice and pro-pain oppose gun control legislation; 75% (110 of 145) of the total sample support the basic

TABLE 3

U.S. House of Representatives Roll Call Vote of Pro-choice and Pro-pain Congressmen
(Average Pro-Child-Life Score equals 79)

Congressman	Party/State	Pro-Child Score	Gun Control	Contra Aid	Congressman	Party/State	Pro-Child Score	Gun Control	Contra Aid
Anderson	D–CA	83	Y	N	MacKay	D–FL	100	N	N
AuCoin	D–OR	67	N	N	Morrison	D–WA	50	N	Y
Boehlert	R–NY	67	N	N	Panetta	D–CA	100	Y	N
Brooks	D–TX	100	N	N	Pursell	R–MI	50	Y	Y
Chandler	R–WA	67	Y	Y	Rangel	D–NY	100	Y	N
Collins	D–IL	100	Y	N	Rose	D–NC	100	Y	N
Crockett	D–MI	83	Y	N	Roukema	R–NJ	33	Y	Y
Fascell	D–FL	100	Y	Y	Rowland	D–GA	100	N	N
Fiedler	R–CA	33	N	Y	Schneider	R–RI	83	Y	N
Gonzalez	D–TX	83	Y	N	Spratt	D–SC	100	Y	N
Gray	D–PA	100	Y	N	Vandergriff	D–TX	50	O	O
Hatcher	D–GA	100	Y	Y	Wyden	D–OR	100	N	N
Levitas	D–GA	67	O	O	Zschau	R–CA	33	Y	Y

Y = Yes; N = No; A = Abstain; O = Not a member of the 99th Congress

psychological relationship between abortion values and human pain with gun control.

More specifically: 69% (47 of 68) of pro-choice and anti-pain congressmen support gun control legislation; 82% (63 of 77) of anti-choice and pro-pain congressmen oppose gun control legislation.

The above data confirm in the U.S. House of Representatives the relationship between abortion and gun control legislation that was previously found in the U.S. Senate. Opposition to abortion is associated with support of legislation that increases the risk to human lives from the violent use of handguns. These data provide no support for and, in fact, contravene the claims of the anti-abortion movement that they have a basic compassion for the victims of violence which they attempt to portray in *The Silent Scream.*

TABLE 7 presents the basic analysis that compares the pro-choice and anti-pain congressmen with the anti-choice and pro-pain congressmen on Contra Aid - this is, support for violent revolution. In brief: 40% (10 of 160) of the total sample who are pro-choice and anti-pain *oppose* Contra Aid - that is, oppose support for violent revolution; 45% (67 of 150) of the total sample who are anti-choice and pro-pain *support* Contra Aid - that is, support violent revolution; 85% (127 of 150) of the total sample support the basic psychological relationship between abortion values and pain with violent revolution.

More specifically: 95% (60 of 63) of pro-choice and anti-pain congressmen oppose Contra Aid - that is, oppose support of human violence; 77% (67 of 87) of anti-choice and pro-pain congressmen support Contra Aid - that is, provide support for human violence.

The above data contravene the claims of the anti-abortion movement that they have a basic compassion for the victims of violence, which they attempt to portray in *The Silent Scream.*

TABLE 4

**U.S. House of Representatives Roll Call Vote of
Anti-choice and Anti-pain Congressmen**
(Average Pro-Child-Life Score equals 80)

Congressman	Party/State	Pro-Child Score	Gun Control	Contra Aid
DeWine	R–OH	17	N	Y
Donnelly	D–MA	100	Y	N
Hamilton	D–IL	83	N	N
Luken	D–OH	100	N	N
Perkins	D–KY	100	N	N

Y = Yes; N = No; A = Abstain; O = Not a member of the 99th Congress

TABLE 5
U.S. House of Representatives Voting Relationships on Freedom of Choice and Freedom from Pain

	Pro-choice	Anti-choice	SUM
Anti-pain	36% N = 68	3% N = 5	73
Pro-pain	14% N = 26	47% N = 88	114
SUM	94	93	**187**

83% Valid Relationship
Chi Square = 88.08; Z = 9.39
N = 187 p < < 0.00001

72% (68 of 94) Pro-choice congressmen support human pain relief
95% (88 of 93) Anti-choice congressmen oppose human pain relief

TABLE 6
U.S. House of Representatives Voting Relationships on Freedom of Choice, Freedom from Pain, and Gun Control

	Pro-choice & Anti-pain	Anti-choice & Pro-pain	SUM
Pro-Gun Control	32% N = 47	10% N = 14	61
Anti-Gun Control	15% N = 21	43% N = 63	84
SUM	68	77	**145**

75% Valid Relationship
Chi Square = 38.44; Z = 6.20
N = 145; p < < 0.00001

69% (47 of 68) Pro-choice and anti-pain congressmen support gun control
82% (63 of 77) Anti-choice and pro-pain congressmen oppose gun control

TABLE 7
U.S. House of Representatives Voting Relationships on Freedom of Choice, Freedom from Pain, and Contra Aid

	Pro-choice & Anti-pain	Anti-choice & Pro-pain	SUM
Pro-Contra Aid	2% N = 3	45% N = 67	70
Anti-Contra Aid	40% N = 60	13% N = 20	80
SUM	63	87	**150**

85% Valid Relationship
Chi Square = 76.64; Z = 8.75
N = 150; p < < 0.00001

95% (60 of 63) Pro-choice and anti-pain congressmen oppose Contra Aid
77% (67 of 87) Anti-choice and pro-pain congressmen support Contra Aid

In summarizing previous and current data on the anti-abortion "personality" and "subculture," a profile emerges from these scientific studies with the following characteristics:

1. Authoritarian control over the personal lives of individuals, as it is reflected in the practice of slavery in primitive cultures, the legislative denial of freedom for women in modern cultures to be mothers by choice, and the imposition of arbitrary police arrests and seizures.

2. Support of human violence and its associated disregard for the dignity and integrity of the human body, as it is reflected in support of such physical assaults against the human body as: torture, mutilation, and killing of enemy captured in warfare; support of capital punishment; support of the war in Vietnam and violent revolution (Contra Aid); opposition to gun control legislation; violent attacks on medical clinics and personnel providing abortion services to women; and participation in the exploitation of a fetus in an abortion procedure to produce a false film "documentary" to serve authoritarian political and religious objectives.

3. Indifference to human pain and suffering, as it is reflected in the refusal to provide effective medicine to control excruciating pain in dying cancer patients.

4. Authoritarian control and denial of the fundamental right of self-determination in sexual expression, as it is reflected in the punishment of prostitution and premarital and extramarital sexuality, in mandatory fornication and adultery as felonious crimes, and in punishment of homosexuality.

5. *Indifference to the quality of life of children*, as it is reflected in the economic exploitation of children (primitive cultures) and failure to provide basic medical care, food, education, and clothing for poor children and their families (legislative actions).

6. *A moral value system that equates human pain, suffering, and violence with moral strength and, conversely, equates sexual pleasure and relief from pain and suffering with moral weakness.*

It is emphasized that the foregoing does not apply to certain individuals who represent 3 to 13 percent of the populations studied. These individuals are characterized by opposition to abortion and physical violence; they respect rights to sexual privacy and choice and have high child and family nurturance scores.

Given the profound moral, psychological, and political dimensions of the abortion controversy, it is unlikely that "data alone" will resolve it. The solution is *prevention*, with which women have complete control over their reproductive state. The prevention of all unintended and unwanted pregnancies should be our common goal.

[Note: As this article was going to press, the House of Representatives voted 221 to 209 (Roll No. 199, June 25, 1986) to support Congressman Edwards' (R-OK) amendment to provide military aid and other assistance to the Contras. This vote reversed the vote on H.J. Res. 540 (Roll no. 64, March 20, 1986) which rejected military and other financial assistance to the Contras. An analysis of this vote for the one hundred pro-choice and one hundred anti-choice congressmen yielded the following results: for the pro-choice and anti-pain congressmen (TABLE 1), only one congressman switched votes from opposing to supporting Contra Aid (Snowe, R-ME); for the anti-choice and pro-pain congressmen (TABLE 2), four congressmen switched votes (Hopkins, R-KY, and Lloyd, D-TN, switched from being opposed to supporting Contra Aid; Yatron, D-PA, and Young, D-MO, switched from supporting to opposing Contra Aid); for the pro-choice and pro-pain congressmen (TABLE 3), only one congressman switched votes from opposing to supporting Contra Aid (Rowland, D-GA); no vote changes were present in the anti-choice and anti-pain congressmen (TABLE 4). These minor changes in voting patterns (of the total of six congressmen, three initially opposed and then supported Contra Aid, while three initially supported then opposed Contra Aid) have had no significant effect on the basic psychological relationship between opposition to abortion and indifference to human pain and suffering that is strongly associated with support of human violence legislation.]

References

Catholics for a Free Choice. 1985. *Reproductive Choice: What It Means and Where Congress Stands.* Washington, DC: Catholics for a Free Choice.

Jaworski, Patricia. 1986 audio tape. "Thinking about *The Silent Scream*." New York: Jaworski Productions.

Prescott, J.W. July/August 1978. "Abortion and the 'Right-to-Life': Facts, Fallacies, and Fraud. I. Cross-Cultural Studies." *The Humanist*, pp. 18-24.

---. March 1976. "Violence, Pleasure, and Religion." *The Bulletin of the Atomic Scientists*, p. 62.

---. April 1975. "Body Pleasure and the Origins of Violence." *The Futurist*, pp. 64-74.

---. March/April 1975. "Abortion or the Unwanted Child: A Choice for a Humanistic Society." *The Humanist*, pp. 11-15.

---. November/December 1972. "Before Ethics and Morality." *The Humanist*; pp. 19-21.

Prescott, J.W., and Wallace, D. November/December 1978. "Abortion and the 'Right-to-Life': Facts, Fallacies, and Fraud. II. Psychometric Studies." *The Humanist*, pp. 36-42.

Appendix D

A Short Directory of Pro-Choice Organizations

Amercians for Religious Liberty
P.O. Box 6656
Silver Spring, MD 20906

American Civil Liberties Union
132 W. 43rd St.
New York, NY 10036

Religious Coalition for Abortion Rights
100 Maryland Ave., NE
Washington, DC 20002

Catholics For A Free Choice
1436 U St. NW
Washington, DC 20009

National Abortion Rights Action League
1101 14th St., NW, Fifth Floor
Washington, DC 20005

Planned Parenthood Federation of America
810 7th Ave.
New York, NY 10019

Abortion Rights Mobilization
175 Fifth Ave. Suite 814
New York NY 10010